PSYCHOLOGY OF RELIGION

A Commentary on the Classic Texts

by John H. Morgan
Ph.D.(Hartford), D.Sc.(London), Psy.D.(FH/Oxford)
Karl Mannheim Professor
of the History and Philosophy of the Social Sciences
Graduate Theological Foundation
Sir Julian Huxley Distinguished Research Professor
Cloverdale College
Senior Fellow of Foundation House/Oxford
Visiting Scholar, Harvard University

PSYCHOLOGY OF RELIGION

A Commentary on the Classic Texts

John H. Morgan
Ph.D.(Hartford), D.Sc.(London), Psy.D.

Rhodes-Fulbright Library

Library of Congress
LOC 2011929802

ISBN 978-155605-435-8
Ebook 978-155605-436-5

Printed in the United States of America

Wyndham Hall Press
5050 Kerr Rd.
Lima, Oh 45806

Dedicated to the Memory of
Peter Homans, friend and colleague.

ACKNOWLEDGEMENTS

All ten classic texts discussed herein are out of print and their copyrights have expired. As most have gone through several editions and multiple publishers, I have chosen not to identify any one edition as the basis for my comments. I have acknowledged, however, with gratitude the various publishing companies and various editions of these primary texts in the primary bibliography section. I trust that both propriety and professional protocol have been honored thereby.

TABLE OF CONTENTS

INTRODUCTION

On the centennial of the death of William James (1842-1910), I approached faculty members at eighteen major theological centers of learning (cf. Appendix) requesting them to identify the ten most important books written between James' 1902 classic *The Varieties of Religious Experience* up to Abraham Maslow's *Religion, Values, and Peak Experiences* (1964). The request was for each faculty member (by agreement to remain anonymous) to identify the ten books during that time period (1902-1970) which, in their opinion, constituted major contributions to the development of the discipline of the psychology of religion. By mutual agreement, James was credited with being the purported founder of the psychology of religion and Maslow the quintessential culmination of the discipline's respectability. Though obviously subjective, the survey did register a consensus of scholars teaching in the field and what follows is a commentary on each of those books which they selected.

Between William James' 1902 *The Varieties of Religious Experience* and Abraham Maslow's 1964 *Religion, Values, and Peak Experiences*, the field of the psychology of religion was born and grew to maturity. About that, there is no serious question or doubt (Beit-Hallahmi; Coe; Gargiulo; Kendler; Strunk). Within these six decades, a discipline came into existence and established itself irrevocably as an indispensable component of the study of the human person. Under the influence of James' pioneering work and culminating in the provocative work of Maslow, ten books proved pivotal in the emergence of the psychology of religion as a respected area of research, study, and specialization within both the disciplines of psychology and theology. Of course, any number of scholars will wish to argue with the selection of these ten titles but few will argue against the merits of those selected here. Another ten could be named and another, but these have been chosen as indicative of the consensus within the academy of their crucial relevance to this collection honoring William James' life and work commemorating the centennial of his death in 1910

(Richardson).

It might prove helpful to the reader for there to be a simple listing of the ten titles selected for consideration here and then, following a brief acknowledgement and assessment of Edwin D. Starbuck's 1899 Scribner's publication, *Psychology of Religion*, wherein the term "psychology of religion" was used for the first time, we will proceed with our commentary on each book and its relevance to the development of the field of study called the psychology of religion. The ten titles which constitute the consensus among the scholars surveyed are as follows and they are listed and considered in chronological order of publication.

(English Translation dates)

James, William (1902) *The Varieties of Religious Experience*
Leuba, James H. (1915) *Psychological Origin and Nature of Religion*
Freud, Sigmund (1927) *The Future of an Illusion*
Jung, Carl (1938) *Psychology and Religion*
Roberts, David E. (1950) *Psychotherapy and A Christian View of Man*
Allport, Gordon (1950) *The Individual and His Religion*
Fromm, Eric (1950) *Psychoanalysis and Religion*
Rank, Otto (1950) *Psychology and the Soul*
Bakan, David (1958) *Sigmund Freud and the Jewish Mystical Tradition*
Maslow, Abraham (1964) *Religion, Values, and Peak-Experiences*

Clearly this collection and the timeframe covered by their publication can be divided into a three-step development, namely, from James to Jung (1092 to 1938), from Roberts the Rank (1950) which constituted the backbone of the discipline's development, and from Bakan to Maslow (1958-1964), when Freud comprised the beginning and ending of the third step. James, Leuba, Freud, and Jung were adventurers in the field of the psychology of religion, exploring where no one had ventured before and attempting an analysis that others would have understandably shied away from, given the problematic nature of the subject matter. Religion was not to be tampered with during this time period except ever so gingerly. But, on the shoulders of the four pioneers of James, Leuba, Freud, and Jung, Roberts, Allport, Fromm, and Rank were at liberty to explore the practical applications of their forebears' insights, speculations, and expostulations. These two, then, launched a monolithic barrage of investigations and applications, the likes of which had never been imagined before and the likes of which will not be seen again as a single moment in time. Finally, and upon the shoulders of the second generation of adventurers, the four members of the third step, i.e., Bakan and Maslow, chose to address the insights of their predecessors relative to Freud and psychoanalysis in a manner that once and for all introduced the viability and effectiveness of the discipline of the psychology of religion for scholars and students of both religion and psychology. Certainly, there were grounds for discussion, argument, and dispute, but that the two fields of study had been brought to a creative synthesis of methodological insights and analyses would not again be seriously disputed by either religionists or psychologists.

The creation of a term, however, is not synonymous with the creation of a scholarly discipline of study. E(dwin) D(iller) Starbuck (1866-1947) was quite clearly aware of that but was, nevertheless, intent upon launching an enquiry with wide sweeping implications for both the discipline of psychology and the general field of religious studies. He did this with countless articles published in the best peer-reviewed journals of the time, but his book, *The Psychology of Religion,* published in New York in 1899 by Charles Scribner's, proved to be the stone that truly rippled the scholarly waters, for it was Starbuck who was the very first to use the actual term "psychology of religion." An Indiana Quaker and a sequential product of Indiana University (B.A.), Harvard University (M.A.) and Clark University (Ph.D.), Starbuck's major influences were William James at Harvard and G. Stanley Hall at Clark. The impetus for his pursuit of the psychology of religion as a lifelong field of study came from F. Max Muller's 1890 classic, *Introduction to the Science of Religion.* Starbuck stayed on at Clark as a research fellow where he worked closely with James H. Leuba (more about whom later). It was during these pivotal years of work that he wrote and published his classic, *The Psychology of Religion,* which went through three editions and was translated into German. Tension with Hall, if not outright jealousy on Hall's part, led Starbuck to move on in both his teaching subjects to include philosophy and education, and to a series of university appointments, including the State University of Iowa and the University of Southern California. It was William James who elevated Starbuck to a national figure by using Starbuck's empirical data in James' own book, which constitutes the formal beginning of our consideration here. "If one attempts an evaluation of Starbuck's work from the perspective of several generations," (Beit-Hallahmi, 1974:86), "one might conclude that it will be remembered more by historians of the field than by practitioners. His work may belong with the classics of the field, but it must be numbered with the unread classics, even among scholars." It was not until a quarter of a century after Starbuck's now classic book, *The Psychology of Religion* (1899), and a year before Freud's pivotal *The Future of an Illusion* (1927), that the Hartford Seminary Foundation in Connecticut hosted a conference entitled, "The Possible Contributions of Modern Psychology to the Theory and Practice of Religion" in October of 1926 (Beit-Hallahmi 1974:86).

In the following, we will introduce each of our ten authors and place him within the context of his time period, and then we will engage in a review of his major contribution to the field of the psychology of religion by way of a systematic reading and commentary of the text itself. Since our intent is to provide a report on the development of the discipline of the psychology of religion and not a critical assessment of the scholarly merits of each book attributed to that development, our consideration of each title will be in terms of a commentary on the book's contents and contribution rather than a critical and scholarly assessment of its intrinsic value itself. We have suggested that these ten books have been identified as pivotal in the emergence of this discipline and, thus, our consideration will be of the text itself rather than a delineated critique of its overall merits. A bibliography of secondary sources will prove to be a major resource for individuals desiring to pursue a critical assessment of each work as judged by the community of scholars. That is not our agenda. Rather, we are offering a summary and commentary on each text in terms of its recognized value in moving the discipline forward in each generation from 1902 to 1964.

NOTE: In the following, the original text will be printed in *Arial Unicode MS* typestyle (as is this illustrative note itself) as an easy and aesthetically pleasing way of identifying the primary source paragraphs. The author's commentary will be in *Times New Roman*. It is hoped that this differentiation between the "primary source" and the "commentary" made by use of differing fonts will prove helpful and not disruptive to the reader. *I have also chosen to use a quadruple asterisk (****) to separate the primary text from the commentary.*

CHAPTER ONE

William James and *The Varieties of Religious Experience*

Historians of the behavioral sciences would all more or less agree that the two volume study published in 1890, *The Principles of Psychology*, by William James constituted one of the most important events in the history of the emerging science of psychology in this country and, some would argue, throughout the European world as well (Richardson 2006:127). Granted the central place of this work by James in the science of psychology, it is the consensus of both psychologists and religionists that his *The Varieties of Religious Experience,* published in 1902, constituted the formal beginnings of the emergence of the sub-field of study in both psychology and religion now established as the psychology of religion. William James (1842-1910) was born into wealth, elegance, and eccentricity, being the son of a Swedenborgian theologian, Henry James, Sr., and the older brother of the subsequently internationally acclaimed novelist, Henry James. The godson of Ralph Waldo Emerson, William James attempted a career as an artist but found science, finally, more to his temperament and liking, discovered as a student at the Lawrence Scientific School of Harvard University, where he continued as a medical student, taking his M.D. degree from Harvard Medical School in 1869, never, alas, to actually practice medicine (Richardson 2006:149).

With no formal training in psychology *per se*, but rather in biology, physiology, and anatomy, he once said that "the first lecture on psychology I ever heard was the first I ever gave" (James 1902:31). Not daunted by this lack of formal training, both James and Harvard pressed on in the creation of an experimental psychology course in 1875 which was attended, over several years, by some of Harvard's subsequently most illustrious students, including G. Stanley Hall. Suffering for years from heart problems, James died at his home in New Hampshire on August 29, 1910, holding out to the very end as a functional psychologist and pragmatic philosopher.

It was *The Varieties of Religious Experience* (1902), however, that established him as a proponent of the value and efficacy of religious experience, making him the darling of laymen everywhere and the bane and nemesis of empirical psychologists throughout the English-speaking world. This book, not approaching the scientific value of his *The Principles of Psychology* (1890), netted him the invitation from the University of Edinburgh to give the 1901 and 1902 Gifford Lectures, a forum wherein he was at liberty to chide the scientific community for its dismissive attitude toward the "value" of religious experience in deference to the "origins and ideas of religion." This criticism took the psychological investigation of religious phenomena into a whole new realm of viability and possibility, for, as Charles Pearce is reported to have said, "James has penetrated into the hearts of people" with his sympathetic approach to the "value of religious experience." Yet, his friend and colleague, George Santayana, responded with a resounding scientific critique of James' work by pointing out that the "great weakness of his (James') position is its tendency to disintegrate the idea of truth" in deference to "belief without reason" (Page 1951:4-5).

As William James is the undisputed father of at least American modern psychology and owing to his central importance in the birth and growth of the psychology of religion, we will spend more time dealing with his biographical information than with any subsequent psychologist considered in this study. We have already suggested and shall soon substantiate James' *The Varieties of Religious Experience* (1902) in the form of the Gifford Lectures in Scotland which proved to be the catalytic and pivotal in the scientific communities interest in and willingness to pursue the application of psychological insights into religious behavior. James was born at the Astor House in New York City on January 11, 1842, and was the oldest of five children, followed by his brother Henry who became an internationally recognized and respected author and literary critic whose novels were particularly celebrated owing to their psychological insights. The family trees on both sides were not distinguished, rather all seem to have been farmers, tradesmen, and merchants. The posterity of James and Henry and their other siblings, likewise, have proven undistinguished.

James's father, Henry, Sr., had graduated from Union College in upstate New York and subsequently attended Princeton Theological Seminary with the intention of seeking ordination in the Presbyterian Church but, owing to a growing sense of what he called "antipathy to all ecclesiasticisms," he diverted his attention to the works of Swedenborg, the Swedish medical mystic, where he seems to have found spiritual solace. Henry, Sr., gradually developed a comprehensive system of thought, inspired if not based on Swedenborgian philosophy, which not only governed the remainder of his life but radically affected the upbringing of all his children. James and Henry were in and out of various schools in America and Europe, for their independently wealthy and eccentric father disparaged and demeaned "traditionalist" education, preferring adventurism and freedom of thought and enquiry as the guiding principles of the truly educated mind. It has been suggested that both James and Henry developed a refined skill of dialogic give-and-take needed to endure the dinner and tea-time discussions foisted off on the family by their demanding father. James' godfather was Ralf Waldo Emerson and James's gift of juggling a variety of ideas, both complimentary and contradictory, was a defining characteristic and quality of all of his writing throughout his career.

The price of such free thinking for James was the experience of being in and out of a variety of pursuits, some taken seriously and other less so. When he was 18 years old, during their residency in Newport, Rhodes Island in the States, James turned his hand to both the study and practice of art but, soon tiring of the discipline and rigor of serious artistic endeavor, he entered the Lawrence Science School of Harvard University. As might have been expected and anticipated by the family, his study of chemistry, biology, and anatomy eventuated in his pursuit of the profession of medicine at the Harvard Medical School. A diversion consisting of an exploring expedition up the Amazon under the tutelage of the famous explorer, Louis Agassiz, resulted in his postponing completion of his medical training and degree in 1869, following a period of studying philosophy and psychology in Germany with Helmholtz, Virchow, and Bernard. Following his venture into Germany and German metaphysics, he returned home where he suffered an emotional breakdown with suicidal tendencies. The practical result of his illness was his inability for a while to commence the practice of medicine, living as a semi-invalid in his father's home under the care of his family. It was during this time that he experienced a "phobic panic" which persisted for nearly a year during which time he turned his attention to Renouvier's work on free will, which resulted in his complete abandonment of determinism and an embracing of free will, saying, "My first act of free will shall be to believe in free will." This turn in his worldview had lasting impact upon all of his mature thought and writing.

Owing to both his own innate abilities and personal reputation established during his years of study at Harvard and with no little assistance from his father's circle of friends, James was appointed an instructor in physiology at Harvard College in 1872, having recovered his emotional and physical health the year before. He taught physiology and anatomy there for four years but his passion was for psychology rather than physiology. The psychology he was driven to pursue, however, was not the "traditional mental science" by what was coming rapidly to the field as "physiological psychology," a psychology which challenged the presumed theological orientation of the colleges in America. Up until this time, psychology had been essentially "mental philosophy" in what Santayana called "the genteel tradition." However, with psychology becoming increasingly a laboratory science, philosophy ceased to be the orientation and, alas, physiological psychology was born. James wrote: "I originally studied medicine in order to be a physiologist, but I drifted into psychology and philosophy from a sort of fatality. I never had any psychological instruction, the first lecture on psychology I ever heard being the first I ever gave."

James' career at Harvard spanned most of his adult life, being appointed an instructor in the spring of 1873 in physiology, then assistant professor of psychology in 1876, assistant professor of philosophy in 1881, full professor in 1885, endowed chair in psychology in 1889, and professor and emeritus professor of philosophy finally in 1907, followed soon thereafter by retirement at the age of 65. His students at Harvard over his teaching career included many famous and not-so-well-known scholars and teachers, including Theodore Roosevelt, George Santayana, W. E.

B. Du Bois, G. Stanley Hall, Gertrude Stein, and Walter Lippmann.

Marrying Alice H. Gibbens of Cambridge, MA, in 1878 at the age of 36, James' whole life and orientation took on a new dimension of expansiveness and exploration. His record of health problems including neurasthenia eventually disappeared. He became much healthier and enthusiastic about his work and writing, including a major step forward into his career by signing a book contract with Henry Holt and Company to produce a textbook in psychology with an anticipated publication date of 1880. Not appearing, however, until 1890, ten years later, the book was *The Principles of Psychology,* and proved much more than a mere textbook in psychology for it was a monumental and monolithic two-volume giant of a contribution to the field, unequivocally establishing James as the authority in this new field of psychology. Indeed, making him, for all practical purposes, the "father of American modern psychology."

Ironically but characteristically, James lost interest in this field of study. Having created the first demonstrational psychology laboratory in America at Harvard, he discovered that he actually disliked laboratory work and felt out of place in the scientific aura of the lab. His preference was for what he called the "adventure of free observation and reflection," preferring to deal with the questions and problems of philosophy and religion rather than with psychology, which seemed to him to be "a nasty little subject." The nature and existence of God, the immortality of the soul, free will and determinism, the value of life, etc., became his driving passions to the surprise and dismay of his psychology colleagues and student followers. In the late 1880s, Harvard had allowed him to teach ethics and religion and though he concluded that scientific evidence was not available to prove life after death, he did contend that religious experience was real. All of this activity, the shifting from the laboratory to observation and speculation, the move from physiological psychology to philosophy, religion, and ethics as his teaching and research field resulted in a plethora of publications, rapidly appearing in succession, including *The Will to Believe and Other Essays in Popular Philosophy (1897); Human Immorality (1898); Talks to Teachers on Psychology and to Students on Some of Life's Ideals*

(1899); and *The Varieties of Religious Experience (1902).* Among Jamesian scholars, this time frame is often called his "religious period" which culminated in his giving the 1902 Gifford Lectures on natural religion at the University of Edinburgh. This last work we will focus our subsequent discussion upon following this general introduction to his life and work. It is this book, more than any other scholar or writings of the time, which is given credit for the establishment of the sub-discipline of the psychology of religion.

Irony not being a stranger to James' life and career, the Gifford Lectures essentially marked the end of his real interest in religious behavior as a field of study for psychology. Having established the legitimacy of the enquiry with the book and Lectures, he now turned his attention explicitly to the philosophical issues and problems always implicit in his earlier works. As early as 1898 in a series of lectures at the University of California, he had developed a philosophical conceptualization of his fundamentally driving principle, developed early in his career, a method which came to be known universally as pragmatism, making James one of the founding fathers along with Dewey and Charles S. Peirce of this school of thought. James defined true beliefs as those that prove useful to the believer in the field of the psychology of religion. His pragmatic theory of truth was a synthesis of "correspondence theory of truth" and "coherence theory of truth." James argued that truth is verifiable to the extent that thoughts and sentiments correspond with actual things, as well as the extent to which they "hang together." The value of any truth, he argued, was dependent upon its use to the person who held it. A thing is true if it is useful to the one who believes it. Thus James and his new pragmatism ushered in the death of "truth as an absolute," rather, "truth is relative to the intensity of the one who believes it and for whom it fills a need and serves a purpose." But unlike Peirce's eccentric genius with its lack of practicality, James transformed this methodology into an operational philosophical modality of analysis of what is provably true. He argued for the centrality of a succession of experiential consequences itself as the litmus test for the truth -- "that truth and error are identical with these consequences or else nothing is." This he called the "pragmatic rule for truth discovery," and some within the professional community attributed James' arguments in this regard for "saving American philosophy" as a university discipline. This work culminated in the 1906 Lowell Lectures at Harvard under the title as a published book, *Pragmatism: A New Name for Old Ways of Thinking.*

James now became the new centre of a philosophical school of thought which was to sweep America and reach deeply into all English-speaking countries *vis a vis* the Europeans generally and the Germans specifically who, however, seemed not to get it or refused to understand it. Championed by Schiller in England and Dewey in the United States, Harvard students in 1907 presented him with a loving silver cup of gratitude for his phenomenally popular course on philosophy, a breaking of precedence at Harvard regarding the honoring of the teaching faculty. He repeated the "Pragmatism" lectures at Columbia University the following year and in 1909 he delivered the Hibbert Lectures at Manchester College of Oxford University, published as *A Pluralistic Universe.* Returning home and exhausted, he died quietly at home in Chocorua, New Hampshire, on August 26, 1910, at the age of 68, survived by his wife, three sons and a daughter.

Our intent in this study is to identify and summarize the ten major books which are recognized as being essentially responsible for establishing the general field of study called the psychology of religion. As has been stated earlier, the consensus of scholars drawn from our survey of the top eighteen theological institutions in the United States is that, without an exception, William James' *The Varieties of Religious Experience* is credited with being the first major work in establishing this discipline. Our interest is not just another critical evaluation of that work but rather, in order to serve the reader with an exposure to the key texts without critical assessments, we intend to offer an overview of each of the ten texts, beginning with James. Critical studies of each of the key texts are cited in the secondary bibliography, but here we will only address the primary sources in our commentary.

The 1902 Gifford Lectures at Saint Andrews University in Edinburgh, Scotland, resulted in the publication of James' quintessential study of religious behavior from a psychological perspective. There were 20 lectures over an eighteen month period and we will comment upon each in the following overview.

Selections from *The Varieties of Religious Experience,* by William James, with commentary.

NOTE: In the following, the original text will be printed in *Arial Unicode MS* typestyle (as is this note itself to illustrate) as an easy and aesthetically pleasing way of identifying the primary source paragraphs. The author's commentary will be in *Times New Roman.* It is hoped that this differentiation between the "primary source" and the "commentary" made by use of differing fonts will prove helpful and not disruptive to the reader. *I have also chosen to use a quadruple asterisk (****) to separate the primary text from the commentary.*

Lecture I Religion and Neurology

If the enquiry be psychological, not religious emotions, but rather religious feelings and religious impulses must be its subject, and I must confine myself to those more developed subjective phenomena recorded in literature produced by articulate and fully self-conscious men in works of piety and autobiography.

This series of lectures, James would have his audience understand, is not anthropological but rather psychological in that, though a cross-cultural selection of data and examples suggest an anthropological orientation, his approach to the selection and his interpretation of the ethnographic illustrations will come from psychology, producing both questions of fact and questions of value. Granted that religious individuals are often neurotic, the medical community's inclination to, therefore, dismiss religious experience as a viable reality is misguided, as are those who attribute religious behavior to repressed sexual drives. The assessment of the legitimacy of religious experience, says James, must be based, not on its origin, but on the value of the resulting behavior of the believer. Therefore, the argument against religion based on the origin criterion is fallacious. He concludes this essay by pointing out the "advantages" of the psychopathic temperament when combined with a superior intellect with illustrations of such to follow in subsequent lectures.

****

Lecture II Circumscription of the Topic

Religious awe is the same organic thrill which we feel in a forest at twilight, or in a mountain gorge; only this time it comes over us at the thought of our supernatural relations. ... There are other things in religion chronologically more primordial than personal devoutness in the moral sense. Fetishism and magic seem to have preceded inward piety historically. ... If fetishism and magic may be regarded as stages of religion, one may say that personal religion in the inward sense and the genuinely spiritual ecclesiasticisms which it founds are phenomena of secondary or even tertiary order.

James here argues against the legitimacy or operational viability of selected definitions of religion and religious behavior. There is no one specific "religious sentiment" that he has been able to identify in all of his research, and there isareecidedly distinctions to be drawn between institutional and personal expressions of religious beliefs and behaviors. He then explores a definition he can live with in his assessment of personal and institutional expressions of religion, viz., "Religion is the feelings, acts, and experiences of individual men in their solitude, so far as they apprehend themselves to stand in relation to whatever they may consider the divine." And, following, we must "interpret the term 'divine' very broadly, as denoting any object that is godlike, whether it be a concrete deity or not." The production of "solemn reactions" in personal experience constitutes his focus on the divine encounter and argues the futility of trying too hard to make the definitions of religion and divinity "too precise and too sharp." The best way in to an appreciative and empathetic understanding of the dynamic of religious behavior is through "extreme cases," that of the mystics, for example. Accepting the universe can be either religious or secular, faith-based or philosophical, and he argues that the religious individual is more enthusiastic about the experience which he characterizes as "enthusiasm in solemn emotion." Religion can, in a way that philosophy or science cannot, overcome unhappiness and it, therefore, serves both a psychological as well as a biological function, soothing the mind and nurturing the body.

****

Lecture III The Reality of the Unseen

It is as if there were in the human consciousness a *sense of reality, a feeling of objective presence, a perception* of what we may call *'something there,'* more deep and more general than any of the special and particular 'senses' by which current psychology supposes existent realities to be originally revealed.

When dealing with religious behavior and reports of religious experience, it is the "perception" rather than the "abstract concepts" which prove function, viable, and legitimizing. Whereas perception validates religious experience, abstractions often are a deterrent to religious belief. For the religious person, there is a "sense of reality" which goes beyond and is transcendent to the regular senses, there is what James says religious experience considers valid as a "sense of presence." There is a sense of reality beyond the phenomenon world of sense experience. This sense of the divine is illustrated by James from the mystics primarily but not exclusively, from the Christian mystical traditions. There is a legitimacy which religious people recognize and accept which is beyond reason, though not considered "unreasonable." Rationalism is devalued, considered inferior, to the validating experience of the religious mystic.

****

Lecture IV & V The Religion of Health-mindedness

> In some individuals optimism may become quasi-pathological. The capacity for even a transient sadness or a momentary humility seems cut off from them as by a kind of congenital anaesthesia. ... To the man actively happy, from whatever cause, evil simply cannot then and there be believed in. He must ignore it; and to the bystander he may then seem perversely to shut his eyes to it and to hush it up. ... In just the degree in which you realize your oneness with the Infinite Spirit, you will exchange dis-ease for ease, in harmony for harmony, suffering for abounding health and strength. ... The mind-curers have demonstrated that a form of regeneration by relaxing, letting go, psychologically indistinguishable from the Lutheran justification by faith and the Wesleyan acceptance of free grace, is within the reach of persons who have no conviction of sin and care nothing for Lutheran theology. It is but giving your little private convulsive self a rest, and finding that a greater Self is there. ... The experiences which we have been studying plainly show the universe to be a more many-sided affair than any sect, even the scientific sect, allows for. ... Science and religion are both of them genuine keys for unlocking the world's treasure-house. ... Primitive thought, with its belief in individualized personal forces, seems at any rate as far as ever from being driven by science from the field to-day. Numbers of educated people still find it the directest experimental channel by which to carry on their intercourse with reality.

Existential happiness, rather than metaphysical truth, is the chief concern of the human person, and religious experience, when had and embraced, brings such happiness. The "born again" experience is self-validating and discounts the interventionist agenda of the rationalist. The reasonableness of the faith experience, the reality of the happiness which comes from "being born again," produces a systematic healthy-mindedness, says James. Walt Whitman is called as a witness and example in this regard. He argues from the perspective of "liberal Christianity" for the efficacy of healthy-minded religion, using such examples as the Lutheran theological doctrine of salvation by grace, salvation as a mechanism for stress-reduction (called by him simply "relaxation"), employing a methodology which includes meditation, recollection, verification, and diversity of adaptation schemes for inducing and enhancing the religious experience. He closes with two "mind-cure cases" as illustrative materials for further discussion.

****

Lecture VI & VII The Sick Soul

There are people for whom evil means only a mal-adjustment with things, a wrong correspondence of one's life with the environment. Such evil as this is curable, in principle, at least, upon the natural plane, for merely by modifying either the self or the things, or both at once. ... But there are others for whom evil is no more relation of the subject to particular outer things, but something more radical and general, a wrongness or vice in his essential nature, which no alteration of the environment, or any superficial rearrangement of the inner self, can cure and which requires a supernatural remedy. ... But the deliverance must come in as strong a form as the complaint, if it is to take effect; and that seems a reason why the coarser religions, revivalist, orgiastic, with blood and miracles and supernatural operations, may possibly never be displaced. Some constitutions need them too much. ... There is no doubt that healthy-mindedness is inadequate as a philosophical doctrine, because the evil facts which it refuses positively to account for are a genuine portion of reality; and they may after all be the best key to life's significance, and possibly the only openers of our eyes to the deepest levels of truth.

On the heels of his thorough-going discussion of healthy-minded religion, James discusses at length the "sick soul" phenomenon. The struggle between the healthy-minded religious person and the reality of the need for repentance often, though not always, leads one into a morbidity of self-negation. The pain one appropriates to oneself in the face of evil in the world and within one's self fosters a sense of the insecurity and uncertainty of natural goodness in the world and in the individual. The world is full of failure and vanity, and pure naturalism leads only to pessimism. Pathological unhappiness characterizes much of western culture in both Greek and Roman thought and history, and melancholy is often the resultsof such reflection. The pure gift of a "zest for life" when lost leads to depression and world-denying behavior illustrated in such individuals as Tolstoy and Bunyan. Supernatural religion offers relief and hope in the midst of pessimistic morbidity for there is always to be the struggle between the healthy-minded and the morbid-minded religious person, for the problem of evil is not escapable in human experience.

****

Lecture VIII The Divided Self and the Process of Its Unification

The psychological basis of the twice-born character seems to be a certain discordancy or heterogeneity in the nature temperament of the subject, an incompletely unified moral and intellectual constitution.

Having in the three previous lectures dealt with both the healthy-minded and the sick soul of the religious believer, James now turns to the "divided self," the religious person's experience of a conflicting personality, what he calls "heterogeneous." The quest of the religious mystic, of course as he points out, is personal unity of the interior life. He lavishly illustrates these struggles with historic figures wrestling with the divided self and the pain and remorse which comes with that experience, an experience which can exacerbate the religious quest and be resolved by the religious journey inward. Though not all quests for soul unity result in a "religious" resolution, as he demonstrates in several illustrations, there is, nevertheless, the anticipation of a gradual or sudden coagulation of personality leading to a deep and abiding sense of interior unity of the self. He uses frequently here and throughout the series the lives of Tolstoy and Bunyan.

****

Lecture IX Conversion

One may say that the whole development of Christianity in inwardness has consisted in little more than the greater and greater emphasis attached to this crisis of self-surrender. From Catholicism to Lutheranism, and then to Calvinism; from that to Wesleyanism; and from this, outside of technical Christianity, to pure 'liberalism' or transcendental idealism, whether or not of the mind-cure type, taking in the medieval mystics, the quietists, the pietists, and Quakers by the way, we can trace the stages of progress towards the idea of an immediate spiritual help, experienced by the individual in his forlornness and standing in no essential need of doctrinal apparatus or propitiatory apparatus.

Using case studies (a methodological approach to psychological research, which was just then coming on the scene as an acceptable mechanism for enquiry within the academy, and one he employed in setting up the psychology laboratory at Harvard), James deals with changes resulting from the experience of conversion in religious behavior. He emphasizes the emotional excitement stimulation which comes as a feature of this experience and how within the person there is also commonly a perceived change in the center of one's personal life, witnessed by others as well as the individual. What is most helpful for the further exploration of the development of the discipline of the psychology of religion is James' uses of the work of Starbuck and Leuba, colleagues who were very active in this same field of research, Starbuck actually using the term "psychology of religion" in a publication for the first time and Leuba writing his classic book, *The Psychological Origin and the Nature of Religion* (about which later in Chapter Two of this study). James deals with the "unconvertible" personality and the two types of conversion regularly encountered in this matrix of behavior. He ventures into the dark and troubled waters of what he calls the "subconscious incubation of motives" as relates to religious conversion, and elaborates on the experience by the believer of "self-surrender" and its overall importance in the history of religious conversion, using case after case as illustrative materials. James was not hesitant or shy about using laboratory examples and case histories to shore up his arguments, especially when venturing into uncharted territory.

****

Lecture X Conversion -- concluded

Nothing in Catholic theology, I imagine, has ever spoken to the sick soul as straight as this message from Luther's personal experience ... The adequacy of his view of Christianity to the deeper parts of our human mental structure is shown by its wildfire contagiousness when it was a new and quickening thing.

Suddenness in conversion is common, but not essential, to the legitimate experience of religious conversion and James uses several illustrations to make his point. The individual personality is the determining factor and where the idiosyncratic components are present, which he attempts to identify and name, then either gradual or sudden conversation can be anticipated. He argues somewhat persuasively that his research has vindicated the reality of "transmarginal and subliminal" consciousness as a factor in this process, discussing even the controversial notion of "automatism." He goes on to contend with illustrative materials that the sudden conversion, or what he also chooses to call "instantaneous conversations" occur more commonly where there is an active, subconscious self involved. James has become famous for his insistence, not just here but throughout his research and writing about religious experience, that the efficacy or value of the religious conversion to the individual does not depend upon that process of conversion but rather upon the fruits of the conversion, in other words, what the converted individual does with his life within the context of the conversion experience. Whether the conversion is sudden or gradual does not affect this argument, says James, but the "sanctified life" as defined and experienced by the converted is the litmus test of validity. James does not nor will not argue for the truthfulness of the reality of God, for that, says he, falls outside his research and responsibility. He is singularly focused upon the validity and reality of the religious experience for the individual who has been converted. He diverts us from an exploration into the relationship between the faith-state of the individual and any intellectual enquiry. Quoting Leuba on this point again, and ending by reciting a litany of faith-states, James indicates that the "sense of truth" has made the world new for the converted individual, ending with comments about the permanency of conversion and instances of lapses to the faith-state.

****

Lectures XI, XII, & XIII Saintliness

The collective name for the ripe fruits of religion in a character is Saintliness. The saintly character is the character for which spiritual emotions are the habitual centre of the personal energy; and there is a certain composite photograph of universal saintliness, the same in all religions, of which the features can easily be traced. ... Since Hindu fakirs, Buddhist monks, and Mohammedan dervishes unite with Jesuits and Franciscans in idealizing poverty as the loftiest individual state, it is worth while to examine it on spiritual grounds for such seemingly unnatural opinion.

Having dwelt at length on the state of "conversion," James now for three full lectures addresses himself to the elevated state of the religiously converted person to what is called "saintliness," commencing with an extended and elaborately detailed characterization of Sainte-Beuve as relates to the "state of grace" in the converted person's life. James enumerates and describes the types of traits among the converted with special reference to the balancing of "impulses and inhibitions" which characterize and burden the converted person approaching saintliness, characteristics that spread the gamut from sovereign excitement to irascibility, noting the range of excitement experiences within the conversion phenomenon. The saintly life, says James, is under the sovereign rule and governance of the spiritual stimulation which comes with conversion which, in some instances, stifles the more human senses and impulses. Where some saints of history have lived lives apparently completely, or nearly so, devoid of the basic human impulses, James suggests that this phenomenon has probably resulted from subconscious influences blocking normal needs and drives including, as some saints have indicated, putting in place artificial mechanisms for blocking such impulses. These are often considered "characteristics of saintliness," and James itemizes them for discussion. There is the sense of reality of a Higher power, an apparent abiding sense of peace of mind, a strong tendency to charity, equanimity, and fortitude in living the saintly life. As he has discussed in a much earlier lecture, there is an apparent connection of the saintly life with an abiding sense of relaxation, stress-free existence and purity of heart combined with a commitment to asceticism, obedience, and poverty imposed by the religious community or church. There is some question regarding the sentiments of democracy and humanity within the context and matrix of this constellation of experiences in the saintly life, all of which do usually lead to an elevated sense of religiously higher excitements than is had by the normal religious person.

****

Lectures XIV & XV The Value of Saintliness

Not only the cruelty, but the paltriness of character of the gods believed in by earlier centuries also strikes later centuries with surprise. We shall see examples of it in the annals of Catholic saintship which make us rub our Protestant eyes. Ritual worship in general appears to the modern transcendentalist, as well as to the ultra-puritanical type of mind, as if addressed to a deity of an almost absurdly childish character, taking delight in toy-shop furniture, tapers and tinsel, costume and mumbling and mummery, and find his 'glory' incomprehensibly enhanced thereby. ... A survey of history shows us that, as a rule, religious geniuses attract disciples, and produce groups of sympathizers. When these groups get strong enough to 'organize' themselves, they become ecclesiastical institutions with corporate ambitions of their own. ... When a religion has become an orthodoxy, its day of inwardness is over: the spring is dry; the faithful live at second hand exclusively and stone the prophets I their turn. ... When Luther, in his immense manly way, swept off by a stroke of his hand the very notion of a debit and credit account kept on individuals by the Almighty, he stretched the soul's imagination and saved theology from puerility. ... St. Paul long ago made our ancestors familiar with the idea that every soul is virtually sacred. ... this belief in the essential sacredness of everyone expresses itself today in all sorts of humane customs, and in a growing aversion to the death penalty and to brutality in punishment. ... Momentarily considered, then, the saint may waste his tenderness and be the dupe and victim of his charitable fever, but the general function of his charity in social evolution is essential.

Once James has established a framework for considering the reality and viability of saintliness as a psychologically worthy topic of enquiry and discussion, he turns specifically to the issue of its value within the human matrix of religious experience. He begins with his standard rule of measure in suggesting that its value to the human community must be determined on the basis of the actions which result from that experience, the "fruits" of saintliness, if you will. Venturing to propose that in this evaluation process there is the need to test the "reality of God" as propounded by the mystic and to discard the "unfit" religions based upon the nature and character of the experiential claims made by such religions, "empiricism," argues James rather persuasively, "is not skepticism," and the enquiry is therefore justified. Distinguishing between individual and tribal religion, the religious mystic is most commonly a loner and the efficacy of the originating experience of a religious movement is corrupted in proportion to its success for followers, not those who have had the experience themselves, but those who follow the one who has, inevitably adulterates the originating mystical experience of the founding saint with extravagances, excessive devoutness, fanaticism, and what James calls "hepatic absorption" in the excesses of purity and charity. Human perfection, not being attainable, is approximated in the saint but misses the mark in the followers so whereas the saint constitutes the stimulus for the religious life among the wider community with excesses of asceticism, which symbolically radiates the heroic life of self-abandonment, the community often responds with the equivalent in the form of militarism and voluntary poverty. The dialectic between saints and strong individuals is discussed, focusing upon the saintly life versus the socially-driven leader of the community, leaders the community often prefer to religious mystics, choosing political governance by the strong leader to a theocracy lead by extremist religious saints. The question of theological truth is raised but not resolved or explored.

****

Lectures XVI & XVII Mysticism

The simplest rudiment of mystical experience would seem to be that deepened sense of the significance of a maxim or formula occasionally sweeps over one. ... The supernaturalism and optimism to which they persuade us may, interpreted in one way or another, be after all the truest of insights into the meaning of this life.

Though James has used the term "mystic" and "mysticism" sparingly but intermittently through the previous 15 lectures, he now turns his attention precisely to the subject of mysticism, beginning with an extended "definitional foray," so as to establish the perimeters of the discussion. There are four marks of the mystic state, says James, and they form a distinct region of human consciousness. Giving examples of their lower levels of existence, he discusses the relationship between mysticism and alcohol and moves on to what he calls "the anaesthetic revelation," known better as religious mysticism. He itemizes and discusses the aspects of nature and the consciousness of God as a "cosmic consciousness," characterizing many of the mystics' own testimonies, not excluding Yoga, the Buddhist mystic, suffism, and with Christian mystics a- plenty. He explores their sense of divine revelation experienced in their mystic states of consciousness and the emotional benefits of the mystic states (called the tonic effects) leading to the mystical *negativa*, the recitation of the negative feature of the mystic state of consciousness. The goal in all mystical traditions is "union with the Divine" or, in some traditions, "union with the Absolute." He discusses the relationship between mysticism and music and draws three conclusions from this exploration into the mystical life: (1) Mystical states carry authority for the mystic personally, (2) such authority is not shared with others, and (3) such authority serves to dissolve the exclusive authority claimed by the rationalistic states of consciousness, thus assuring the "primacy" of the mystical experience as experienced and extrapolated by the mystic personally to the subscribing community of followers.

****

Lecture XVIII Philosophy

I do believe that feeling is the deeper source of religion, and that philosophic and theological formulas are secondary products. ... The spontaneous intellect of man always defines the divine which it feels in ways that harmonize with its temporary intellectual prepossessions. Philosophy can by comparison eliminate the local and the accidental from these definitions. ...Both from dogma and from worship she (a new science) can remove historic incrustations. By confronting the spontaneous religious constructions with the results of natural science, philosophy can also eliminate doctrines that are now known to be scientifically absurd or incongruous. ... Sifting out in this way unworthy formulations, she can leave a residuum of conceptions that at least are possible. ... She can perhaps become the champion of one which she picks out as being the most closely verified or verifiable. ... She can offer mediation between different believers, and help bring about consensus of opinion. ... I do not see why a critical Science of Religions of this sort might not eventually command as general a public adhesion as is commanded by a physical science.

Ever the philosopher even when doing psychology and physiology, James puts forth his philosophical orientation here in a formal and systematic fashion offering, for those interested, a thoroughgoing illustration and demonstration of his system of thought called "pragmatism." Contending that "feeling" in religious experience is primary and must, therefore, take precedence over philosophical considerations which are necessarily secondary, he criticizes "intellectualism" for professing to escape the inevitable subjectivism of religious experience. A theological construction, including dogmatic theology, must be critiqued in its recitation of the attributes of God. "Pragmatism" is the basis upon which "valuation" can be assessed when considering religious behavior and religious testimony. The metaphysical attributes of God as propounded by dogmatic theology have no practical significance in the pragmatic agenda of valuation, and every attempt to "prove" the moral attributes of God and to establish a "systematic" theology fail under scrutiny when valuation is employed as the criterion for viability and utility. He calls into question transcendental idealism as he learned it in Germany and, drawing from John Caird, argues against the utility of that system of thought as "reasoned proof" for God. What philosophy can do in the field of religious studies is to develop a "science of religions" which, interestingly enough, is what much of the philosophy of religion has become in the past fifty years, particularly as a "phenomenology of religion," as expounded by G. Van Der Leeuw.

****

Lecture XIX Other Characteristics

The strength of these aesthetic sentiments makes it rigorously impossible, it seems to me, that Protestantism, however superior in spiritual profundity it may be to Catholicism, should at the present day succeed in making many converts from the more venerable ecclesiasticism. ... The religious phenomenon, studied as an inner fact, and apart from ecclesiastical or theological complications, has shown itself to consist everywhere, and in all its stages, in the consciousness which individuals have of an intercourse between themselves and higher powers with which they feel themselves to e related. ... At all stages of the prayerful life we find the persuasion that in the process of communion energy from on high flows in to meet demand, and becomes operative within the phenomenal world. So long as this operativeness is admitted to be real, it makes no essential difference whether its immediate effects be subjective or objective. The fundamental religious point is that in prayer, spiritual energy, which otherwise would slumber, does become active, and spiritual work of some kind is effected really. ... In persons deep in the religious life, as we have abundantly seen, -- and this is my conclusion, -- the door into this region seems unusually wide open; at any rate, experiences making their entrance through that door have had emphatic influence in shaping religious history.

Anticipating his final lecture, James addresses himself to a variety of topics related to religious phenomena, including the aesthetic elements in religion which had to this point been sadly ignored. He contrasts, as best the untrained scholar can in these situations, the Catholic and the Protestant versions of religious understanding and behavior. He discusses the religious concept of sacrifice and of confession in both major traditions including a nice interlude on the meaning and nature of prayer. Because religion itself claims that spiritual work is effected in and by prayer, he identifies three types and levels of opinion as to what this might actually mean and discusses each degree in some detail. He ventures once again to momentarily discuss "automatism," looking at religious leaders and illustrative characters from Judaism, Islam, and Mormonism, ending with a salvo once again into the nature and scope of the relationship between religious experience and the subconscious.

****

Lecture XX Conclusions

(The Characteristics of the religious life as summarized by James in his concluding Lecture XX.)
1. That the visible world is part of a more spiritual universe from which it draws its chief significance.
2. That union or harmonious relation with that higher universe is our true end.
3. That prayer or inner communion, with the spirit thereof - be that spirit 'God' or 'law' - is a process wherein work is really done, and spiritual energy flows in and produces effects, psychological or material, within the phenomenal world.
4. A new zest which adds itself like a gift to life, and takes the form either of lyrical enchantment or of appeal to earnestness and heroism.
5. An assurance of safety and a temper of peace, and, in relation to others, a preponderance of loving affections.

If we are peevish and jealous, destruction of self must be an element of our religion; why need it be if we are good and sympathetic from the outset? If we are sick souls, we require a religion of deliverance; but why think so much of deliverance, if we are healthy-minded? Unquestionably, some men have the completer experience and the higher vocation, here just as in the social world; but for each man to stay in his own experience, whatever it be, and for others to tolerate him there, is surely best. ... Religion, occupying herself with personal destinies and keeping thus in contact with the only absolute realities which we know, must necessarily play an eternal part in human history. ... When we survey the whole field of religion, we find a greater variety in the thoughts that have prevailed there; but the feelings on the one hand and the conduct on the other are almost always the same, for the Stoic, Christian, and Buddhist saints are practically indistinguishable in their lives. The theories which Religion generates, being thus variable, are secondary; and if you wish to grasp her essence, you must look to the feelings and the conduct as being the more constant elements. ... God is the natural appellation, for us Christians at least, for the supreme reality, so I will call this higher part of the universe by the name of God. ... I only translate into schematic language what I may call the instinctive belief of mankind: God is real since he produces real effects. ... What the more characteristically divine facts are, apart from the actual inflow of energy in the faith-state and the prayer-state, I know not. But the over-belief on which I am ready to make my personal venture is that they exist. ... If asked just where the differences in fact which are due to God's existence come in, I should have to say that in general I have no hypothesis to offer beyond what the phenomenon of 'prayerful communion,' especially when certain kinds of incursion from the subconscious region take part in it, immediately suggests. ... The only thing that it unequivocally testifies to is that we experience union with *something* larger than ourselves and in that union find our greatest peace.

His concluding lecture (only followed in the publication with a "Postscript") functions almost as a potpourri of the entire series. He begins by summarizing the already-discussed-at- length many characteristics of religious experience and behavior, pointing out the radical diversity of religious experiences and traditions in the world, and arguing that such diversity does not impinge upon the meaning and efficacy of the religious experience itself. Diversity does not mean dubious! He makes a strong and mature suggestion for the "science of religions" to function, not as the basis for proclaiming a religious creed but for offering a phenomenologically responsible address to an analysis of the matrix of religious experience and behavior itself. Arguing against the popular secular notion that religion is a primordial vestige of by-gone days of primitive peoples, polished up and marketed by religious institutions as a viable address to the modern world. He suggests that modern science has unfortunately and too hastily discounted the anthropomorphized world of the pre-scientific religious mind, equally discounting the viability of individual and personal experience as a valid basis for assessment of the meaning and purpose of life. He argues, as a scientist, that scientific objects are abstractions and that only individualized experiences are concretely verifiable and real, and religion, by definition and example, does precisely that. Religion offers a deliverance mechanism from a world fraught with uncertainty and intractable ethical dilemmas. Religion functions to provide answers to the ambiguities and uncertainties of life which allow individuals to go on. Religion works, contends James; whether one argues its truthfulness or not is irrelevant so long as it "bears the fruit of peace and tranquility."

****

Postscript

James' concluding remarks provided him with an opportunity to proclaim without fear of interruption or public contradiction things he chose not to say but wished finally to say in the Gifford Lectures of 1902. He restates his own philosophical orientation dealing with the concept of universalistic supernaturalism and argues for the responsible discussion of the use of facts in discussing the existence, uniqueness, and infinity of God, the question of immortality, suggesting that religious experience does not settle these questions but provides opportunities for enquiry, nevertheless. He concludes by stating plainly his own position that the "pluralistic hypothesis is more conformed to common sense" than any other presently recognized system of thought as relates to the "varieties of religious experience."

===============

Note: Owing to the numerous editions of James' Gifford Lectures, published in a number of English-speaking countries and periodically throughout the past century, I have chosen NOT to identify a single "authorized" edition for quoting. Therefore, I have used "illustrative quotes" from various editions but always identifying the Lecture number in which the quote occurs.

CHAPTER TWO

James H. Leuba and *Psychological Origin and Nature of Religion*

Just over a dozen years after the publication of James' Gifford Lectures, J. H. Leuba published the book that would take James' work into a whole new and higher dimension of scientific respectability within the psychological community. Leuba's book, *The Psychological Origin and Nature of Religion* (London: Constable and Company, 1915), constituted a culmination of countless minor and esoteric studies of various religious phenomena by a plethora of psychologists, most being former students of both James and G. Stanley Hall at Harvard, Leuba (1868-1948) being among the most prolific researchers and writers in the field. A Swiss by birth and early education, Leuba studied under G. Stanley Hall at Clark University where he graduated in 1895 and stayed on as a research fellow until moving to Bryn Mawr College to become head of the psychology department (Leuba 1896).

A prolific researcher and writer, he eventually participated in the 1926 International Congress of Psychology in Germany, in which he contributed a paper on a panel he shared with Ernest Jones, Freud's authorized biographer and distinguished psychoanalyst in his own right (Leuba 1926b:729). Of major significance was the fact that Leuba was consistently a student and faculty colleague of E. D. Starbuck, both at Clark under G. Stanley Hall, and at Harvard under William James. The two, Starbuck and Leuba, worked closely together throughout their careers and it was only by chance that Starbuck, rather than Leuba, actually coined the term "psychology of religion" for they both were early and key players in its development. Besides his major books (1915; 1926a), Leuba's significant contribution to the advancement of the study of the psychology of religion as a scientific researcher came when he presented a paper at the Hartford Seminary Foundation's 1926 Congress on the possible contributions of modern psychology to the theory and practice of religion (Leuba 1926a), a gathering of scholars which included Starbuck and Hall as well. Unlike James' work, which argued for the "value of religion" without attempting an assessment as to its etiology, Leuba brought to bear all of the available analytical tools of scientific enquiry into the meaning and nature of human behavioral responses to perceived and experienced encounter with what was thought, by the subject, to be of a "religious" nature. Here was the application of the psychological science of behavior gone well beyond James' sympathetic and empathetic embrace of the *sui generis* character of religious experience. From Leuba onward, the psychology of religion focused upon the empirical evidence of behavior, and the *Psychological Origin and Nature of Religion* (1915) took its place at the head of the class.

James Leuba, a student of William James, but one who moves well beyond James' analysis of religious behavior, produced this little book precisely to scope out the perimeters of what he perceived to certainly be a new field of psychological enquiry coming on the heels of James' Gifford Lectures. Here, Leuba writes six short chapters in a book with less than 100 pages, categorizing his enquiry into (1) The Fundamental Nature of Religion, (2) Three Types of Behaviour* Differentiated, (3) Origin of the Ideas of Ghosts, Nature-Beings, and Gods; (4) Magic and Religion; (5) The Original Emotion of Primitive Religious Life, and (6) Concluding Remarks on the Nature and the Function of Religion.

Selections from *Psychological Origin and Nature of Religion,* by James Leuba, with commentary.

NOTE: In the following, the original text will be printed in *Arial Unicode MS* typestyle (as is this note itself to illustrate) as an easy and aesthetically pleasing way of identifying the primary source paragraphs. The author's commentary will be in *Times New Roman.* It is hoped that this differentiation between the "primary source" and the "commentary" made by use of differing fonts will prove helpful and not disruptive to the reader. *I have also chosen to use a quadruple asterisk (****) to separate the primary text from the commentary.*

Chapter I The Fundamental Nature of Religion

The opinions advanced in this essay and the arguments with which they are supported will be more readily appreciated if the fundamental nature of Religion is set forth in a few introductory pages. The students of Religion have usually been content to describe it either in intellectual or in affective terms. 'This particular idea or belief,' or 'this particular feeling or emotion,' is, they have said, 'the essence' or the 'vital element' of Religion. So that most of the hundreds of definitions which have been proposed fall into two classes. We have, on the one hand, the definitions of Spencer, Max Muller, Romanes, Goblet d'Alviella, and others, for whom Religion is 'the recognition of a mystery pressing for interpretation,' or 'a department of thought,' or 'a belief in superhuman beings'; and, on the other, the formulas of Schleiermacher, the Ritschlian theologians, Tiele, etc., who hold that Religion is 'a feeling of absolute dependence upon God,' or 'that pure and reverential disposition or frame of mind we call piety.' According to Tiele, 'the essence of piety, and, therefore, the essence of Religion, is adoration.'

It will be another dozen years before Freud writes his little classic, *The Future of an Illusion*, wherein he pursues relentlessly the application of psychoanalytic theory to the study of the origins of religion. But Leuba has chosen already to take on that discussion from a more traditionalist psychological perspective, challenging anthropology and philosophy alike in limiting "religion" too exclusivistically to either "emotional" or "cognitive" characteristics. Leuba wishes to argue for a broader, more psychologically sophisticated multi-tiered definition of religious experience and behavior. Religion, he argues, is not merely or simply a belief in superhuman beings as portrayed in the writings of Spencer and Muller and others, nor, he argues further, is it strictly and solely a "feeling" or "emotional affectation," according to the theological school of Schleiermacher (the father of modern liberal Protestant theology).

****

To-day it has become customary to admit that 'in Religion all sides of the personality participate. Will, feeling, and intelligence are necessary and inseparable constituents of Religion.' But statements such as this one do not necessarily imply a correct understanding of the functional relation of the three aspects of psychic life. (In looking at the critical texts of such scholars as Max Muller and Schleiermacher and Feuerbach), the reader discovers that the opinion(s) defend 'Religion as the outcome of an effort to explain all things -- physical, metaphysical, and moral -- by analogies drawn from human society, imaginatively and symbolically considered. In short, it is a universal, sociological hypothesis, mythical in form.' What is this but once more the intellectualistic position? Religion arising from an effort to explain; Religion as hypothesis! It is Herbert Spencer over again with an additional statement concerning the way in which man attempt to explain 'the mystery pressing for interpretation.'

The maturing thought of the investigative psychologist, says Leuba, has come to a sound understanding that the core of religious experience and behavior includes the whole dynamic of the human personality, not just the cognitive nor just the emotive dimensions of personhood. Leuba will suggest in more detail later that religion calls upon the tripartite dynamic of willing, feeling, and thinking, not just one of these characteristics, thus refuting the tendency at the time (in the social and behavioral sciences) to reduce religion to a socially-induced worldview and ethos, however sophisticated the presentation in myth and symbol it might have been perpetrated on society. Religion, in essence, is not merely an attempt of the untutored mind to explain the way things are and how they came to be, even if these are legitimate features of religious cognizance.

****

It must be admitted, however, that several of the more

recent definitions have completely broken with this bad psychology. Among these are those of J. G. Frazer, of A. Sabatier, and of William James. The first understands by Religion 'propitiation, or conciliation of powers superior to man, which are believed to direct and control the course of nature and of human life.' For Sabatier, Religion 'is a commerce, a conscious and willed relation into which the soul in distress enters with the mysterious power or which it feels that it and its destiny depend.' William James (says) ' ... one might say that religious life consists in the belief that there is an unseen order, and that our supreme good lies in harmoniously adjusting ourselves thereto.' ... But the battle against intellectualistic and affectivity conceptions of Religion is not yet won. The recent definitions ... show only too clearly how strong the tendency remains to identify Religion with some feeling or emotion.

The bad psychology, or at least the less mature psychological insights into religious experience and behavior, suggests Leuba, have been surpassed by the works of such anthropologists as Sir James Frazer and psychologists such as William James. These maturing anthropological insights, based usually upon tribal societies described in ethnographic studies which were just beginning to appear in literature, emphasized the centrality of a belief in super- human powers, whether personal or impersonal, resulting in ritual acts of propitiation or reconciliation when individuals and societies felt themselves in jeopardy or danger, or in need of outside and superior assistance in dealing with the varieties of life. This reliance upon an "unseen order" of superior power and intellect constitutes a central feature in religious consciousness. The danger in these analyses is, still, according to Leuba, too intellectualistically focused upon "religion as feeling."

****

As the amazing discrepancies and contradictions offered by authorized definitions of Religion arise, in my opinion, primarily from a faulty psychology, a moment may profitably be devoted to an unethical statement of the present teaching of that science upon the relation existing between the three acknowledged modes of consciousness -- willing, feeling, and thinking. Aristotle characterized man as *thinking-desire*. In swinging back from Intellectualism to Voluntarism, modern psychology has accepted the fundamental truth excellently expressed by the Greek philosopher. (In his *Ethics*, Aristotle wrote) 'Will is not merely a function which sometimes accrues to consciousness, and is sometimes lacking; it is an integral property of consciousness.' … 'The one thing that stands out,' says Professor Dewey, 'is that thinking is inquiry, and that knowledge as science is the outcome of systematically directed inquiry.' … It is *the intention, the purpose,* which makes thought what it is; that is to say, significant. We think because we will. Thought does not exist for itself; it is the instrument of desire.

The "faulty psychology" implicit in these reductionistic definitions can be improved by drawing from the insights of Aristotle and early Greek philosophy, says Leuba. An informed and sophisticated modern psychology recognizes the modes of consciousness to not be merely reduced to "feeling" or "emotion" but consisting of willing and thinking as well. Aristotle and the early Greeks called this "thinking-desire." Dewey, joining with James and Leuba and other modern psychologists, will have us know that the thinking inclination and capacity of the human person involves inquiry, and inquiry is motivated by desire. We think because we will to think, and our thinking is driven by our desire, a desire to know, to be, to have. To reduce religion to merely a feeling is to cut it off from the broader and deeper dynamic of human experience involving willing and thinking as well as feeling.

****

The psychologist speaks, therefore, of the *instrumental* character of thought, and considers cognition to be a function of conduct. The mastery of desire over thought is abundantly illustrated in the history of belief, and nowhere so strikingly as in Religion. ... As to sentiments and emotions, they involve ideas and conative elements in addition to sensations and feelings. An emotion is a reaction, the response of an organism to a situation. It is a form of action. Aristotle's characterisation of man is thus seen to be adequate; it does not leave out the feelings, as it might seem at first. Thinking-desire includes the affection since it is included in desire. Every pulse of consciousness is psychically compounded of will, feeling, and thought.

Modern psychology, Leuba would have us understand, is intent upon mobilizing the instrumental or action quality of thought, not holding it hostage merely to self-reflective cognition. The relationship between thought and action and thought and desire is illustrated profoundly and profusely in the history of religious experience and behavior. Religious emotions, says he, are derivatives of cognitive activity, thought processes, as well as and in complimentarity to feelings and emotions. Feeling is a central, but not *the* central, part of religious experience, for it derives from and compliments thought, ideation, cognition, and self-reflectivity.

****

This, then, is the double teaching of psychology in this matter: (1) Will, feeling, and thought enter in some degree into every moment of consciousness which can be looked upon as an actuality, and not merely as an abstraction; they are necessary constituents of consciousness. The unit of conscious life is neither thought, nor feeling, nor will, but all three in movement towards an object. (2) The will is primal; or, in other words, conscious life is always oriented towards something to be secured or avoided immediately or ultimately. If, with this conception in mind, we turn to Religion, we shall understand it to be compounded of will, thought and feeling ... And it will, moreover, be clear that a purpose or an ideal, i.e., something to be attained or maintained, must always be at the root of it. The outcome of the application of current psychological teaching to religious life is, then, to lead us to regard Religion as a particular kind of activity, as a mode or type of behaviour, and to make it as impossible for us to identify it with a particular emotion or with a particular belief, as it would be to identify, let us say, family life with affection, or to define trade as 'belief in the productivity of exchange'; or commerce as 'geed touched with a feeling of dependence upon society.'

Neither anthropology nor philosophy has brought us to this deeper understanding of the role and function of willing, feeling, and thinking in the matrix of religious experience and behavior. It is modern psychology which has done so, for earlier schools of anthropology have focused too exclusively upon the "feelings and emotions" of tribal societies, and philosophy, provoked by theological reflection, has over-emphasized cognitive thought processes, i.e., religion as idea and explanation. Modern psychology has placed willing, feeling, and thinking as central components of human consciousness, not just as mere abstractions. The emphasis is upon the integrality of these three characteristics of human cognition. The primeval nature of human will is demonstrated in early human desire to know and control, and there is no better illustration than in the world of religion. Religion is action, it is a complex of behavioral configurations, including objective movement in ritual, and subjective reflection in myth and symbol. It is not reducible to one form of behavior or one ideational configuration of human thought. It is, indeed, a consummate coagulation of willing, thinking, and feeling in response to a desire to know from whence we came and whither we go.

****

In speaking of Religion as an activity, or as a type of behaviour, I would not be understood to exclude from it whatever does not express itself in overt acts, in rites of propitiation, submission, or adoration ... For (man's) relations which gods, or their impersonal substitutes, may not have any visible form; they may remain purely subjective and none the less exercise a definite guiding and inspiring influence over his life. The adjectives *passive* and *active* might be used to separate amorphous from organized Religion, i.e., the feeling-attitude from the behavior. 'Passive," used in this connection, would mean simply that the person does not actively seek those advantages the gods might procure, but is content to be acted upon by them. *Unorganised religiosity* must be, it seems, the necessary precursor of organized Religion; it is its larval stage. But it does not by any means disappear from society when a system of definite relations with gods, or with impersonal sources of religious inspiration, has been developed. In all societies there is always a large number of people who live in the limbo of organized Religion. They are open to the influence of religious agents, in which they believe more or less cold-heartedly, without ever entering into definite and fixed relations with them.

Religion is, indeed, an activity, a behavioral complex of human responses to thought or imagined worlds of supernaturalism, but not solely action, not only behavioral in nature. Religion also suggests a subjective component wherein, even in the absence of overt ritual actions, there is the function of religious awareness on the part of the individual, a subjective passivity which, nevertheless, affects and influences human behavior and thought. There is both "passivity" and "activity" in religion, says Leuba. "Passivity," he suggests, implies a submission to or subjective resignation under the mandate of a religious worldview without implying or requiring a behavioral response, resulting in what Leuba suggests is "unorganized religiosity." All societies, argues Leuba, have a large component of its constituency, whether simple villagers or industrialized modern society dwellers, who live under the mandate of religion without themselves responding to its demands.

****

CHAPTER II Three Types of Behaviour Differentiated

In his dealings with the different kinds of objects or forces with which he is, or thinks himself, in relation, man has developed three distinct types of behaviour. ... We may designate them as -- (1) The mechanical behaviour, (2) The coercitive behaviour, or Magic, and (3) The *anthropopathic behaviour, which includes Religion. The mechanical behaviour differs from the anthropopathy by the absence of any reference to personal beings. ... If science is to be provided with an ancestor, and only with one, it should be this first type of behaviour rather than Magic. ... Magic separates itself, on the one hand, from the mechanical behaviour by the absence of implied quantitative relations, and, on the other hand, from anthropopathy behaviour by the failure to use means of personal influence; punishment and reward are just as foreign to Magic as to mechanical behaviour. ... As one ascends from the lowest stages of culture, Magic gradually loses official recognition. ... (However) So-called 'religious' practices may really be magical. The cross, the rosary, relics, and other accessories of Religion, acquire in the mind of many Christians a power of the coercitive type; that is, for instance, the case when the sign of the cross, of itself, without the mediation of God or Saint, is felt to have power; or when 'saying one's beads' is held to possess a curative virtue of the kind ascribed to sacred relics by the superstitious.

*NOTE: Anthropopathy is the attribution of human emotion to a non-human being, generally a god. By comparison, the term anthropomorphism originally referred to the attribution of human *form* to a non- human being -- although in modern usage, anthropomorphism has come to encompass both meanings.

Ever the psychologist, Leuba is eager to nuance the behavioral matrices of religious experience by differentiating what he considers to be three related but distinct types of human behavior. Detailing them at length with countless examples and illustrations, he is keen to label behavior specifically by these terms -- mechanical, coercive, and anthropomorphic. The first is a specifically non-human referential and, therefore, says he, mechanical behavior constitutes the ancestor to what is today modern science. Coercive behavior is synonymous with magic as it does not imply any use of a "reasonable" explanation for the action done and the result found. Furthermore, it is distinct from "religion" in that it employs no consequential results such as punishment or reward and, suggests Leuba, as one moves from less complex to greater complex cultures, magic itself becomes decreasingly important and operative within the worldview of those peoples. That is not to say, in closing this recitation of the three types of behavior, that religious behavior does not infrequently carry with it strong instances of magic and superstition (and he recites numerous examples within Christianity for illustration).

****

It has been the habit of most students of the origin of Religion to concern themselves exclusively with the origin of the god-idea, as if belief in the existence of gods was identical with Religion. They have ignored its other essential components: the motives or desires and the feelings, as well as the means by which, in Religion, the gratification of desire is sought. ... It is the Agent or the Power with which man thinks himself in relation, and through whom he endeavours to secure the gratification of his desires, which alone is distinctive of religious life. ... it is assumed that the god-concept precedes, in the mind of man, the establishment of Religion. This opinion is ... the correct one.

Leuba is eager to emphasize the tripartite character of human experience and behavior as a composite of willing, feeling, and thinking. In every instance of psychological assessment and analysis, these three components of the human person must always be present. Religion's origin is not merely the "god-idea," but is a composition of coagulated components of desire and feelings, thought and action.

****

Our first problem is to discover how Religion arose, and what psychological capacities and conceptions it implies. A comparative study of the three modes of behaviour (willing, thinking, feeling) is, after all, the shortest way of gaining a satisfactory understanding of the origin of Religion. (A) point of psychology: animals establish habits under the guidance of immediate results while man develops the magical art and Religion *despite* the usual absence of the results sought after. The very possibility of deceiving himself reveals the superiority of man over animals, for self-deception requires a degree of independence from sense-observation, a capacity of constructive imagination, a susceptibility to auto-suggestion, to be to found in animals.

In the absence of a faith-based science, which is an impossibility, and, therefore, the absence of a theologically driven psychology, modern science must begin its analysis of religion with origins -- its historical origins and the psychological components within the human species which brought religion about. Religion, naturally, grew out of a need, a desire, an experience, and a self-reflective assessment of the human encounter with the external world. Religion did not just happen; it did not fall from the sky. It arose within the experiential matrix of human emotion, thought, and desire. Whereas animals respond on the basis of instincts, the human animal has a capacity for self-deception, an ability to postpone and even to deny sense observations owing to the human inclination to deny what is not desirable, and to claim ownership over that which is not yet owned. Whether the human animal employs self-deception in the form of magic or religion, his ability to conjure up and respond to auto-suggested images is boundless.

****

The intended results of the gains to be credited to the practice of Magic and of Religion are (1) The gratification of the lust for power. The Magician and the Priest are mediators between superior, mysterious powers and their fellow-men. The sense of mastery over, or communion with, these powers, and the respect and fear with which Magicians and Priests are regarded, are, of themselves, almost sufficient to keep up these practices. (2) Both these modes of behavior, but especially Magic, appeal to the gambling instinct. (3) Less obvious, perhaps, than the preceding advantages, but not less valuable, is the general mental stimulation induced by magic and Religion. Magic is the great social play of the savage.

Both magic and religion, as human products created by self-deception and auto-suggestion, serve more than one function and are found universally within every human community. They function, first, for the gratification of the lust for power within the human character, power to rule the environment, both physical and social. Both magicians and clergy attempt to exercise power through the use of their presumed mastery over the world and their hidden abilities at communion with the powers outside normal human channels of relationship. Besides the wielding of power over the community and individuals within it, both magic and religion seem to fill the gambling instinct within the human heart as well as the sense of play and the fostering of excitement in conjuring the powers of the super-human for manipulation of the environment of world and people.

****

CHAPTER III Origin of the Ideas of Ghosts, Nature-Beings and Gods

Every savage tribe known to us has already passed beyond the naturistic stage of development. The living savages believe in ghosts, in spirits, and all of them, perhaps, also in particular spirits elevated to the dignity of gods. Whence these ideas of unseen personal beings? They may be traced to four independent sources. (1) States of temporary loss of

> consciousness -- trances, swoons, sleep, etc. -- seem in themselves sufficient to suggest to ignorant observers the existence of 'doubles,' i.e., of beings dwelling within the body, animating it, and able to absent themselves from it for a time or permanently. The belief in a second life of the dead would also spring easily enough from these observations. (2) Apparitions in sleep, in the hallucinations of fever, of insanity, etc., of persons still living or dead, seem also sufficient to lead to a belief in ghosts and in survival after death. These two distinct classes of facts have no doubt co-operated in the production of the belief in ghosts, so that I shall refer to them in the sequel as the double origin of the ghost-belief. Echoes, and reflections in water and in polished surfaces may have played a subsidiary role in establishing, or confirming, the belief in ghosts and in spirits. (3) The third independent source of belief in unseen personal agents is the *spontaneous personification of striking natural phenomena, storms, tornadoes, thunder, sudden spring-vegitation, etc.* ... What we mean to assert here is merely that the systematized belief can have arisen out of the impulsive and occasional personification of awe-striking and frightening spectacles. (4) *The necessity of a Maker is, no doubt, borne in upon the savage at a very early time,* not upon every member of a tribe, but upon some peculiarly gifted individual, who imparts to his fellows the awe-striking idea of a mysterious, all-powerful Creator.

Leuba, being a man of his time, refers to traditional societies in the then acceptable nomenclature of "savage tribes," terms no longer acceptable yet still understandable today. He believed, as did his academic peers of the time, that there exists nowhere on earth a society of people that are not expressive of a spirit-centered religious sensibility. Whereas once it was believed by earlier anthropologists that pre-spirit consciousness conjured a "naturalistic" notion of power in the world, now only belief in spirits, ghosts, etc., exist and the origins of these unseen spiritual non-human entities come from several sources. First, variations on differing levels of consciousness, including trances and swooning, have led to a belief in spiritual powers and life after death among traditional societies of "primitive" peoples. Also, dream states, hallucinations due to illness and fever, and even insanity have fostered spiritual beliefs and hope and expectations regarding the dead and life after death. Not least as a source of belief in the spiritual dynamics of human life is the presence of unexplained and unexplainable natural disasters, events, and happenings such as storms, thunder, lightning, etc. Finally, all of these things must have a "cause," there must be a "source," someone or something must "make" these things happen, whether bad or good, serviceable or disastrous to the community. The one who claims to control them, whether magician or priest, is the one to whom the community must look for safety and understanding. The one who wields this power over the community is destined to rule that community with more stories, elaborate explanations, and sophisticated conjuring rituals whereby this special person controls the Maker of these things, the Creator of the Universe, The God or pantheon of gods which rule the world and are at the beck and call of the conjuror personally, whether magician or priest.

****

Belief in the existence of unseen, anthropopathy beings is not Religion. It is only when man enters into relation with them that Religion comes into existence. The passage from the animistic interpretation of nature, or from the merely belief in ghosts, or in a creator, to Active Religion is not to be taken as a matter of course, fir it may require on the one hand, as we have said, a transformation of the man-like or animal-like unseen beings, such as will make entering into relation with them possible and worth while, and, on the other, the invention of ways an means to that end, or, at least, the adaptation of old habits of behaviour to the requirements of the new relation. ... That a belief in ghosts may coincide with only a pre-religious stage of culture is not a mere supposition. There are tribes (according to anthropologist Alfred William Howitt in his *The Native Tribes of South-East Australia, 1904/London: Macmillan),* in South-East Australia among which it is customary to make fires in the graves, and to place in them water, food, and weapons. Yet we are told that these people have no system of propitiation or of worship. It appears probable that in certain instances of this sort, the only motive of action is benevolence. They wish the ghost to be able to warm himself, eat, drink, and defend himself against enemies. ... I see here an instance of what I have called *Passive Religion.*

Leuba is at his best when he nuances human experience in the realm of emotion and cognition, feeling and thinking. It is not, says he, the belief in the unseen and its multiplicity of manifestations which is the origin and nature of religion. Many peoples have acknowledged the existence of those natural occurrences which have seemingly no reasonable explanation for occurring. It is the individual and communities which establish a relationship to these experiences that results in the formation of religion. It is the leader of the community who purports to explain the meaning and nature of these natural events and deeply felt human experiences in terms of his and their relationship to the spirit world behind these events that leads to the creation of religion. The eventual institutionalization of ritual, myth, and symbol, controlled by the conjuror, and imposed upon the community results in the gradual but inevitable emergence of faith-based communities with their rules of conduct and obedience. Where there is no allegiance to the conjuror's portrayal of the relationship which he and they have with the spirit world, there is no formalized religion; there is only the passivity of religiosity according to Leuba, a recognition of the presence of the spiritual realities without an obligation to respond to or establish a relationship with them. When response and relationship occur, religion of an active nature is born, ushering in the institutionalization process.

****

CHAPTER IV Magic and Religion

In the preceding section, I have ... attempted to single out the psychological traits whose presence in man accounts for his possession of Religion and Magic. The relation obtaining between

Magic and Religion has been variously understood. Most authorities hold that Magic preceded Religion, and that they are in some way genetically related. In the following pages we shall argue in support of two opinions: (1) the primary forms of Magic probably antedated Religion; (2) whether Magic antedated Religion or not, Religion arose independently of Magic, they are different in principle and independent in origin. ... Three classifications of Magic we will consider ... *Class I* is characterized by the absence of any idea of a power belonging to the operator or his instrument and passing from either one of them to the object of the magical art. To this class belong many instances of so-called sympathetic Magic; a good many of the taboo customs; most charms; the casting of lots,; most modern superstitions... *Class 2* A power, not itself personal, is supposed to belong to the magician, to his instrument, or to particular substances, and to pass into, or act upon, the object. ... *Class 3* Perhaps a special class should be made of the cases in which the magician feels as if his will-effort was the efficient factor. This is often true of spells, of incantations, and of solemn curses.

Having versed himself rather extensively in the ethnographic documents evidenced in the field notes produced by contemporary anthropologists of the time as relates to the lives of traditional societies (what Leuba and the academic world at the time unfortunately referred to as "savage tribes"), Leuba set out to both recite the origin and characteristics of magic and religion and to explain the complexity of their relationship to each other. Contrary to popular scholarly opinion within the anthropological community of the time, Leuba did not believe that religion was a "natural development" of magic but that, rather, though they shared similar features in responding to the demands of the human community for explanation and manipulation of their environment, magic may have predated religion but was not its natural precursor. Leuba suggests that there are three classifications for magic worthy of our attention. First is characterized by no notion of power within the conjuror himself; second is the power of magic which is, indeed, the sole possession of the conjuror and no one else but over which he himself is not the proprietor; and third, that unique classification of magic which, in the mind of the conjuror, is endemic to his own person, solely his and resulting from who he is as magician. In short, the three classifications of magic according to Leuba are: (1) power not belonging to the magician but known to him; (2) power over which he is the steward but which is not coterminous with his person; and (3) power which is inseparable from the magician himself. The similarities of the magician and the priest were mentioned and worthy of examination, but were not pursued by Leuba at this juncture.

****

According to J. H. Frazer (*The Golden Bough),* 'Magic is nothing but a mistaken application of the very simplest and most elementary process of the mind, namely, the association of ideas by virtue of resemblance or contiguity.' ... 'Among the aborigines of Australia,' Frazer suggests, 'the rudest savages as to whom we possess accurate information, Magic is universally practiced, whereas Religion, in the sense of a propitiation or conciliation of the higher powers, seems to be nearly unknown. Roughly speaking, all men in Australia are magicians, but not one is a priest ...'

This little vignette has been included here owing to its clarity and simplicity and, recognizing who Sir James Frazer was as an Oxford scholar and anthropological authority, the statement merits our careful acknowledgment. The suggestion that magic is merely a misunderstanding of natural processes and a misapplication of ideas to action reduces magic to something less than what we have come to expect of religious experience and behavior. Using the Australian aborigines as the best ethnographic illustration of his point, Sir James points out the presence and function of magic amongst these traditional peoples but the singular absence of "religion," if by which we mean experiences and ideas related to a superpower to which or to whom propitiation and conciliation action is required or desirable from the human person and community.

****

The Independence of Religion from Magic. The following psychological arguments appear to me to go a long way towards proving that *magical behaviour has had an origin independent of the animistic belief,* and that some of its forms, at least, antedated it, and therefore also Religion. (a) The absorbing interest found by young children in the *use* of things, and their complete indifference at first to the *modus operandi*, point, it would seem, to a stage in human development at which the explanation of things is not yet desire. It is well known that long before a child asks 'how?' he wearies his guardians with the question, 'what for?' ... A mental attitude such as this would make Religion impossible, while it would provide the essential condition for a Magic of our first class. (b) Children like to amuse themselves by setting up prohibitions and backing them up with threats of punishment. 'If you do this,' they will say, 'that will happen to you.' The 'this' and the 'that' have usually no logical connection with each other, neither is there in the mind of the child any thought of a particular kind of power, or agent, meting out the punishment. This kind of play is strikingly similar to a large number of magical practices. (c) It is a fact of common observation that in passionate moments, men of every degree of culture act, in the absence of the object of their passion, more or less as if it was present. ... by the sick-bed of one beloved, one must do something, however useless to him. ... The less a person is under the control of reason, the more likely is he, not only to yield to promptings of this order, but also to be seduced by his wish into a belief in their efficacy. ... the effect of repetition, and of the tribal sanction obtained by magical customs ... then to make doubt and criticism next to impossible.

Leuba proposes three illustrative examples of why he wishes, with his psychology colleagues in their dialogue with ethnographers and anthropologists of primitive religions, to make an indisputable distinction between magic and religion, emphasizing specifically that magic is not necessarily a precursor of religion, nor religion a sophisticated development of magic. Granted the similarities of character in both when found in traditional societies, both magic and religion ,can and do stand alone in the absence of the other without any loss of their unique integrity as behavioral matrices within the human community. First, by way of illustrating his argument, Leuba, with his contemporaries within the psychological and anthropological community, assumed the similarity of mental function of the traditionalist and the modern child. Today, this parallel is essentially discounted, but at the time it was more or less an unchallenged domain assumption. Therefore, Leuba's first point as to the child's (and, thus, the "savage's") early disinterest in the "what for" of function but rather only the "how" of a thing reflects the human susceptibility to "magic" as the mechanism for doing a thing without the necessity of the "reason" behind it. Second, suggests Leuba, children (like the "savage") are prone to establish rules of rewards and punishments regarding action for which there is no logical connection between the deed and the results, not unlike magical actions. Finally, the presence of "phantom" experiences is of a "thing in its absence," a feeling the presence of a thing or idea even amidst the realization of its not being really physically present at the time. Thus, says Leuba, the "how" of an action, the disconnect between deed and reward, and the experienced reality of phantom power, these phenomena (deed and reward) characterize magic but not necessarily religion.

****

However closely interwoven they may be, Magic and Religion remain distinct ... Our conclusions are ... that Magic has had an independent origin, that it very probably antedated Religion, and that they associate for common purposes without ever fusing, for they are referable to different principles. ... what magic shares with science is not the belief in the fundamental principle ... but the desire to gain the mastery over the powers of nature and the practice of the experimental method. ... The essential presupposition of science -- the one that differentiates it alike from Magic and from Religion -- is the acknowledgment of definite and constant *quantitative* relationships between causes and effects, relations which completely exclude the personal element and the occult.

Religion advances the human capacity to offer explanations for happenings in the world, whereas magic simply demonstrates them without explanation. Thus, the improvement on each of three distinguishing characteristics of magic -- the how, the disconnect, and the phantom experience -- is easily demonstrated through traditional as well as contemporary religious experience and behavior. The "what for" rather than merely the "how" of an action is for the religious person central, as is the explanation of the connection between an action and its reward or punishment. The experience of a thing without it actually being present is, of course, central to religion and in all three of these examples, religion provides a simple yet operative explanation by using the superhuman power referent! These things can all be explained on the basis of a belief in a god or the experience of the reality of a super power source in the universe. Magic, rather than religion, is akin to science and its precursor owing to both their desire to master the universe by the experimental method but science, unlike either magic or religion, seeks a reasoned explanation of cause and effect (magic cares nothing for it and religion says it comes from god) in the specific absence of the personal element of human involvement. Magic and religion insist upon the personal.

****

CHAPTER V THE Original Emotion of Primitive Religious Life

The failure to recognise in Religion three functionally related constituents -- willing, feeling, and thought -- is responsible for a confusing use of the term 'origin.' Some have said that Religion began with the belief in superhuman, mysterious beings; others that it had its origin in the emotional life, and these usually specified fear; while a third group have declared that its genesis is to be found in the will-to-live. ... Two opposed opinions divide the field. The more widely held is that fear is the beginning of Religion; the other, accepted by a small but weighty minority, that it has its origin in a loving reverence for known gods.' ... these two views, instead of opposing, supplement each other. ... 'Fear begets gods,' said Lucretius. ... fear are presents only one of the three constituents of Religion, that it is not in virtue of a particular quality or property that fear is the primitive emotional form of Religion ... Religion requires nothing found in fear that is not also present in other emotions ... The place of fear in primitive Religion is, then, due not to its intrinsic qualities, but simply to circumstances which made it appear first as a well-organized emotion vitally connected with the maintenance of life.

Showing his reliance upon the Greek philosophers, and particularly Aristotle, in proposing the origin of religion to center in the tripartite human characteristics of willing, feeling, and thinking, Leuba points to the abiding two schools of competing thought regarding religious origins. One school argues that religion begins with a belief in a superior power, the mysterious superhuman entities, whereas the other argues for the primacy of primordial fears conjured in the untutored mind of the primitive "savage." A third school, however, proposes a human drive known as the "will-to-live" as the abiding feature of religious origins. A fourth and final school, dear to Leuba's thought, is that small group of scholars who wish to emphasis awe, wonder, and reverence for a loving deity, conjured and experienced in the human community itself which is devoid of fear but infused with loving reference. Whereas Lucretius suggests that "fear begets gods," Leuba would counter by saying that love also begets gods. Nothing in the experience of fear itself implies, suggests, or requires a belief in a superhuman power but the primitive experience in the world devoid of explanations as to the varieties of life created a situation in which fear and belief were conjoined without being synonymous. Love and belief might, suggests Leuba, likewise converge in producing religion.

****

In certain peoples a feeling of dependence upon benevolent gods, regarded probably as Creators and all-fathers, eliciting admiration rather than fear or selfish desire, would have characterized its beginnings ... W. Robertson Smith in his *The Religion of the Semites (1901),* denies that the attempt to appease evil begins is the foundation of Religion. 'From the earliest times religion, as distinct from magic or sorcery, addresses itself to kindred and friendly beings, who may indeed be angry with their people for a time, but are always placable except to the enemies of their worshippers or to renegade members of the community. It is not with a vague fear of unknown powers but with a loving reverence for known gods who are knit to their worshippers by strong bonds of kinship, that religion, in the only sense of the word, begins.' ... What he denies is that the attempt to propitiate, in dread, evil spirits, is Religion. ... Negative Religion may be used to designate man's dealings with radically bad spirits, and Positive Religion his relations with fundamentally benevolent ones. ... The more striking development of religious life is the gradual substitution of love for fear in worship. This is one more reason for not completely dissociating the propitiation of evil spirits from the worship of kindly gods.

Just as a life situation fraught with danger from the environment, deadly predators, severe weather conditions, hunger, cold and heat, etc., would naturally nurture an abiding fear of what life held in store for the individual and the community in such life situations, a different life situation wherein there were no deadly predators, the absence of severe weather, plenty of food and comfortable environment might just as readily foster a sense of well-being, satisfaction, and contentment in the world. Either fear or contentment, therefore, could be sources of religious sensibilities -- a loving god or a vengeful god are equally possible, viable, and operative. These options, says W. Robertson Smith (1901) in his little classic on the Semites of Palestine, are both in evidence in the world -- the one a "negative" religious experience and expression and the other a "positive" one. Yet and still, says Leuba, the ultimate primacy of fear over love and the practice of propitiation to the evil powers over the worship of the kindly powers is a universal characteristic of religion. In these situations, it does seem that fear is more powerful than love when speaking of religion, so that even when a "loving god" is promoted by the priests, there is always the "vengeful god" standing in the shadows.

****

CHAPTER VI Concluding Remarks on the Nature and the Function of Religion

The organized, historical Religions are sufficiently described, in their objective aspect, as systems of practical relations with unseen, hyper human, and personal Beings. ... Judged according to this definition, several savage tribes and a very large number of persons among civilized peoples would have to be accounted non-religious. Most of them may, however, lay claim to what we have called Passive Religiosity. ... we propose to give increased precision and coherence to the conception of Religion ... (1) Passive and (2) Godless Religions. ... (Howitt on Australian religions) 'If Religion is defined as being the formulated worship of a divinity, then these savages (Australian aborigines) have no Religion; but I venture to assert that it can be no longer maintained that they have no belief which can be called Religion, that is, in the sense of beliefs which govern tribal and individual morality under a supernatural sanction.' ... What has 'the speculative faculty' to do with Religion? ... The outcome of speculative thinking is *philosophy* of which Religion may make use, but that is not a reason for confusing it with philosophy. The religious experience consists not in seeking to understand God, but in fearing Him, in feeding upon Him, in finding strength and joy in Him. If believers in Ruling Powers may be called religious, it is not because they possess *an idea* of these powers, but in virtue of the guiding and inspiring influence these powers exert upon them.

As psychologist, Leuba is eager to point to the nature and

function of human behavior and a definition of religion, especially the historic institutionalized forms of religious belief and practice, he is keen to characterize as a system built upon a belief in the superhuman powers of the gods. In doing so, he is quick to point out that in many societies there is a large number of people who themselves do not practice nor, indeed, even appear to experience the driving force of such religious sensibilities. Using Howitt as an anthropological witness to this phenomenon found strikingly present among the Australian aborigines, a people who do not seem to demonstrate any behavioral evidence of religion as defined in this study, Leuba has chosen to address the issue of what he calls passive religion and godless religion, the latter term not being intended at all to imply disparagement in the way modern society has used the expression "godless communism," or "godless atheism" for example. Explanation of the world, says Leuba, is not the domain of religion but of philosophy, whereas the providing of mechanisms for the worshipping of the super-human power source in the universe, whether personal or non-personal, constitutes the religious agenda.

****

The Godless Religions -- We have found it convenient up to this point to speak as if Power had to be personal in order to become the centre of a Religion. That view would exclude original Buddhism, the Religion of Humanity, and several other varieties of mental attitudes generally regarded as religious. The significant fact that until recently every existing historical Religion was a worship of a personal Divinity, is not a sufficient reason for refusing to recognise other types. The affinity between the worship of a God and certain relations maintained with non-personal sources of power is substantial enough to be recognizes by the use of a name common to both. .. The term Religion is used by some in a still wider sense. Professor J. R. Seeley (*Natural Religion,* Macmillan, 1882) bestows that valued name upon 'any habitual and permanent admiration.' ... Should we concur in this extension, it would be difficult to stop anywhere. ... We should have to admit almost anything ... But since the function of words is to delimitate, one defeats the purpose of language by stretching the meaning of a word until it has lost all precision and unity of meaning. We would therefore throw out of our definition anything which did not include: (1) A belief in a great and superior psychic power -- whether personal or not. (2) A dynamic relation -- formal and organized or otherwise -- between man and that Higher Power tending to the preservation, the increase, and the ennobling of life. This conception is broad enough to include even the uncrystallised form of Religion conditioned, in the words of Professor James, by 'an assurance that this natural order is not ultimate, but a mere sign or vision, the external staging of a many-storied universe, in which spiritual forces have the last word and are eternal.'

Leuba is eager to circumscribe the perimeters of a definition of religion which is actually usable in scholarly discussions. A definition that includes everything, for example, "religion as any habitual and permanent admiration," as proposed by Professor Seeley (1882), gets us nowhere because that definition seems to have no boundaries whatsoever. If a word has a definition, that definition must circumscribe the boundaries, establish the perimeters, in order for reasonable use in dialogue and enquiry is to occur. Therefore, and here Leuba finally shows his colors, any use of the term religion in any meaningful enquiry or scholarly discussion must include at least the following items: A belief in a superior power and an interactive and meaningful relationship between the human and that power. How that power is experienced and defined and how that relationship configures itself in the mind of the worshipping community is not part of the definition -- when these two simple characteristics are present, there is religion. In some instances, that power source is personalized and made into a few or even one entity. Also, that relationship which must have meaning for the practitioners may be in the form of a simple or sophisticated complex of myths, rituals, and symbols. When these two features are present, there is something to study, and something to discuss. The sciences have data upon which to practice their analytical skills, and the philosophers and theologians have ideas and concepts worthy of discussion and debate.

****

Active Religion may properly be looked upon as that portion of the struggle for life, in which use is made of the Power we have roughly characterized as psychic and superhuman, and for which other adjectives, 'spiritual,' 'divine,' for instance, are commonly used. ... The current terms, 'religious feeling,' 'religious desire,' 'religious purpose,' are deceptive if they are supposed to designate affective experiences, desires and purposes met with only in religious life. ... The conception of the Source of Psychic Energy, without the belief in which no Religion can exist, has undergone very interesting transformations in the course of historical development. (From animism to polytheism to monotheism) in which the One, Eternal, Creator and Sustainer of life ... with sympathy, love, and justice among his attributes. In a second phase, this formless, but personal, God was gradually shorn of all the qualities and defects which make individuality. He became the passionless Absolute in which all things move and have their being. ... the personifying work of centuries is undone, and humanity, after having, as it were, lived throughout its infancy and youth under the controlling eye and with the active assistance of personal divinities, on reaching maturity, finds itself bereft of these sources of life. The present religious crisis marks the difficulty in the way of an adaptation to the new situation. As belief in a God seems no longer possible, man seeks an impersonal, efficient substitute, belief in which will not mean disloyalty to science. ... Any solution will have the right to the name Religion that provides for the preservation and the perfectioning of life by means of faith in a superhuman psychic Power.

For Leuba, the psychologist, it is "active" religion, its experience and behavior, which constitutes the focus of his research interests. Passive religion, magic, and pre-science are all somewhat interesting but in the development of a school of thought focusing upon the "psychology of religion," it is religious behavior and ideology which constitutes the orientation of the research psychologist. Leuba wrote at a time of great interest in this newly emerging field of study, but he was limited in terms of available psychological research. Rather, he was dependent, often to his own detriment, on the ethnographic documentation of often marginally trained anthropologists and lay psychologists, scholars dependent upon a 19th century cosmology centered around a firm belief in unilinear evolution, with western culture (and particularly English culture) at the pinnacle. Talk of the "savage" was common and never questioned. Scholarly and even, alas, anthropological notions about "lower" cultures and "higher" cultures were presumed an unimpeachable domain assumption. The presumption that religion evolved from animistic to polytheistic to monotheistic sophistication went without saying, without argument, without enquiry. But in his closing remarks, Leuba does raise the issue of a secularization of religious society and the inevitability of a world experienced without God, throwing down the gauntlet to the wider community to address this emerging reality with insight and responsibility. Within a dozen years, Sigmund Freud is to drop a bomb on the complacent religious community with his little classic, *The Future of an Illusion.*

---

*Note: Spelling in Leuba's book is in the English tradition owing to the book being published in London by the renowned publisher, Constable & Company in Leister Square.

CHAPTER THREE

Sigmund Freud and *The Future of an Illusion*

No case needs to be made for the lofty ranking of Sigmund Freud in the study of either psychology or religion, for whether one is in favor of his system of thought or not, no one would be so irresponsible as to deny his primacy in such discussions as these. Whether early in his career writing *Totem and Taboo* (1918) or late in his career writing *Moses and Monotheism* (1939), Freud was always there and ready to contribute to and critique any serious discussion of religious behavior. An Austrian born neurologist driven by a desire to break from the oppression of anti-Semitism among his colleagues and to establish himself as a pioneer in medical research, Freud (1856 - 1939) set out to establish a school of thought and enquiry, and he succeeded far beyond his greatest expectations. After finishing medical school and studying with some of the great minds of the day, including the Parisian Jean Martin Charcot, he set up on his own a psychiatric practice in his hometown of Vienna and eventually established a system of analysis and treatment, viz., psychoanalysis, which was to sweep Europe and America with such profundity and comprehensiveness that, even today, it is impossible to think of social criticism, counseling psychology, or psychiatric practice without having to deal with Freudian theory (Gay 1988:7). At the end of his life, Freud and psychoanalysis were household words and professional juggernauts in the world of psychiatry and psychotherapy. And, to be honest about it, they both still are.

Between *Totem and Taboo* and *Moses and Monotheism* however, Freud wrote a little book, *The Future of an Illusion* (1927) which, without question, placed him front and center in all current and future discussions of the psychology of religion. If his *Civilization and Its Discontents* (1930) is one of the great 20th century critiques of western civilization, then his book on the future of an illusion is comparably one of the greatest criticisms of popularly practiced religion in western civilization. From William James, who wished to emphasize the "value" of religious experience, whether or not the experience is real and true, to

Leuba, who wished to emphasize the analytical requirement of a scientific methodology in studying experience described as religious behavior, the psychology of religion took a giant leap into respectability. With Freud, empowered by this liberated spirit of scientific enquiry into religious experience and behavior itself, he was able to employ his psychoanalytic methodology without restraint. Proposing that society is established upon the fundamental renunciation of instinct, Freud contends that religion is simultaneously an "instrument of coercion" and a "compensation for the stifled desires of mankind." Religion, he argues, functions as a substitute for the repressed desires which cannot be satisfied due to social restrictions on instinctual human behavior.

Freud is quick, even eager, to identify the benefits of the socialization of the human animal through the cultivation of culture, including our moral development, our artistic and ideological refinements, and even our religious systems, illusory though they prove to be. Particularly with religion, Freud, as a psychoanalyst and social critic, is keen to draw poignant attention to the functions and values of religion to society and to the inevitable future of these functions and values as mechanisms of sublimation and repression of our natural instincts. Granted, religion provides a worldview and ethos of explanation as to the verities of life -- where we come from, who we are, where we are going -- but, says Freud, all of these function to stifle and inhibit natural aspirations which are contradictory to the needs and interests of society. Religion, then, provides an optional substitute for our desires which is socially acceptable. But the price is great. In exchange for an All-Seeing God, a father-image, who looks over us and sees after us, humanity relinquishes our right to pursue our own fulfillment as individuals, ever stifled and inhibited by the rules laid down by the Overseer. The conflict between the individual and society is matched and surpassed by the conflict between individual desires and the constraints derived and administered by God. Religion is humanity's formalized response to our own feelings of insecurity, incompetence, and lack of control over the environment. The only genuine solution, says Freud, is for humanity to throw off this illusory source of an All-Powerful God and assert our own independence, with all of the dangers and risks implied by doing so.

Selections from *The Future of an Illusion,* by Sigmund Freud, with commentary.

NOTE: In the following, the original text will be printed in *Arial Unicode MS* typestyle (as is this note itself to illustrate) as an easy and aesthetically pleasing way of identifying the primary source paragraphs. The author's commentary will be in *Times New Roman*. It is hoped that this differentiation between the "primary source" and the "commentary" made by use of differing typestyles will prove helpful and not disruptive to the reader. (Note: The edition of Freud's book used here was published in England and, thus, the English rather than American spellings.)

CHAPTER I

Human civilization, by which I mean all those respects in which human life has raised itself above its animal status and differs from the life of beasts -- and I scorn to distinguish between culture and civilization -- presents, as we know, two aspects to the observer. It includes on the one hand all the knowledge and capacity that men have acquired in order to control the forces of nature and extract its wealth for the satisfaction of human needs, and, on the other hand, all the regulations necessary in order to adjust the relations of men to one another and especially the distribution of the available wealth.

The brilliance of Freud's social critique has never been seriously challenged, even by his most outspoken detractors and towards the end of his professional life he spent most of his time writing such books and articles, including his greatest classic in this field, *Civilization and Its Discontents* (1930). Others in this same social critical genre included *Totem and Taboo* (1927) and *Moses and Monotheism* (1939). But our attention will focus upon this little work of fewer than 100 pages, *The Future of an Illusion.* Freud knew he would make no new friends with this work, and anticipated alienating even further his critics on the theistic side of the equation. It seemed not to bother him, for he was intent upon demonstrating the acute application of psychoanalytic theory to the practice of religion. To do that, he begins with an extensive probing enquiry into the meaning and nature of culture and civilization, both terms meaning the same thing throughout this work. Civilization (read 'culture' if you like) requires all knowledge and human capacity as well as all humanly contrived regulations in order to make social relationships tenable. This constitutes the starting point for Freud's social critique.

****

The two trends of civilization are not independent of each other: firstly, because the mutual relations of men are profoundly influenced by the amount of instinctual satisfaction which the existing wealth makes possible; secondly, because an individual man can himself come to function as wealth in relation to another one, in so far as the other person makes use of his capacity for work, or chooses him as a sexual object; and thirdly, moreover, because every individual is virtually an enemy of civilization, though civilization is supposed to be an object of universal human interest. ... civilization has to be defended against the individual.

Three components constitute the make up of the human person in relationship to culture, namely, gratification of one's instincts through wealth (and does he have it and if so how much), the wealth potential of an individual based on his capacities, and the individual's capacity to defend himself against the demands of civilization. If Freud is going to get us to face and embrace his criticism of religion as mere illusion, he is compelled to place his critical analysis within our "weltanschauung," i.e., our worldview. This he set out to do with precision and acuity.

****

One thus gets an impression that civilization is something which was imposed on a resisting majority by a minority which understood how to obtain possession of the means to power and coercion. ... While mankind has made continual advances in its control over nature and may expect to make still greater ones, it is not possible to establish with certainty that a similar advance has been made in the management of human affairs ... many people have asked themselves whether what little civilization has thus acquired is indeed worth defending at all.

Freud, ever wary of the purported benefits of civilization to the well-being of the individual, is keen to emphasize that, whereas there have been great advances in the physical manipulation of the environment with its concomitant proliferation of technology, power, and the sophisticated uses of coercion of both the physical and social environment, there has been essentially no advancement in the "management of human affairs." Wars and rumors of wars, pestilence and disease, etc., and the list goes on all bespeak a desperate situation worthy of ponder.

****

One would think that a re-ordering of human relations should be possible, which would remove the sources of dissatisfaction with civilization by renouncing coercion and the suppression of the instincts, so that, undisturbed by internal discord, men might devote themselves to the acquisition of wealth and its enjoyment. That would be the golden age, but it is questionable if such a state of affairs can be realized. It seems rather that every civilization must be built up on coercion and renunciation of instinct ...

Never a romantic and always the realist, Freud despairs of and disparages the notion of a "golden age" where all is peace and tranquility while humankind is left to pursue wealth and enjoyment in the absence of the coercive demands of civilization which readily exercises its relentless power over every individual by stifling their instinctual drives and urges. Freud is not hopeful that the human community nor the individual is sufficiently in control of life's situations, precipitated by civilization, to be able to alter the very fabric of culture. Coercion and stiflement are essential components of the phenomenon of culture and it is culture which has made human society possible and yet, while making it possible, has necessarily introduced the exercise of power over every individual in it.

****

One has, I think, to reckon with the fact that there are present in all men destructive, and therefore anti-social and anti-cultural, trends and that in a great number of people these are strong enough to determine their behaviour in human society ... This psychological fact has a decisive importance for our judgement of human civilization ... The decisive question is whether and to what extent it is possible to lessen the burden of the instinctual sacrifices imposed on men, to reconcile men to those which must necessarily remain and to provide a compensation for them. It is just as impossible to do without control of the mass by a minority as it is to dispense with coercion in the work of civilization.

The psychological fact of humankind's propensity to destruction exacerbated by anti-social and anti-cultural inclinations and fed by selfish and libido-driven instincts has both produced civilization as a mechanism to assure social continuity and survival while concurrently stifling human inclinations to seek self interests and personal satisfaction. This situation leads the human community to what Freud has chosen to call "the decisive question," namely, how to make the demands of civilization more palatable by both lightening the burden of instinctual starvation while providing acceptable alternatives and substitutes for instinctual gratification.

****

CHAPTER II

We have slipped unawares out of the economic field into the field of psychology ... Alongside of wealth we now come upon the means by which civilization can be defended -- measure of coercion and other measures that are intended to reconcile men to it and to recompense them for their sacrifices. These latter may be described as the mental assets of civilization. ... For the same of a uniform terminology we will describe the fact that an instinct cannot be satisfied as a "frustration," the regulation by which this frustration is established as a "prohibition" and the condition which is produced by the prohibition as a "privation."

Freud, ever eager to offer the psychoanalytic critique of civilization (and particularly western culture), draws back at the beginning of this chapter from pursuing an aggressive attack upon the economic factors driving human psychology towards the pursuit of wealth and its pleasure-seeking self-aggrandizement. Drawing back, Freud re-emphasizes the necessity of defending the existence of civilization, grants its oppressive nature in stifling human instinct, as the only mechanism which assures social survival. What must happen, explains Freud, is a creative deployment of "substitutes" and "alternatives" which society has approved and provided for those instinctual drives which otherwise are destructive and counter-productive to social cohesion. Addressing the complex relational matrix of frustration, prohibition, and privation as affects instinctual gratification, Freud pushes towards a discussion of what he has chosen to call the "mental assets of civilization."

****

It is not true that the human mind has undergone no development since the earliest times and that, in contrast to the advances of science and technology, it is the same to-day as it was at the beginning of history. We can point out one of these mental advances at once. It is in keeping with the course of human development that external coercion gradually becomes internalized; for a special mental agency, man's super-ego, takes it over and includes it among its commandments. Every child presents this process of transformation to us; only by that means does it become a moral and social being. Such a strengthening of the super-ego is a most precious cultural asset in the psychological field.

Early in Freud's intellectual development, he embraced Darwinian evolution as the scientifically responsible posture towards the emergence of the universe and life on the earth. A scientist through and through, Freud was always eager to demonstrate how his own understanding of the human psyche through psychoanalysis was true science employing scientific methodology and application. In his psycho-cartography of the mind, he contends against those who would say that the human mind has been the same "from the beginning." From man as animal to man as intellect has been an evolution. His mind has, indeed, undergone advances and Freud demonstrates this fact by pointing to the human trend to "internalize" what otherwise had been external socially-created coercive mechanisms within culture. Only in this way have external factors controlling human behavior become moral mandates fostering social cohesiveness within the human community.

****

...we observe with surprise and concern that a majority of people obey the cultural prohibitions on these points only under the pressure of external coercion -- that is, only where that coercion can make itself effective and so long as it is to be feared. This is also true of what are known as the moral demands of civilization, which likewise apply to everyone. ... there are countless civilized people who would shrink from murder or incest but who do not deny themselves the satisfaction of their avarice ... sexual lusts ... lies, fraud and calumny, so long as they can remain unpunished for it, and this, no doubt, has always been so through many ages of civilization.

Though Jewish, Freud was no believer in the essential and natural goodness of humankind. Owing possibly to his work in psychotherapy as a counselor to troubled people struggling with mental illness, Freud was ever aware of the darker side of human nature. Believing that people, more or less, follow the rules owing to the ever presence of the external mechanism for rule enforcement rather than the interior governance of a moral code of ethics, civilization endures primarily relying upon strict and enforceable restrictions to human behavior. If good people can get away with things, they usually will, says Freud. In the absence of punishment, chaos looms large on the horizon of all civilizations.

****

The moral level of a civilization's participants is not the only form of mental wealth that comes into consideration in estimating a civilization's value. There are in addition its assets in the shape of ideals and artistic creations -- that is, the satisfactions that can be derived from those sources. ... People will be only too readily inclined to include among the psychical assets of a culture its ideals -- its estimates of what achievements are the highest and the most to be striven after. ... The satisfaction which the ideal offers to the participants in the culture is thus of a narcissistic nature; it rests on their pride in what has already been successfully achieved. ... On the strength of these differences every culture claims the right to look down on the rest. ... No mention has yet been made of what is perhaps the most important item in the psychical inventory of a civilization. This consists in its religious ideas in the widest sense -- in other words in its illusions.

Civilizations (or cultures), according to Freud, have been variously valued on the basis of their "moral wealth," that is, the sophistication of the ethical behavioral mechanism in place governing members of each particular society. But "moral wealth" is not the only standard of measurement. There are what Freud calls the "ideals" of a society and its "artistic creations." Each of these, in its own way, generates a nurturing quality to society so long as members of that society are willing to relinquish their own selfish instinctual drives for the substituted value implicit in the ideals and the artistic endeavors of the culture. These ideals are narcissistic in nature owing to the fact that they feed a self-interest while functioning as a transformative substitute for more primordial instincts. Each culture's ideals validate its own individual claim to greatness and priority over all others. The ultimate "psychical inventory of civilization," however, says Freud, is not merely the social ideals but most decidedly its "religious ideals," what Freud will henceforth call "illusions."

****

CHAPTER III

We have spoken of the hostility to civilization which is produced by the pressure that civilization exercises, the renunciations of instinct which it demands. ... It is true that nature would not demand any restrictions of instinct from us, she would let us do as we liked; but she has her own particularly effective method of restricting us. She destroys us -- coldly, cruelly, relentlessly, as it seems to us, and possibly through the very things that occasioned our satisfaction. It was precisely because of these dangers with which nature threatens us that we came together and created civilization, which is also, among other things, intended to make our communal life possible. For the principal task of civilization, its actual *raison d'etre*, is to defend us against nature.

Civilization, Freud is contending, both provides the mechanism for social cohesion and survival while simultaneously providing the mechanisms needed to stifle and divert individual self-interests. The irony, says Freud, is that the very thing that assures our endurance is the very thing that is the source of our psychic illness brought on by the required renunciation of instinctual desires and behavior. Civilization, none the less, was the result of the human species recognition that survival depended upon the creation of these stifling mechanisms to protect us from the destructive power of Nature itself for, says Freud, this is the primary purpose of culture and civilization, a mechanism of protection from a cold, cruel, relentlessly destructive Nature.

****

We know already how the individual reacts to the injuries which civilization and other men inflict on him: he develops a corresponding degree of resistance to the regulations of civilization and of hostility to it. But how does he defend himself against the superior powers of nature, of Fate, which threaten him as they threaten all the rest? ... Civilization relieves him of this task. ... Man's self-regard, seriously menaced, calls for consolation; life and the universe must be robbed of their terrors ... and his curiosity demands an answer. ... the humanization of nature (is the answer). ... if the elements have passions that rage as they do in our own souls ... perhaps we are not even defenseless. ... A replacement like this of natural science by psychology no only provides immediate relief, but also points the way to a further mastering of the situation. For this situation is nothing new. It has an infantile prototype...

While the individual, explains Freud, has creatively and quite ingeniously developed personal capabilities to insulate himself from the overbearing demands and pressures of civilization, all the while complying with the essentials of that cultural matrix, the bigger question is how has he, individually and collectively, managed to cope with the superior powers of Nature, of Fate itself, which, as we know, impinges upon our well-being at every juncture of daily life. Freud suggests that it is the process of the "humanization of nature" itself which has brought about the possibility of "managing the verities of life." This shift from natural science to psychology in the human mind, from the external realities to the internal imaginative cogitations, has produced a mechanism for managing and understanding the external realities of nature, a mechanism not unlike what we conjured as infants in coping with a loving yet fearing relationship with our fathers.

****

A man makes the forces of nature not simply into persons with whom he can associate as he would with his equals but he gives them the character of a father. He turns them into gods, following in this, as I have tried to show, not only an infantile prototype, but a phylogenetic one. ... Man's helplessness remains and along with it his longing for his father, and the gods. The gods retain their threefold task: they must exorcize the terrors of nature, they must reconcile men to the cruelty of Fate ... and they must compensate them for the sufferings and privations which a civilized life in common has imposed on them.

As infants and children, we relied upon the power and governance of our fathers over things beyond our capacity to control or understand. In adulthood, we have resorted to the same mechanism but because we now know, in adulthood, that our fathers individually or collectively cannot do what we as children assumed they could, namely, control the world, we have infused our father-ideal with deity. In other words, we have elevated our own fathers to the idea of a singular monolithic Father God! We are, indeed, helpless, yet, against the verities of life, we have attributed to our Father God the three fundamental tasks of deity: control the dangers of nature, reconcile us to the inevitable, and offer solace and comfort in the face of civilization's relentless demands upon us.

****

The precepts of civilization themselves were credited with a divine origin; they were elevated beyond human society and were extended to nature and the universe. And thus a store of ideas is created, born from man's need to make his helplessness tolerable and built up from the material of memories of the helplessness of his own childhood and the childhood of the human race. It can clearly be seen that the possession of these ideas protects him in two directions -- against the dangers of nature and Fate, and against the injuries that threaten him from human society itself.

Religion, explains Freud, functions to protect us on two fronts and, thus, its amazing attractiveness to the human species throughout the world and throughout time up to the present day. First, this elevated reliance upon the Father God provides us with a mechanism of explanation for the unexplainable in life -- tragedy, disaster, pain, etc., as well as presenting us with an "escape" hatch from the oppressions of civilization itself. In order to make our "helplessness tolerable," explains Freud, we have elevated our corporate fathers into a Father God who, like our individuals fathers when we were infants, now has the capacity to control the universe, protect us, reward us, and punish us for non-compliance with His Will (the corporate will of society writ large).

****

CHAPTER IV

I have tried to show that religious ideas have arisen from the same need as have all the other achievements of civilization; from the necessity of defending oneself against the crushingly superior force of nature. ... the relation of the child's helplessness to the helplessness of the adult which continues ... The child's attitude to its father is colored by a pecular ambivalence. The father himself constitutes a danger for the child ... but his longing for a father is a motive identical which his need for protection against the consequences of his human weakness. ... what we are concerned with here is the finished body of religious ideas as it is transmitted by civilization to the individual.

Freud is eager to minimize the presumed, and falsely conceived, distinctions in fundamentals between the major ideas of civilization and those of religion. Religious ideas, just like all other operative ideas within a surviving culture, derive from the same fundamental cause and source, namely, the desire to protect ourselves from the ravages of nature and the oppressions of social life. The feelings of helplessness in infancy are exaggerated and carried forth into both the adulthood of the individual and the maturity of the human race in the form of an elevated conception of father. If the child's father is both powerful and loving as well as capable of punishment, so in maturity the human race has produced a Father God who is all of those things, but exponentially greater. Though the Father-figure God is capable of love, his deployment of power with abiding terror is an equally characteristic feature, and the ideologies which surround this transmogrification are perpetrated by civilization and infused in each individual, thereby making religion an indispensable component of human culture.

****

CHAPTER V

What, then, is the psychological significance of religious ideas and under what heading are we to classify them? ... Religious ideas are teachings and assertions about facts and conditions of external (or internal) reality which tell one something one has not discovered for oneself and which lay claim to one's belief. Since they give us information about what is most important and interesting to us in life, they are particularly highly prized. ... the teachings of religion. When we ask on what their claim to be believed is founded, we are met with three answers, which harmonize remarkably badly with one another. Firstly, these teachings deserve to be believed because they were already believed by our primal ancestors; secondly, we possess proofs which have been handed down to us from those same primeval times; and thirdly, it is forbidden to raise the question of their authentication at all.

The significance of religious ideas (doctrines of faith) from a psychological point of view occupies Freud's attention at this juncture. These "teachings and assertions," as he calls the theological postulates of the great religions of the world (but here specifically western-style Christianity), are purported to be and are perpetrated as "factual information" beyond that known by any individual but embodied in the essence of one's own culture and civilization. Highly prized facts because they provide information to each individual in the absence of verifiability, enquiries as to the origin of the "religious factions" from the fool who would venture where angels fear to tread are met with three types of responses, differing in kind, essence, and function from each other. First, religious teachings are worthy of adherence because they were believed by our forbears; second, religious truths are worthy of embracing because of their ancient origins; and third, these "religious facts" must be believed but under no circumstances questioned as to their validity. To question them is to deny them their primacy within the hierarchy of cultural ideas and ideals.

****

We ought to believe because our forefathers believed. But these ancestors of ours were far more ignorant than we are. They believed in things we could not possibly accept today ... It does not help much to have it asserted that their wording, or even their content only, originates from divine revelation; for this assertion is itself one of the doctrines whose authenticity is under examination, and no proposition can be a proof of itself. Thus we arrive at the singular conclusion that of all the information provided by our cultural assets it is precisely the elements which might be of the greatest importance to us and which have the task of solving the riddles of the universe and of reconciling us to the sufferings of life -- it is precisely those elements that are the least well authenticated of any. ... This state of affairs is in itself a very remarkable psychological problem.

The essence of the validity in the absence of verifiability of all religious truths lies in the argument that we must, says Freud, believe them because our ancestors believed them. That is sufficient evidence and proof of their truthfulness. The fact that our ancestors, those who early demonstrated religious sensibilities beginning even with Paleolithic peoples, believed things about the world which are to us today blatantly childish and naive, does not mitigate the mandate to believe in their religious ideologies. To argue for the "divine" origin of these religious beliefs does not move their legitimacy forward, says Freud, for this is a proof which cannot be questioned nor validated. One cannot use an unproven proof to prove a point, for no proposition can be a proof of itself! The irony of cultural assets, Freud points out, is the reality that those facts which are most needed to validate our experience are the very ones which are forbidden to be questioned or tested.

****

Chapter VI

...We turn our attention to the psychical origin of religious ideas. These, which are given out as teachings, are not precipitates of experience or end-results of thinking: they are illusions, fulfillments of the oldest, strongest and most urgent wishes of mankind. The secret of their strength lies in the strength of those wishes. As we already know, the terrifying impression of helplessness in childhood aroused the need for protection -- for protection through love -- which was provided by the father; and the recognition that this helplessness lasts throughout life made it necessary to cling to the existence of a father, but this time a more powerful one.

When finally Freud gets to it, he is clear and poignant and bold. The psychological origins of religious ideas (doctrines of faith) are not, says he, the result of critical thinking, analytical probing of experiential evident, or logical deductions. Religious ideas are clearly "illusions," as they serve to fulfill the oldest, strongest and most urgent wishes of humankind. Wishes which have come down through the eons of human evolution as well as from the individual maturation of the human person -- ontogeny recapitulating phylogeny! What one person experiences from infancy to adulthood is like what the human species has experienced through the evolution of our species (our *speciel* evolution). Our wishes for a loving and powerful father as individuals now exaggerated to the wishes for a loving and powerful Father-God for, explains Freud, society itself now constitutes the present reality.

****

When I say that these things are all illusions, I must define the meaning of the word. An illusion is not the same thing as an error; nor is it necessarily an error. ... What is characteristic of illusions is that they are derived from human wishes. In this respect they come near to psychiatric delusions. ... In the case of delusions (however), we emphasize as essential their being in contradiction with reality. Illusions need not necessarily be false -- that is to say, unrealizable or in contradiction to reality. ... Thus we call a belief an illusion when a wish-fulfillment is a prominent factor in its motivation, and in doing so we disregard its relations to reality, just as the illusion itself sets no store by verification.

An "illusion," explains Freud, is the exaggerated manifestation of an individual or social wish, a desire so strong as to consume the individual's imagination as well as that of society. The stronger the wish, the stronger the illusion. It is not necessarily an error and it is certainly not a "delusion," for whereas an illusion is a strong wish for what could or might be possible, a delusion is anti-reality, opposed to all that is reasonable and logical. A defining feature of an illusion, however, is that it is impervious to verification, as in the case of religious ideas.

****

Let us return once more to the question of religious doctrines. We can now repeat that all of them are illusions and insusceptible of proof. ... some of them are so improbable ... we may compare then to delusions. .. Where questions of religion are concerned, people are guilty of every possible sort of dishonesty and intellectual misdemeanor. Philosophers stretch the meaning of words until they retain scarcely anything of their original sense. They give the name of 'God' to some value abstraction which they have created for themselves; having done so they can pose before all the world as deists, as believers in God, and they can even boast that they have recognized a higher, purer concept of God, notwithstanding that their God is now nothing more than an insubstantial shadow and no longer the mighty personality of religious doctrines.

Religious ideologies or faith-statements or theological doctrines are the epitome of illusion in that they are the exaggerated manifestation of wish fulfillments of individuals and societies, wishes for a protective Father, a powerful super human being, standing between the individual and the verities of life. And, these illusions are not, because they are illusions, susceptible to verification as to authenticity. You cannot prove a religious doctrine, you can only accept and believe it or not. As reason and logic as well as verifiable experience are gradually applied to a roster of theological doctrines, theologians and philosophers are pressed to prevaricate linguistically by the slight of tongue, the twisting and turning of phrases and terms to mean what ever is necessary to protect and promote the doctrine in question. The notion of a Virgin Birth is only one of a thousand examples. The term itself is an oxymoron. Proof of the truth of such incongruities is "beyond" and "above" reason and logic, they are defended by such notions as "it is a mystery," "only those who believe can understand," etc.

****

It is enough for us that we have recognized religious doctrines as being, in their psychological nature, illusions. But we do not have to conceal the fact that this discovery also strongly influences our attitude to the question which must appear to many to be the most important of all. We know approximately at what periods and by what kind of men religious doctrines were created. If in addition we discover the motives which led to this, our attitude to the problem of religion will undergo a marked displacement. We shall tell ourselves that it would be very nice if there were a God who created the world and was a benevolent Providence, and if there were a moral order in the universe and an after-life; but it is a very striking fact that this is exactly as we are bound to wish it to be.

For the reasonable person, to have identified religious doctrines as illusions, instances of supreme wish fulfillments without factual verification or the possibility of such, as well as to have traced the "origin" of such ideologies to both the individual maturation process (infancy to adulthood) and *speciel* evolution (pre-human to modern man), would be sufficient to dispense with further discussion. We would simply dismiss religious belief out of hand with no need of further probing. But for Freud the psychoanalyst, there is a strong desire to seek out the "motives which led to" religious beliefs in the first place. But wishing does not make it happen and does not make it so; as with religion, just because the individual wishes for a supreme Father, all-powerful and loving, or just because civilization requires such a belief to maintain its existence does not make it true. Motives as relates to the exercise of power and control fascinated Freud and so he plies his wares in analyzing religion within this context.

****

CHAPTER VII

Nothing that I have said here against the truth-value of religions needed the support of psychoanalysis. ... the application of the psychoanalytic method makes it possible to find a new argument against the truths of religion ... but defenders of religion will by the same right make use of psychoanalysis in order to give full value to the affective significance of religious doctrines ... Religion has clearly performed great services for human civilization. It has contributed much towards the taming of the asocial instincts. But not enough. .. If it had succeeded in making the majority of mankind happy, in comforting them, in reconciling them to life and in making them into vehicles of civilization, no one would dream of attempting to alter the existing conditions. But what do we see instead? We see that an appallingly large number of people are dissatisfied with civilization and unhappy in it, and feel it as a yoke which must be shaken off ... it will be objected against us that this state of affairs is due to the very fact that religion has lost a part of its influence over human masses precisely because of the deplorable effect of the advances of science.

Freud was not naïve in realizing early in his developmental period that the very thing he was attacking would itself use his own tools for its defense. The emergence of "Christian psychoanalysis" was close behind the establishment of Freud's own international association of psychoanalysts. Many clergy were attracted to the insightfulness of his psychological theories of personality development and wished to use his insights without adopting the premises for his work. Freud is quick to credit religion for having contributed substantially to the creation and maintenance of civilization, especially its capacity to stifle the instinctual urges of the normal person. But culture has failed in carrying through, for, says Freud, if it was completely successful in stifling the primordial *libido* of the human animal there would not be the need and attraction to move beyond, leaving behind religion as we know it. The present situation demonstrates the failure of religion to answer the demands of civilization, for there is, says Freud, an "appallingly large number" of individuals who are unhappy, dissatisfied, unfulfilled, and wish yet to divest themselves of the yoke and burden of religion's moral demands and culture's strangle hold on individual freedom. It is science, ironically, says Freud, that is both blamed and credited with this present situation.

****

We have heard the admission that religion no longer has the same influence on people that it used to. (We are here concerned with European Christian civilization). And this is not because its promises have grown less but because people find them less credible. Let us admit that the reason -- though perhaps not the only reason -- for this change is the increase of the scientific spirit in the higher strata of human society. If the sole reason why you must not kill your neighbour is because God has forbidden it and will severely punish you for it in this or the next life -- then, when you learn that there is no God and that you need not fear His punishment, you will certainly kill your neighbour without hesitation, and you can only be prevented from doing so by mundane force (the law). Thus, either these dangerous masses must be held down most severely and kept most carefully away from any chance of intellectual awakening, or else the relationship between civilization and religion must undergo a fundamental revision.

Religion, says Freud, (that is specifically western Christianity) is on the decline not because of its failure to offer promises of unbelievable happiness in the after-life, but because these very promises are incrementally losing their credibility. The promise to children of a happy future can only hold their attention and allegiance so long and then they despair. With religion, the reason the promises are losing ground daily is that they pale in the face of modern science, reason, and experience. Like Pandora's Box, when the questions begin to be asked about the verifiability of religious claims to universal truth and the Box is necessarily opened for examination, then everything is lost. The secret is out and the religious answers are reduced to fairy tales and superstition. The impact upon personal ethics is profound and individuals and societies must find a firmer basis for moral behavior than "mandates from God found in a book and proclaimed by priests!" To do the right thing because God said to do it is less mature than to do the right thing because it is the right thing to do.

****

CHAPTER VIII

When civilization laid down the commandment that a man shall not kill the neighbour whom he hates or who is in his way or whose property he covets, this was clearly done in the interest of man's communal existence, which would not otherwise be practicable. For the murderer would draw down on himself the vengeance of the murdered man's kinsmen and the secret envy of others, who within themselves feel as much inclined as he does for such acts of violence. ... But we do not publish this rational explanation of the prohibition against murder. We assert that the prohibition has been issued by God. ... In behaving in this way we are investing the cultural prohibition with a quite special solemnity, but at the same time we risk making its observance dependent on belief in God ... we no longer attribute to God what is our own will and if we content ourselves with giving the social reason ... we gain something else as well. ... the character of sanctity and inviolability ... has spread from a few major prohibitions on to every other cultural regulation, law and ordinance.

Freud here challenges and criticizes civilization for having "hidden" the real origin of ethical behavior. Ethical codes and moral conduct did not, contrary to the teachings of the religious establishment, descend from a transcendent source of super power and authority, even though leaders of the religious institutions would have members of society believe they did. Morality and its resulting codes of ethics have derived from tried and proven standards of behavior necessary for the survival of the human species. As these behavioral experiments proved their value and worth to our corporate social life, they were codified in our minds and subsequently in our books. However, owing to humankind's propensity to question and challenge any and all rules, it became necessary for society to infuse a deeper source of power and validation to these tried and proven rules of behavior and, alas, religion came to the rescue by identifying the source of these rules (and their elaboration by the religious leaders themselves) as from the Father God. By "sanctifying" and making inviolable these rules, and by further elaborating them for the benefit of religious jurisdiction and control, civilization has relinquished its freedom of assessment and capitulated its own right of reason to the God of religion and the Bible.

****

Since it is an awkward task to separate what God Himself has demanded from what can be traced to the authority of an all-powerful parliament or a high judiciary, it would be an undoubted advantage if we were to leave God out altogether and honestly admit the purely human origin of all the regulations and precepts of civilization. ... these commandments and laws would lose their rigidity and unchangeableness as well. People could understand that they are made ... to serve their interests; and they would adopt a more friendly attitude to them, and ... would aim only at their improvement.

With the slightest detection of sarcasm in Freud's tone, he suggests that if the human community were to re-own the human origins of ethical codes and moral behavior and divest itself of this child-like dependence upon the rules enforced by the power and authority of the Father God, civilization would mature to a higher level of freedom and personal as well as corporate responsibility. If the rules did not come from God, they, then, came from human ingenuity and, thus, we hold within our own hands the power and right as well as the reason for creating, altering, and even dispensing with ethical codes of behavior which we ourselves have made. The improvement of human society would, then, be vested entirely in our hands and not in an intervening power source outside the universe, a transcendent being as outside agitator.

****

But, as we have shown by arguments which I need not repeat here, the primal father was the original image of God, the model on which later generations have shaped the figure of God. ... We now observe that the store of religious ideas includes not only wish-fulfillments but important historical recollections. This concurrent influence of past and present must give religion a truly incomparable wealth of power. ... We know that a human child cannot successfully complete its development to the civilized stage without passing through a phase of neurosis sometimes of greater and sometimes of less distinctness. .. Most of these infantile neuroses are overcome spontaneously in the course of growing up, and this is especially true of the obsessional neuroses of childhood. ... Religion would thus be the universal obsessional neurosis of humanity; like the obsessional neurosis of children ,,, out of the relation to the father.

But, explains Freud, the religious ideologues and theological fabricators have been very creative and ingenious in their development not only of moral codes, which they themselves have been invested with the power to enforce by God Himself, but they have also reconstructed our human origins with an historical recreation which, not surprisingly, validates all of their claims of authenticity. The power which comes from both creating and then self-validating moral behavior and historical factuality is great, indeed, says Freud. Religion, then, in psychoanalytical thought, has become the "universal obsessional neurosis of humanity," an obsession with obedience to power out of love and fear and a neurotic adherence to whatever is demanded by the power source which validates and authenticates the existence and meaning of life, viz., religion.

****

Our knowledge of the historical worth of certain religious doctrines increases our respect for them, but does not invalidate our proposal that they should cease to be put forward as the reasons for the precepts of civilization. ... Those historical residues have helped us to view religious teachings, as it were, as neurotic relics, and we may now argue that the time has probably come, as it does in an analytic treatment, for replacing the effects of repression by the results of the rational operation of the intellect.

Freud, at this point, is rather generous in crediting civilization and its strong-arm companion, religion, with having made survival possible. The moral behavior and the ethical codes fostered by religious leaders and institutions, which produce and govern such behavior, contribute to the cohesive functioning of social and corporate life. Without it, there is reason to believe we might not have survived. But now, admonishes Freud, since we understand the origin of this power to validate and punish, to authenticate and chastise, we must as an act of our own social maturity re-assert our own reason, logic, and experience. We now understand the phylogenetic origins of the ontogenetic experience of the father projected into a socially created Father God. Now that we understand its *speciel* origins, we must divest ourselves of its irrationality and embrace our own freedom, our own capacity to govern ourselves without the fictional God in Heaven.

****

CHAPTER IX

Think of the depressing contrast between the radiant intelligence of a healthy child and the feeble intellectual powers of the average adult. Can we be quite certain that it is not precisely religious education which bears a large share of the blame for this relative atrophy? I think it would be a very long time before a child who was not influenced began to trouble himself about God and things in another world ... But we do not wait for such a development; we introduce him to the doctrines of religion at an age when he is neither interested in them nor capable of grasping their import. Is it not true that the two main points in the programme for the education of children today are retardation of sexual development and premature religious influence?

Pressing his argument to its logical conclusion, Freud argues that the stifling of creativity and ingenuity evidenced in the adult suffering under the burden of a religious worldview and ethos pales in the presence of the unadulterated child of innocence, devoid of and protected from the strangling effect of religious instruction. If left alone, children will not pursue questions to which religious educators have prepared answers dealing with God and another world designed to curb their curiosity and to snare their creative imagination. The stifling of sexual development and religious teachings about heaven and hell constitute the two driving principles of religious education and, explains Freud, civilization does not await the maturity of the individual, a maturity vested with the capacity for reason and logic, because bludgeoning the child with its moral mandates is what religion does best.

****

When a man has once brought himself to accept uncritically all the absurdities that religious doctrines put before him and even to overlook the contradictions between them, we need not be greatly surprised at the weakness of his intellect. ... How can we expect people who are under the dominance of prohibitions of thought to attain the psychological ideal, the primacy of the intelligence? So long as a person's early years are influenced not only by a sexual inhibition of thought but also by a religious inhibition and by a loyal inhibition derived from this, we cannot really tell what in fact he is like. ... But surely infantilism is destined to be surmounted. Men cannot remain children for ever; they must in the end go out into 'hostile life.' We may call this 'education to reality.' Need I confess to you that the sole purpose of my book is to point out the necessity for this forward step?

Modern man, explains Freud, is essentially intellectually weakened, owing to the stifling of the use of logic and reason in the governance of his life and decisions, a stifling brought on by religion. Richard Dawkins in this century has called it a "mind virus," but Freud simply suggests that it is the control of the human mind by religious institutions and leaders which constitutes the bane and burden of civilization. The crippling of logic and reason, the diverting of critical thinking into a mantra of religious litanies will one day, some day, and probably sooner than later, be surpassed and psychological maturity will then be a real possibility for the human community. Freud says this is his "sole purpose" in the writing of this book, namely, to usher in the new day of reason and logic divested of religious entanglements.

****

You (the religious person) would have the state of bliss begin directly after death ... On the way to this distant goal your religious doctrines will have to be discarded, no matter whether the first attempts fail, or whether the first substitutes prove to be untenable. Your know why: in the long run nothing can withstand reason and experience, and the contradiction which religion offers to both is all too palpable. ... No doubt if they confine themselves to a belief in a higher spiritual being, whose qualities are indefinable and whose purposes cannot be discerned, they will be proof against the challenge of science; but then they will also lose their hold on human interest. ... Observe the difference between your attitude (believer) to illusions and mine (non-believer). You have to defend the religious illusion with all your might. If it becomes discredited -- and indeed the threat to it is great enough -- then your world collapses. There is nothing left for you but to despair of everything, of civilization and the future of mankind. From that bondage I am, we are, free. Since we are prepared to renounce a good part of our infantile wishes, we can bear it if a few of our expectations turn out to be illusions.

In the long run, explains Freud, in almost a pastoral mode of comportment, everyone will have to succumb to reason and experience. There is no escaping it. And when this happens, the contradictions, the irrationalities, the *non sequiturs*, the superstitions and magic of religious ideology will come to naught. So long as religion insists on holding to a worldview and ethos which defies logic and reason, which denies the role of science in understanding and interpreting the world and our place in it, the human community will be conflicted with divided loyalties -- civilization which began with belief in the power of a Father God, but is now the mechanism itself for producing a scientific explanation of the world. Despair is the final destination of those who cling to a religion in decline. Freedom of thought and action, however, is the journey being trod by those who have let go of God and have embraced modern science.

****

We shall not on that account (the loss of some of our non-believers' illusions) lose our interest in the world and in life, for we have one sure support which you (believers) lack. We believe that it is possible for scientific work to gain some knowledge about the reality of the world, by means of which we can increase our power and in accordance with which we can arrange our life. If this belief is an illusion, then we are in the same position as you. But science has given us evidence by its numerous and important successes that it is no illusion. … No, our science is no illusion. But an illusion it would be to suppose that what science cannot give us we can get elsewhere.

CHAPTER FOUR

Carl Jung and *Psychology and Religion*

From James to Freud is no simple nor easy jump, but once made, there is no turning back. Freud demonstrated both the destructive and constructive power of psychological analysis of religious ideology and behavior. Whether one agreed with his psychoanalytic assessment, and many did not then nor do they now, nevertheless, the astuteness and acuteness of his analysis and critique set the psychological and religious world on its heels, and what followed proved to be provocative and creative in the scholarly world. However, it took Carl Gustav Jung (1875-1961) of Zurich to recapture the religious world's interest in depth psychology's analysis of religion after the devastating blow dealt by Freud. Jung was an avid, though somewhat and sometimes less than traditionally orthodox, Christian and the son of a Swiss Reformed Church pastor. Though early on he was attracted to and influenced by Freud and psychoanalysis, Jung subsequently branched out on his own, "and that has made all the difference." He took his medical degree from the University of Basel and launched his professional career in the Burgholzli, a psychiatric hospital in Zurich, alongside none other than Eugene Bleuler, a colleague who was early on to prove to be an important confidant and collaborator. Following a period of close collegiality with Freud, during which time Freud anticipated Jung becoming his protégé, Jung broke with him over issues related to infantile sexuality and dream interpretation. As prolific a writer as Freud himself, Jung's career as a therapist was paralleled by his career as a writer, and though his book, *Psychology of the Unconscious* (1912) launched him into international notoriety, his little book, *Psychology and Religion,* based on the Terry Lectures given at Yale University in 1938, undoubtedly established him and his school of thought, called "analytical psychology," as a major player in the psychological study of religion, competing with Freud and psychoanalysis as the major school of depth psychology.

Unlike Freud, who seemed to have a personal agenda regarding the negative influences of religion on human freedom and personal development, Jung came with a positive assessment of the phenomenon, albeit somewhat unorthodox in his characterization of the impetus and motivation for the religious life. In 1952, during his declining years as a then-popular sage, he wrote: "I find that all my thoughts circle around God like the planets around the sun, and are as irresistibly attracted by Him. I would feel it to be the grossest sin if I were to oppose any resistance to this force" (1963:xi). It is only here in his autobiography that Jung ever spoke of his personal relationship to God, choosing rather, as in his Terry Lectures, to maintain a professional distance and what he considered to be a scientifically respectable posture. "Notwithstanding the fact that I have often been called a philosopher, I am an empiricist and adhere to the phenomenological standpoint" he said in his opening remarks in the Terry Lectures at Yale University (1938:1).

Jung, differing radically from Freud on this analytical point, argued that the increase in western society of the scientific understanding of the world has led us into a dehumanization of the natural and social environments in which we live and, thus, our prehistoric and primitive responsiveness to occurrences in the natural world have lost their "symbolic efficacy." Therefore, he suggested, modern man has lost touch, has become alienated, from his natural environment. This loss, contended Jung, has led humanity away from a belief in God and has produced a lack of awareness of powers implicit within human nature. Modern society has, therefore, fallen into the grip of psychological disorder and chaos. We are in desperate need, says Jung, of a religious mooring, a religiously-based worldview and ethos, to re-align ourselves with the "collective unconscious," which infuses all of our conscious and unconscious thoughts, actions, and dreams. While religion cannot be proven either true or false, it is quite apparent that the pragmatic value of religious ideology and its resulting belief system served the psychological needs of man "in search of his soul" (Jung 1933:12) While contending vociferously for the universality of the collective unconscious, Jung is quick to point out that there is no possibility of empirically verifying its reality other than in the effectiveness of its use in the treatment of psychological disorders. "At the root of the problem," says Edward (1967:389), "lies an ambiguous set of ontological claims. … it is worth noting that we possess no statistical evidence of a worthwhile kind about the efficacy of Jungian psychotherapy." Be that as it may, the acclaim Jung's Terry Lectures received, particularly from the religious establishment and theological community of the time, was profoundly instrumental in placing Jungian psychology front and center in the development of what would eventuate into a pastoral psychology embraced by virtually every seminary in the country.

Selections from *Psychology and Religion,* by Carl Gustav Jung, with commentary.

NOTE: In the following, the original text will be printed in *Arial Unicode MS* typestyle (as is this note itself to illustrate) as an easy and aesthetically pleasing way of identifying the primary source paragraphs. The author's commentary will be in *Times New Roman*. It is hoped that this differentiation between the "primary source" and the "commentary" made by use of differing typestyles will prove helpful and not disruptive to the reader. *I have also chosen to use a quadruple asterisk (****) to separate the primary text from the commentary.*

Chapter I The Autonomy of the Unconscious Mind

Since religion is incontestably one of the earliest and most universal activities of the human mind, it is self-evident that any kind of psychology which touches upon the psychological structure of human personality cannot avoid at least observing that the fact that religion is not only a sociological or historical phenomenon, but also something of considerable personal concern to a great number of individuals.

Jung had early gained notoriety in America, owing to his having come with Freud to Clark University, from which Freud received an honorary doctorate. However, he subsequently established himself with the encouragement and support of friends and followers at both Yale and Princeton. Jung, unlike his counterpart in depth psychology Sigmund Freud, was keen to elevate a discussion of religion beyond the precariousness of reductionism, which he saw and critiqued in Freudian psychoanalytic theory. Religion, says Jung, is a universal phenomenon bespeaking a universal experience and, therefore, worthy of psychology's close scrutiny. This was the focus of his Terry Lectures and the reason Yale invited him to come.

****

Notwithstanding the fact that I have often been called a philosopher, I am an empiricist and adhere to the phenomenological standpoint. I trust that it does not collide with the principles of scientific empiricism if one occasionally makes certain reflections which go beyond a mere accumulation and classification of experience. ... I approach psychological matters from a scientific and not from a philosophical standpoint. In as much as religion has a very important psychological aspect, I am dealing with it from a purely empirical point of view, that is, I restrict myself to the observation of phenomena and I refrain from any application of metaphysical or philosophical considerations.

Jung early, as he did late, defend himself against what he thought were false accusations of being a philosophical speculator rather than a research psychologist. Riding on the fact that he had, actually, earned a medical degree and was a licensed physician, he used that credential to validate what most research scientists at the time and still today consider Jung's mystical speculating based on eccentric episodic dream-life of neurotic and psychotic patients. He refused to allow the dismissiveness of the scientific community to go unchallenged.

****

I am aware that most people believe they know all there is to be known about psychology, because they think that psychology is nothing but what they know of themselves. But I am afraid psychology is a good deal more than that. While having little to do with philosophy, it has much to do with empirical facts, many of which are not easily accessible to the average experience. It is my intention in this book to give a few glimpses, at least, of the way in which practical psychology becomes confronted with the problem of religion.

Jung became, over the years, more and more critical of Freud and psychoanalysis as Freud became more and more aggressively dismissive of Jung and what Jung had come to call "analytical psychology," with Freud's retort that it was neither analytical nor psychology. Jung dismissed Freud because, as he pointed out, Freud based his theories on his own self-analysis! But, argues Jung, there is a great deal more about the human personality than can be found out by examining one person thoroughly. Freud, too, moved away from self-analysis in his further developmental theories. Jung, rather, chose to select carefully random case histories from his patients of esoteric and exotic dreams to demonstrate his analytical theories, as did Freud, but, Jung pointed out, with a real difference of interpretation.

****

Since I am going to present a rather unusual argument, I cannot assume that my audience is completely aware of the methodological standpoint of that kind of psychology which I represent. This standpoint is exclusively phenomenological, that is, it is concerned with occurrences, events, experiences, in a word, with facts. Its truth is a fact and not a judgment. Speaking for instance of the motive of the virginn birth, psychology is only concerned with the fact that there is such an idea, but it is not concerned with the question whether such an idea is true or false in any other sense. It is psychologically true in as much as it exists. Psychological existence is subjective in so far as an idea occurs in only one individual. But it is objective in so far as it is established by a society -- by a *consensus gentium*.

Jung was aware, if not defensive, about the uniqueness of his analytical approach and interpretation. And, to fend off scientific criticism, which was ever present, he was keen to delineate carefully the methodological approach he employed in his analytical psychology. Always insisting upon the "phenomenological" nature of his analytical approach, a philosophical school of thought which was then and still is very popular, commencing with Hegel and Husserl and not stopping with Heidegger and Merleau-Ponty, his science was defended by his philosophical orientation, which constituted the basis of the scientific criticism in the first place. Nevertheless, Jung was a scientist as he defined science.

****

In speaking of religion I must make clear from the start what I mean by that term. Religion, as the Latin word denotes, is a careful and scrupulous observation of what Rudolf Otto aptly termed the "numinous," that is, a dynamic existence or effect, not caused by an arbitrary act of will. On the contrary, it seizes and controls the human subject, which is always rather its victim than its creator. ... The numinous is either a quality of a visible object or the influence of an invisible presence causing a peculiar alteration of consciousness. ... there are, however, certain exceptions when it comes to the question of practice or ritual. A great many ritualistic performances are carried out for the sole purpose of producing at will the effect of the numinous by certain devices of a magic nature, such as invocation, incantation, sacrifice, meditation and other yoga practices, self-inflicted tortures of various descriptions and so forth. But a religious belief in an external and objective divine cause always precedes any such performance.

Shifting from a defense of his science and its methodology, Jung attribute the operative definition of religion to Rudolf Otto who, in his little classic, *Das Heilige*, 1917 (trans. *The Idea of the Holy,* 1938), had defined religion as the *mysterium tremendous et fascinans*. Religion is not the agenda of man, says Jung, but man is the agenda of religion for religion, or the driving experience owned and perpetrated by religious sensibilities, grips man and holds him captive to the experience of mystery and fascination. In its core, it is a numinal rather than phenomenal encounter. To produce this numinous effect is the motivating force in ritual and liturgy, says Jung, but these are "manifestations" rather than the essence of religion.

****

Religion appears to me to be a peculiar attitude of the human mind, which could be formulated in accordance with the original use of the term "religio," that is, a careful consideration and observation of certain dynamic factors, understood to be "powers," spirits, demons, gods, laws, ideas, ideals or whatever name man has given to such factors as he has found in his world powerful, dangerous or helpful enough to be taken into careful consideration, or grand, beautiful and meaningful enough to be devoutly adored and loved.

Jung does not presume to dismiss religious experience as merely or strictly a human construct, though Jungians may do so without impunity. Jung considers religious experience to be the result of a particular attitude of the human mind in response to the actual experience of powerful factors in the world. Whether those powerful factors as experienced are real or strictly a product of human reflection upon those experiences is a question he does not address nor can it be answered, according to Jung. That the experience is real is without question, says Jung, following in the footsteps of William James, the father of such enquiries. Whether those experiences are the result of an encounter with that which is real cannot be answered. The experience, however, is real.

****

I want to make clear that by the term "religion" I do not mean a creed. ... Religion, it might be said, is the term that designates the attitude peculiar to a consciousness which has been altered by the experience of the numinous. ... Creeds are codified and dogmatized forms of original religious experience. The contents of the experience have become sanctified and usually congealed in a rigid, often elaborate, structure. The practice and the

> reproduction of the original experience have become a ritual and an unchangeable institution. ... the psychologist, in as much as he assumes a scientific attitude, has to disregard the claim of every creed to be the unique and eternal truth. He must keep his eye on the human side of the religious problem, in that he is concerned with the original religious experience quite apart from what the creeds have made of it.

Whereas Freud and company were as eager to challenge the doctrine of religion as the claimed experience of religion, Jung is not. The systematic formulations and systematizations of religious experience and reflection are of no interest to Jung. His interest is solely in the reported and reportable experiential encounter itself. The codification and dogmatization of formulas devised by religious leaders is post-experience and, therefore, far outside the purview of psychological analysis and assessment.

****

> Being a doctor and a specialist in nervous and mental diseases my point of departure is not any creed, but the psychology of the homo religious, the man who takes into account and carefully observes certain factors which influence him and, through him, his general condition. It is easy to denominate and define those factors according to historical tradition or anthropological knowledge, but to do the same thing from the standpoint of psychology is an uncommonly difficult task. What I can contribute to the question of religion is derived entirely from my practical experience, both with my patients and with so-called normal beings.

Jung takes the high road as a practicing physician and clinical researcher in that creeds and dogmas are of no consequence in the assessment of the reported experience of a religious nature. Tradition and cultural conditioning, as well as socially-induced responses to purported religious phenomenon, fall outside the range of psychological analysis, for those things are to be left to historians, anthropologists, sociologists, and theologians. It is the experience itself prior to formulations that constitutes the raw data for psychological assessment. When a human being reports having had an experiential encounter with a religious phenomenon, there begins the psychological analysis.

****

We should not forget that any neurosis means a corresponding amount of demoralization. In so far as man is neurotic, he has lost confidence in himself. A neurosis is a humiliating defeat and is felt as such by people who are not entirely unconscious of their own psychology. ... Our usual materialistic conception of the psyche is, I am afraid, not particularly helpful in neurotic cases. ... Medicine feels a strong dislike toward anything of a psychical nature -- either the body is ill or there is nothing the matter. And if you cannot prove that the body is really diseased, that is because our present means do not enable the physician to find the true nature of the undoubtedly organic trouble.

In his drive to probe the human psyche through dream analysis, particularly in this instance, of having had a religious encounter, Jung is not reluctant to make a key distinction between the practice of medicine, particularly psychiatric pharmacology, and depth psychology, particularly psychotherapy. Whereas medicine must define a situation in terms of ill or well, psychology will more precisely address the issue of functional or dysfunctional. The psyche, says Jung, is an illusive phenomenon for medicine, whereas for psychology it is the focus and substance of that science.

****

But what is the psyche after all? A materialistic prejudice explains it as a merely epiphenomenal by-product of organic processes in the brain. Any psychic disturbance must be an organic or physical disorder which is undiscoverable only because of the insufficiency of our actual diagnostic means. The undeniable connection between psyche and brain gives this point of view a certain strength, but not enough to make it an unshakable truth ... On the other hand, it is indubitable that the real causes of neuroses are psychological. It is indeed very difficult to imagine that an organic or physical disorder can be cured in a moment by a mere confession. But I have seen a just such a case.

Jung will not let pass the general medical definition of the psyche in its traditional dismissive manner, for it is the psyche precisely that constitutes the focus and basis of his life's work. Jung was then and would be even more so now, highly critical of psychopharmacology's domain assumption that to chemically alter the imbalance of a neurotic patient could and does bring about the desired behavioral change for the better. It is not just the behavior of a patient that concerns Jung. It is his overall sense of well-being. This, Jung contends, must go beyond chemistry and address the fundamental composition of the psyche itself.

****

It is, to my mind, a fatal mistake to consider the human psyche as a merely personal affair and to explain it exclusively from a personal point of view. Such a mode of explanation is only application to the individual in his ordinary everyday occupations and relationships. If, however, some slight trouble occurs, perhaps in the form of an unforeseen and somewhat extraordinary event, instantly instinctive forces are called up, forces which appear to be wholly unexpected, new, and even strange. .. The change of character that is brought about by the up-rush of collective forces is amazing. ... it needs as little as a neurosis to conjure up a force that cannot be dealt with by reasonable means. ...

To press his point further for the universality of psychic content and function, Jung refuses to allow the mental disturbances of a neurotic to be dismissed as merely and solely an individual and personal phenomenon. He wishes to elevate such data to a universality of content and function. Jung is so taken with the profundity of this universal content lodged in the human psyche that he expounds on its power and strength, its pervasiveness through time and history, and argues against a dismissal of its reality by the use of the orthodox rules of reason and logic. It is meta-reason, it is meta-logic, says Jung, but it is indubitably real and present in the psyche of every human being, ill or well.

****

Dreams are the voice of the Unknown, that ever threatens with new schemes, new dangers, sacrifices, warfare and other troublesome things. ... There are any amount of creeds and ceremonies that exist for the sole purpose of forming a defense against the unexpected, dangerous tendencies of the unconscious. ... In the last two thousand years we find the institution of the Christian church assuming a mediating and protective function between these influences and man. It is not denied in medieval ecclesiastical writings that a divine influx could take place in dreams, for instance, but this view is not exactly encouraged and the church reserves the right to decide whether a revelation is to be considered authentic or not.

But how to tap into this power source was Jung's ever-abiding question and constituted the basis for his drive to probe and prod the human psyche for the key for entry. He believed he found it in dreams! This "voice of the Unknown," as Jung referred to it, preceded all creeds and rituals, all rational and logical thought, but was present in every human activity from our earliest existence as individuals and as a species. Religious institutions, with their creeds and dogmas, function as a wall between us and that voice, mediating access through approved channels of control and governance. Jung believed that the Christian church (and other religious institutions as well) knew of this power source, knew its uses and abuses, knew its dangers when let loose in the masses without proper control and supervision. Thus, these institutions of religion have evolved as management mechanisms to control and direct and limit access to the voice of the Unknown. Now, depth psychology, particularly in the form of analytical psychology, has come with a way to access this "voice of the Unknown" (but not unknowable) through the analysis of the dream. This was Jung's work, his mission, his service to the troubled and mentally crippled masses laboring under the inordinate governance of religious leaders, authorities, creeds, dogmas, and institutions.

****

There are numerous works ... concerning the phenomenology of dreams, but very few that deal with their psychology. This for the obvious reason that it is a most ticklish and risky business. Freud has made a courageous effort to elucidate the intricacies of dream psychology by the aid of views which he has gathered in the field of psychopathology. Much as I admire the boldness of his attempt, I cannot agree with his method and its results. He explains the dream as a mere façade, behind which something has been carefully hidden. There is no doubt that neurotics hide disagreeable things, probably just as much as normal people do. But it is a serious question whether this category can be applied to such a normal and world-wide phenomenon as the dream. I am doubtful whether we can assume that a dream is something else than it appears to be.

Jung discounts the phenomenology of dream studies which are in reality, he argues, not psychological in nature. He goes further to seemingly compliment Freud for his pioneering work, while likewise discounting or discrediting Freud's psychoanalytic approach to dream analysis as not doing justice to the raw data of dreams itself. Freud's material, explains Jung in a condescending tone, comes from his work in psychopathology, not a particularly satisfying venue in which to mine good dream materials, according to Jung. Believing Freud to have reduced dream content to merely a veneer placed over reality which, then, must be stripped away and interpreted, Jung is quick to argue that his approach takes the actual content of the dream seriously in its own right. Dream symbols are not designed, contrary to Freud's analysis, to disguise and hide from consciousness things better left hidden. Dream imagery is precisely what it purports to be, images of that which it intends.

****

The dream is such a difficult and intricate subject, that I do not dare to make any assumptions about its possible cunning. The dream is a natural even and there is no reason under the sun why we should assume that it is a crafty device to lead us astray. The dream occurs when consciousness and will are to a great extent extinguished. It seems to be a natural product which is also to be found in people who are not neurotic. Moreover, we know so little about the psychology of the dream process that we must be more than careful when we introduce elements foreign to the dream itself into its explanation. For all of these reasons I hold that our dream really speaks of religion and that it means to do so. Since the dream is elaborate and consistent it suggests a certain logic and a certain intention, that is, it is preceded by a motivation in the unconsciousness which finds direct expression the dream content.

The clarity of the imagery, however, does not imply the clarity of the dream's message or intention, explains Jung. The data is intricate, detailed, ancient, and even primordial in origin and purpose. It is "natural" to dream, the imagery is natural to the dreamer, and these images come during sleep, when consciousness and human intentionality are at rest, freeing the psyche to explore its inner chambers. The beauty of dreams is that they occur in both the healthy as well as the mentally disturbed mind and, thus, constitute a fair terrain for exploration without the distractions of psychopathological analysis. Freud's patients were mentally ill; Jung's patients were mentally healthy (for the most part), but adventurers on a pilgrimage into the unconscious chambers of the human psyche. And, concludes Jung, it is the dream journey that leads us to explore religion, for religion, not creeds and dogmas, have to do with the human experience of power and wonder in our universe, our exterior, but more precisely our interior universe of the unconscious archives of human history.

****

Chapter II Dogma and Natural Symbols

I differentiate between that which I have produced or acquired by my own conscious effort and that which is clearly and unmistakably a product of the unconscious mind. Someone may object that the so-called unconscious mind is merely my own mind and that, therefore, such a differentiation is superfluous. But I am not at all certain whether the unconscious mind is merely *my* mind, because the term "unconscious" means that I am not even conscious of it.

It is at this juncture that Jung brings down upon his head the criticisms of the scientific community for it is here that he leaves the hallowed halls of recognized research methodology and moves ever so closely to mysticism. Jung, as clinical practitioner and physician, held his rightful place within the academy and the laboratory so long as he stayed on the beaten path of generally accepted protocol when it came to dream analysis. However, when he ventured into a notion of a universal unconsciousness which each individual mind participated in but was not synonymous with, there he was abandoned by his medical colleagues.

****

We may assume that human personality consists of two things: first, of consciousness and whatever this covers, and second, of an indefinitely large hinterland of unconscious psyche. So far as the former is concerned it can be more or less clearly defined and delimited, but so far as the sum total of human personality is concerned one has to admit the impossibility of a complete description or definition. In other words, there is unavoidably an illimitable and indefinable addition to every personality, because the latter consists of a conscious and observable part which does no contain certain factors whose existence, however, we are forced to assume in order to explain certain observable facts. The unknown factors form what we call the unconscious.

Jung has been credited with great creativity in the study of human personality (so long as he steered clear of anything approaching a "universal unconsciousness," which, alas, was his real interest). His work on the notions of the introverted personality and the extroverted personality and similar explorations merited him a sizeable acclaim within a variety of schools of thought (though some histories of personality theory still omit him as a serious contributor). To claim that the human personality consists of both consciousness and unconsciousness fell in line with Freud and traditional depth psychology, but he pressed the issue in claiming that this unconscious psyche was connected in some way (not genetically but archetypically) to a universe of symbols and images held by all human beings, and it was through these that he would lead his followers to a discussion of the meaning and place of religious experience within the human psyche, both individually and corporately.

****

My psychological experience has shown time and again that certain contents issue from a psyche more complete than consciousness. They often contain a superior analysis or insight or knowledge which consciousness has not been able to produce. We have a suitable word for such occurrences -- intuition. In pronouncing it, most people have an agreeable feeling as if something had been settled. But they never take into account the fact that you do not *make* an intuition. On the contrary it always comes to you; you *have* a hunch, it has produced itself and you only catch it if you are clever or quick enough. Consequently I explain the voice ... as a product of the more complete personality to which the dreamer's conscious self belongs as a part, and I hold that this is the reason why the voice shows an intelligence and a clarity superior to the dreamer's actual consciousness. This superiority is the reason for the unconditioned authority of the voice.

Unquestionably, Jung has moved away from laboratory science and into the darkened chambers of the self-indulging mystic. Whether his insights are of merit remains to be seen, but clearly Jung is not being scientifically orthodox at this juncture; even his language is poetic and mystical in tone and character. The connectedness of the dreamer's consciousness with a universal unconsciousness of symbols and archetypes was the kind of claim that stimulated a tremendous following, particularly among the clergy and the laity, but lost Jung his reputation among the medical and scientific community. He seemed not to care. He had a great following, and clergy flocked to his insistence upon this universal world of the unconscious, plumbed by way of dream analysis. His suggestion that intuition was an empirical indicator of this connectedness of individual consciousness with corporate unconsciousness seemed to have merited him a great deal of attention from the non-scientific community, but lost a comparable amount of ground among medical practitioners.

****

What is usually and generally called "religion" is to such an amazing degree a substitute that I ask myself seriously whether this kind of "religion," which I prefer to call a creed, has not an important function in human society. The substitution has the obvious purpose of replacing immediate experience by a choice of suitable symbols invested in a solidly organized dogma and ritual. The Catholic church maintains them by her indisputable authority, the Protestant church (if this term is still applicable) by insistence upon faith and the evangelical message. As long as those two principles work, people are effectively defended and shielded against immediate religious experience. Even if something of the sort should happen to them, they can refer to the church, for it would know whether the experience came from God or from the devil, whether it was to be accepted or to be rejected.

Jung distinguishes himself as a social psychologist and even sociologist in his particular assessment and characterization of religious institutionalization *vis a vis* religious experience. Creeds and dogmas are not religion, explains Jung, but *manifestations* of religion and, more particularly and to the point, evidence of religious leaders' attempts to control and govern the religious experiences of individuals seeking some authentic expression of that encounter with the power source of the universe. Religious institutions, Jung goes on to explain in a very insightful and provocative matter, serve the ironic function of protecting people from authentic religious experience on the principle that such experience cannot normally be managed by the untrained and untutored, excepting, of course, the occasional mystic or prophet which the religious establishment attempts to control, manage, and eventually institutionalize. When an individual does, indeed, have an authentic encounter with the power source of the universe, a truly "religious experience," they are usually directed to the institutional church to take possession of that experience for explanation and proper management. All of this has disenfranchised the human individual and the human community from having a true encounter with the Divine Source. It is the dream which still escapes the governance of the Church but, alas, with so many clergy following after Jungian analysis, it is only a matter of time until even the dream is appropriated by religious leaders!

****

Chapter III The History and Psychology of a Natural Symbol

Freud has discovered repression as one of the main mechanisms in the making of a neurosis. Suppression amounts to a conscious moral choice, but repression is a rather immoral "penchant" for getting rid of disagreeable decisions. Suppression may cause worry, conflict and suffering, but never causes a neurosis of one of the usual patterns. Neurosis is a substitute for legitimate suffering. ... Unfortunately there is no doubt about the fact that man is, as a whole, less good than he imagines himself or wants to be. Everyone carries a shadow, and the less it is embodied in the individual's conscious life, the blacker and denser it is.

This was radically new stuff in 1938 to be presented in a traditional setting at Yale University under the aegis and blessings of the Terry Lectures. Jung was not unaware of it and took advantage of the opportunity at every juncture. The study of religion from the discipline of psychology was on the move, thanks to James and Freud and lesser lights, but Jung had introduced yet another way into the subject matter, namely, dreams as symbols and archetypes of the universal unconscious. What great excitement he caused with this suggestion. Driven by Jung's own Calvinist upbringing by a father and grandfather and uncles who were all in the Protestant ministry, he had no difficulty identifying and embracing the notion of a "shadow" within the human psyche, the blacker and denser element of human consciousness.

****

We carry our past with us, to wit, the primitive and inferior man with his desires and emotions, and it is only by a considerable effort that we can detach ourselves from this burden. If it comes to a neurosis, we have invariably to deal with a considerably intensified shadow. And if such a case wants to be cured it is necessary to find a way in which man's conscious personality and his shadow can live together. This is a very serious problem for all those who are either themselves in such a predicament, or who have to help other people to live. A mere suppression of the shadow is just as little of a remedy as is beheading against headache. To destroy a man's morality does not help either, because it would kill his better self, without which even the shadow makes no sense.

That ontogeny recapitulates phylogeny was earlier formulated by Freud, meaning only that the individual maturation process was reciprocally reflected in the evolution of the human species. However, Jung takes that notion one giant step forward by suggesting, based on his analysis of dream content, that the individual person's unconscious participates in and carries with it the full mass of primordial content of all humanity. This was going too far for much of the scientific community, the notion that "somehow" symbols and archetypes are carried from one generation to another through individual unconsciousness. He did not claim this to be genetic or related to the DNA. Nevertheless, that it occurred was without question. The how of the thing was impossible to address or answer, but the fact of the thing, Jung argued, was not to be questioned. Mental health, explained Jung, requires a balance of the waking personality with the shadow of the unconscious. This was the work of analytical psychology and its dream-analysis methodology.

****

Religion is a relationship to the highest or strongest value, be it positive or negative. The relationship is voluntary as well as involuntary, that is, you can accept, consciously, the value by which you are possessed unconsciously. That psychological fact which is the greatest power in your system is the god, since it is always the overwhelming psychic factor which is called god. As soon as a god ceases to be an overwhelming factor, he becomes a mere name. His essence is dead and his power is gone. Why have the antique gods lose their prestige and their effect upon human souls? It was because the Olympic gods had served their time and a new mystery began: God became man.

Like William James, Jung will not be caught professing a personal belief in a personal God, but he does come close here and throughout his writings, especially during his waning years. The fact, however, that religion was the mechanism to foster ethical behavior and provide a venue for moral conduct, was, for Jung, an essential component of civilization (Freud's term for culture) and, argued Jung, without this reliance upon religion as the mechanism to foster and direct access to the power source of the universe, the human community would be cut adrift without any psychic moorings. This must not happen in the evolutionary process of "man coming of age." Man, Jung suggests in another place, is in search of his soul, and it is religion which provides the map for the journey.

****

When we now speak of man we mean the indefinable whole of him, an ineffable totality, which can only be formulated symbolically. I have chosen the term "self" to designate the totality of man, the sum total of conscious and unconscious existence. I have chosen this term in accordance with Eastern philosophy, which for centuries has occupied itself with those problems that arise when even the gods cease to become human. The philosophy of the Upanishads corresponds to a psychology that long ago recognized the relativity of the gods. This is not to be confounded with such a stupid error as atheism.

Jung's blatant discounting of atheism as stupid was a cheap shot across the bow at Freud and psychoanalysis, which had built its critique of religion on a non-theistic assessment of man's place in the universe. Jung, on the other hand, held back from making faith professions of his own, allowing his followers, particularly the eager clergy and the naïve laity, to assume and presume a theism implicit in analytical psychology. The "self" constituted Jung's beginning and ending when dealing with the human person, for it encompassed everything of relevance to humankind: his psyche, his conscious state, his unconsciousness. There is nothing about humankind outside the self and he took his inspiration from the Indian classical literature of the East for symbolic representations. Jung's drift towards Hindu and Buddhist symbolism and artistic expressions in the form of the Mandela and poetic recitations of the lesser gods became a distinguishing characteristic of his later writings and the Terry Lectures provided the forum for his early announcement of this trajectory in his thought.

****

In remote times the main body of psychical life was apparently in human and in nonhuman objects; it was projected, as we should say now. Consciousness can hardly exist in a state of complete projection. At most it would be nothing but a heap of emotions. Through the withdrawal of projections, conscious knowledge slowly developed. Science, curiously enough, practically began with the discovery of astronomical laws, which was a first stage in the de-spiritualization of the world. One step slowly followed another. Already in antiquity they removed the gods from mountains and rivers, from trees and animals. Our science has subtiliated its projections to an almost unrecognizable degree. But our ordinary psychological life is still swarming with projections. You can find them spread out in the newspapers, books, rumors and in ordinary social gossip. All gaps in actual knowledge are still filled with projections. We are still almost certain we know what other people think or what their true character is.

The "de-spiritualization of the world," was a favorite topic of Jung and constituted, for him, a great lament over the loss of our pristine preoccupation with mystery and superstition fostered by dreams and environmental events such as lightning and thunder. But, alas, the emergence of the scientific propensity of man, our desire to really know the reason for things, produced a suppression of these earlier primordial sensitivities within the human psyche. This was particularly lamentable in that we displaced the gods of antiquity with the science of modernity. But, rejoices Jung, our psychological lives, our psyche, is still susceptible to and in possession of these primordial data of experience. We still possess the capacity to "project" our recollected past onto the present through art, literature, music, rumors, and gossip. Our past is still alive in our unconscious present.

****

Modern psychological development leads to a much better understanding as to what man really consists of. The gods first lived in superhuman power and beauty on the top of snow-clad mountains or in the darkness of caves, woods, and seas. Later on they drew together into one god, and then that god became man. But the gods in our time assemble in the lap of the ordinary individual and are as powerful and as awe-inspiring as ever, in spite of their new disguise -- the so-called psychical functions.

Jung's confidence in the insightfulness of modern psychology was reassuring to many of his colleagues, who wondered whether he was drifting into a mystic's fascination with the esoteric and exotic phenomena of the dream-world of the mentally insane. Whether Jung was insinuating the Christian doctrine of the Incarnation when he consistently spoke of "god becoming man" is an open argument, but that modern man is able to wrestle with the superhuman powers and beauties of the primordial world of mountain-inhabiting gods can only occur, says Jung, through an analysis of the unconscious, for we have stifled our sensitivities to the ancients with modern science and technology. The work to be done in aligning our modern psyche with the legacy of primordial phenomenon is left now to depth psychology as the science of dream interpretation.

****

Man thinks of himself as holding the psyche in the hollow of his hand. He dreams even of making a science of her. But in reality she is the mother and the maker, the physical subject and even the possibility of consciousness itself. The psyche reaches so far beyond the boundary line of consciousness that the latter could be easily compared to an island in the ocean. While the island is small and narrow, the ocean is immensely wide and deep, so that if it is a question of space, it does not matter whether the gods are inside or outside. But if the historical process of the de-spiritualization of the world -- the withdrawal of projections --- is going on as hitherto, then everything of a divine or demonic character must return to the soul, to the inside of the unknown man. At first the materialistic error seems to be inevitable. Since the throne of god could not be discovered among the galactic systems, the inference was that god had never existed. The second inevitable mistake is psychologism: if god is anything, he must be an illusion derived from certain motives, from fear, for instance, from will to power, or from repressed sexuality. These arguments are not new.

Jung is as quick to criticize contemporary civilization as was Freud, but with a difference: Freud's criticism was culture's suppression of human freedom through the use of mechanisms for the stifling of creativity and freedom of expression, particularly the role of religion as that mechanism, whereas Jung is critical of our contemporary dismissal of our primordial moorings embodied in our dream world of symbols and archetypes. They are, in essence, as far away from each others' reasons for social criticism as night from day. Jung believed that the only way to retrieve what has been de-spiritualized through modern science and technology is through tapping into the repository of the unconscious, and this can only be done through dream analysis. Jung believed we had psychologized ourselves out of a capacity to believe in God, and had presumed that all there is to human life is the phenomenal. There is no god so there is no soul of man or numinal side to the universe.

****

Since the idea of God represents an important, even overwhelming, psychical intensity, it is, in a way, safer to believe that such an autonomous intensity is a non-ego, perhaps an altogether different or superhuman entity, "totaliter-aliter." Confronted with such a belief man must needs feel small, just about his own size. But if he declares the "tremendous" to be dead, then he should find out at once where this considerable energy, which was once invested in an existence as great as God, has disappeared.

Jung would settle for a belief in God to be a belief in the Totally Other, a God that is still so very overwhelming as a psychic phenomenon that when embraced it would stabilize human individuals and society itself. To declare the absence of such a power source is to deny man's own future, his own sense of well-being. If God does not exist, then mankind is smaller than he once believed himself to be. There is no power source, no mystery, no beckoning to man to come up higher. Whether or not God is real does not concern Jung so much as the necessity of man believing that God is real, for in such a belief, man becomes greater than himself and embraces the future with hope.

****

If I am right in assuming that every religion is a spontaneous expression of a certain predominant psychological condition, then Christianity was the formulation of a condition that predominated in the beginning of our era and that was valid for many subsequent centuries. But it expressed one condition predominant just then, which does not exclude the existence of other conditions that are equally capable of religious expression. Christianity had to fight for its life for a while against Gnosticism which, for all we know, was another condition almost tantamount to the "Christian" precondition. Gnosticism was stamped out completely and its remnants are so badly mangled that special study is needed to get any insight at all into its inner meaning. But if the historical roots of our symbols extend beyond the Middle Ages they are certainly to be found in Gnosticism.

Jung's fascination with Gnosticism was no secret. In fact, he wrote extensively upon the subject, and his passion for the subject constituted a major portion of his energy later in life. Religion, as Jung always contended, was not creeds and dogmas nor institutionalized forms of ritual expression. Those things bespoke the original religious experience, an experience of individuals and societies as they encountered the power source of the universe. It is fundamentally a psychological condition, a situation of the human mind, experienced by the conscious mind and mediated through the symbols of the unconscious, particularly the dream world. But before Christianity, there was the gnosis! The Gnostics were susceptible to the unconscious world of symbol and ritual, and that susceptibility was carried on in the Christian tradition, its creeds and dogmas providing authenticity and legitimacy to the shadow of human consciousness, and that power continues somewhat unabated to modern times.

****

Religious experience is absolute. It is indisputable. You can only say that you have never had such an experience, and your opponent will say: "Sorry, I have." And there your discussion will come to an end. No matter what the world thinks about religious experience, the one who has it possesses the great treasure of a thing that has provided him with a source of life, meaning and beauty and that has given a new splendor to the world and to mankind. He has pistis and peace. Where is the criterium by which you could say that such a life is not legitimate, that such experience is not valid and that such pistis is mere illusion? Is there, as a matter of fact, any better truth about ultimate things than the one that helps you to life?

Again, Jung with William James defended the "experience" of religion without having to defend the "truth" of the religious claim about God. Many have had that experience while others have not. Those who have need not defend it and those who have not are hardly in a position to deny to others what they themselves have not had (though the same could be said of a mental breakdown or a psychiatric episode of insanity). Yet and still, Jung and James defended the legitimacy of the experience without attempting to defend the truth of the religious claims made from that experience. Jung goes so far as to ask, since a kind of abiding peace comes with such experiences, why would anyone wish to forbid or deny the experience? The only justification needed for religion is that it makes life easier!

****

The thing that cures a neurosis must be as convincing as the neurosis; and since the latter is only too real, the helpful experience must be of equal reality. It must be a very real illusion, if you want to put it pessimistically. But what is the difference between a real illusion and a healing religious experience? It is merely a difference in words. You can say, for instance, that life is a disease with a very bad prognosis, it lingers on for years to end with death; or that normality is a generally prevailing constitutional defect; or that man is an animal with a fatally overgrown brain. This kind of thinking is the prerogative of habitual grumblers with bad digestions. Nobody can know what the ultimate things are. We must, therefore, take them as we experience them. And if such experience helps to make your life healthier, more beautiful, more complete and more satisfactory to yourself and to those you love, you may safely say: "This was the grace of God."

Jung ceases to be a representative of the medical profession and takes on the guise of a minister and pastoral counselor in this closing remark about the value and function of religion. There is no argument offered by the scientific community, only a sigh of dismissal.

****

CHAPTER FIVE

David E. Roberts and *Psychotherapy and A Christian View of Man*

By the middle of the 20th century, the touchstones of the development of the psychology of religion as a *bona fide,* however yet fledgling, discipline of study, though many had contributed, were clearly the pivotal works of James, Leuba, Freud, and Jung. From respectable curiosity to depth analysis, the "psychological" nature of religious ideology and behavior was well established, thanks to these four individuals who were, of course, buttressed by the works of many, though lesser, researchers and writers of the time (Beit-Hallahmi 1974; Henry 1938; page 1951; Schaud 1923; Schaud 1924; Strunk 1957). And, though Jung was unabashed in his allegiance to Christianity, being the son of a Christian minister and himself a psychiatrist who did not fail to traffic in Christianity nomenclature, nevertheless, a full fledged address to the relationship between the Christian view of the human condition and the relevance of a scientific psychology had not yet occurred. All of that changed profoundly in 1950 with the publication of *Psychotherapy and a Christian View of Man,* by David E. Roberts of Union Theological Seminary in New York City. That same year, three leading psychologists would publish their contributions to the field of psychology of religion and, with these four books, the discipline of psychology of religion was well positioned to claim a rightful place at the table in both academies of psychology and religious studies.

David E. Roberts (1911 - 1955) was an Omaha, Nebraska, native and the son of the Rev. Dr. William E. Roberts. He graduated in 1931 from Occidental College and went on to earn his Bachelor of Divinity *magna cum laude* from the Union Theological Seminary in New York City. Having earned a traveling fellowship from the Seminary, he traveled and studied extensively in Germany and England, earning his Ph.D. from the University of Edinburgh in Scotland, and returning to the Seminary in 1936 as a member of the faculty, first as instructor, and then, in rapid succession, assistant professor, associate professor, the Marcellus Hartley Professor of the Philosophy of Religion and Dean of Students by 1950, dying in his sleep at the early age of 44 in 1955. A Phi Beta Kappa and prolific writer of scholarly articles for the leading journals of the day, his only book was the now classic and at the time internationally acclaimed *Psychotherapy and a Christian View of Man,* published in New York by Charles Scribner's Sons in 1950. A brief 161 page study, it was poised to change the face of psychological studies of Christian thought in every major seminary in the United States. Both Rollo May, a leading psychotherapist of the time, and Paul Tillich, the leading liberal Protestant theologian of the 20th century, joined in touting the originality of Roberts' study, and Seward Hiltner of Princeton, the leading authority at the time in the fledgling field of pastoral care and counseling, mandated in his endorsement that all pastors and theologians, as well as psychologists and psychotherapists, owed it to themselves and their profession to become acquainted with "this remarkable book."

Roberts' work was cut out for him in this study because, on the one hand, he had to tread lightly, but confidently, amidst the psychological nomenclature and analysis of religious behavior, satisfying both psychiatry and secular psychologists, while simultaneously threading his way through the theological maze of fundamental Christian concepts such as creation, the Fall, sin, grace, predestination, and salvation. To please the medical and psychological community was ominous, but to complicate that by attempting to at least stay clear of major battles with divergent theologies within the Christian camp was quite another. He did it with aplomb to, seemingly, the satisfaction and commendation of both disciplines of psychology and theology.

Granted that Roberts' theocentricism and, sometimes quite conspicuously, his christocentrism took a major hand in setting the agenda for discussion of the interrelatedness of psychotherapy (and its seasoned partner, psychoanalysis) and Christian theology, nevertheless, he was eager to demonstrate that a mature theological methodology would and should incorporate psychological components in its concept of the human person. Sin and depression, therapy and forgiveness, salvation and wholeness constitute parallels in psychology and religion, and his attempt was to demonstrate how both professions can work together for the benefit of the individual without necessarily relinquishing the unique domain of each. Whether he succeeded or not is not so important for us here as to realize that the discipline of the psychology of religion took a major stride forward in fostering dialogue between the two disciplines and the two professions of clergy and psychologists in a way that all previous attempts had neither tried nor succeeded at doing. To even place the terms "psychotherapy" and "Christian" within the same title of the book was monumental and set the stage for the next twenty-five years of dialogue between the professions.

Selections from *Psychotherapy and A Christian View of Man,* by David E. Roberts, with commentary.

NOTE: In the following, the original text will be printed in *Arial Unicode MS* typestyle (as is this note itself to illustrate) as an easy and aesthetically pleasing way of identifying the primary source paragraphs. The author's commentary will be in *Times New Roman*. It is hoped that this differentiation between the "primary source" and the "commentary" made by use of differing typestyles will prove helpful and not disruptive to the reader. *I have also chosen to use a quadruple asterisk (****) to separate the primary text from the commentary.*

PREFACE

In this book I use "psychiatry," "psychotherapy" and "psycho-analysis" more or less interchangeably because, in view of the non-technical character of the chapters on psychology, no useful purpose would be served in making the necessary distinctions. Strictly speaking, however, "psychiatry" involves the whole range of medical care for the mentally ill. "Psychotherapy" is one specific technique within that range. And if the wishes of Freudians were followed, "psycho-analysis" would be used only in connection with their form of psychotherapy. It would be cumbersome, however, to use a different word or phrase whenever a departure from Freudianism is involved, even though both Jung and Adler have taken the trouble to furnish distinctive labels for their theories. Instead, I have simply called attention to modifications of Freud's doctrines, or disagreements with them at relevant points in the text.

Though not intended as an apology from a layman to the professionals, Roberts does from the very start indicate his ready willingness to "lump" the various branches of the science of psychology and its practice into a generalized category without the subtle distinctions employed among psychologists themselves. This is, of course, acceptable for a self-professed layman who is a trained theologian and not a professional psychologist. What is amazing about this little book is that it constitutes the first effort within the theological community to speak to and with professional psychologists in a manner in which and a hope of which to be received as professional peers. That it received the enthusiastic endorsement of no less than Paul Tillich himself is indication enough of its pioneering endeavor.

****

CHAPTER I Co-operation between Religion and Psychotherapy

The effects of the initial hostility with which religious thinkers greeted Freud and the effects, in turn, of his remarks about religion, have not completely disappeared by any means. Nevertheless, within both psychiatric and Christian groups there are some who have found a harmonization between religious faith and mental health not only possible, but well-nigh inescapable. … probably the one salutary lesson to be learned from irresponsible attacks upon psychotherapy is that it does need uniform standards of licensure in order to weed out quacks. … Through clinical training and through courses in counseling, the theological seminaries are extending the facilities whereby pastors may acquire greater knowledge and competence in helping people who suffer from emotional conflicts. Indeed, a significant proportion of the clergy now have a favorable, even an eager, attitude towards obtaining whatever enlightenment and assistance they can from psychotherapy.

Roberts, as theologian, is a pioneer, and some might venture even to say a hero, for both the professions of ministry and psychology for he will commence a conversation in this little work that will endure through six decades without abatement and with much productivity for both professions. He is the first major voice within the seminary culture establishment to both praise and call for more work in psychology by those in ministry education training. Furthermore, he calls for a "standardization" of nomenclature and licensure requirements and practices which, up to this point, had not been formally and publicly solicited from the professional schools and practitioners. It was a landmark call and the result, though mixed to be sure, have precipitated a plethora of professional associations, societies, bodies of all faith-stances, and educational standards.

****

There are not enough psychiatrists to staff our mental hospitals, at a time when public opinion is clamoring for expansion and improvement of such facilities. ... It needs maximum help from schools, courts, social service agencies, and from every other institution or profession that deals with people in their family relationships and their personal troubles. The Church and its ministers are much more aware of the problem and much more willing to co-operate in meeting it than was the case a generation ago. ... Therefore the Church should be looked upon by the psychiatric profession as a potential ally of enormous importance. ... The pastor himself -- again, if properly trained -- can deal with many pressing personal problems which will never reach a psychiatrist's office.

Roberts, of course, is writing at a time when nationally there were countless state hospitals for the mentally insane! Those days are gone, since Ronald Reagan essentially closed most of them on the grounds that the incarceration of the patients was a violation of their civil rights. Since then, homelessness and street-side mental illness goes fundamentally untreated. But when Roberts was writing, there were many understaffed such institutions. He wrote between the Korean War and the Vietnam War, when the need for mental health services was definitely on the rise. This was, says he, the propitious moment for the religious community, the Church establishment, to step up and take the lead in both training of professionals and providing of such services to those in need. The clergy could, Roberts argued, become the "friend" of mental health professionals, at the time an innovative idea.

****

> Because the Church plays an important role in shaping the moral assumptions of a community, it is bound to exercise a steady influence either *in the prevention* or *in the aggravation* of mental illness. Part of its task, in learning increasingly how to exert a beneficent instead of a harmful influence, involves examining its own beliefs and practices in the light of what psychotherapy has to offer. ... Among the expedients available, aside from "education," there are only two which can *directly* transform man's internal character-structure; only two which can thus assist him to bring forth from within himself the resources for changing the patterns of contemporary civilization. Those two resources are psychotherapy and religion. Quite conceivably they may not succeed.

Roberts is bold and clear in pointing to the Church as both the purveyor of mental health and its antagonist! To early on acknowledge the possibility, if not actuality, of the religious community itself being responsible for the psychiatric fallout of religious faith is strong medicine to the clergy, administered by one of their own. Yet, says he, the cure for the ailment is in learning what is available from the professional community of psychologists, particularly those in the practice of psychotherapy. Both the profession of ministry and the profession of psychotherapy are uniquely situated in society to offer help to those suffering from mental illness, but the help will be greatly enhanced if there is professional collaboration rather than antagonism between the two.

****

Evolution has produced a few crucial "leaps"; one where life emerged and gained a foothold; another where rational self-consciousness developed and managed to maintain itself. ... But it does not follow that we should leave matters to chance, in the blind faith that "evolution" or "man's fundamental will-to-live" or his intelligence or his goodness will enable us to rise to the emergency somehow. ... The curing of psychological and spiritual ills makes a direct contribution to the building of a better world; but one does not have to believe that the advent of this better world is either possible or likely in order to justify such cures.

The courage of Roberts is seemingly unlimited, for he early embraced evolution as the way of understanding the world and our place in it, then proceeds to suggest that the two pivotal "leaps" in that process was first, the appearance of life on the planet, and second, the emergence of self-reflective awareness within the human animal. That being said, he suggests that the human community needs not necessarily presume that chance will continue to provide solutions to our problems of living in the world. A better world, says he, can come from a concerted and joint effort between psychology and religion.

****

CHAPTER II THE NEED FOR THERAPY

The most important discoveries of psycho-analysis have been connected with the manner in which it has been able to gain access to unconscious factors and to study their role in mental conflict. Generally speaking, insofar as we are conscious of what is involved in a conflict or tension, serious psychological harm does not result ...When we are aware of putting aside or restricting an impulse, that is called "suppression." We deliberately relinquish or limit a given desire for the sake of serving a purpose which we regard as worth the cost involved. By and large, suppression does not cause psychological harm. ... However, when we reject an impulse in such a way that we are largely or wholly unconscious of it, that is called "repression," and, by and large, it is harmful.

Roberts is aware, of course, that his readership is not, by and large, the professional community of psychologists, but rather the clergy. On occasion, the simplicity of his remarks must be justified with this point painfully in mind lest one think Roberts is either talking down to his reader or is simply a naïve layman when it comes to psychology. Roberts is doing neither. His emphasis upon what psychology does and can offer is, however, presented to the professional clergyperson who is, by default, a layman in the school of psychology and psychotherapy. Thus, his summary of the distinction between "suppression" and "repression" must be taken in this context. It is a sophomoric assessment in psychology but must not be ignored by the clergy in their pastoral duties where counseling is required.

****

How does harmful (neurotic) conflict get started? In the family situation; but well-night everything, healthy a well as unhealthy, gets started in the family situation. ... We cannot have the high potentialities of human nature without the attendant risks. If the goods of a cultural heritage must be transmitted through the development of each new person, then evils -- emotional disorders, prejudices, unjust social and economic patterns, deeply rooted national hatreds -- can be transmitted and perpetuated in the same way. ... Often it is only after one has become an adult, with considerable experience of diversified patterns of living, that one can look back upon his own parents and trace adequately within himself what they have "done to him"' and such a retracing of the past does not usually occur on a full scale outside psycho-analysis.

Roberts' interplay between technical and common terminology, such as using "harmful" and "neurotic" as synonyms, is a heuristic tool for his readers and it proves effective. In this particular instance, he is eager for the reader to understand the etiology of conflict within the context of family and personality maturation. The "tracing" of the origins of conflict, he explains, falls within the purview of psychoanalysis and psychotherapeutic practice and not commonly with the clergy. However, pastors who understand this issue are better prepared to assess and refer.

****

A large proportion of the self-rejection which takes place in the growing child is centered around his biological equipment in general and his sexual equipment in particular. Stupid handling of toilet training and of sexual curiosity is disastrous because repudiation of the body injures one's capacity for deep feeling, for affection, and for a sense of organic relatedness with nature and with other human beings. An especially baffling problem is posed by the fact that even when parents are intelligent about such matters they cannot safeguard the child from adverse surrounding influences. However, if he has been allowed to take a healthy attitude toward his own body, it may "roll off his back" when an old maid of either sex calls him "dirty" for manifesting the curiosities that are normal in growing children. At least his chances are much better than those of a child who grows up in a family where silence, embarrassment or severity surround the subject.

Eager to challenge the naïve and often destructive practices of the well-meaning but poorly informed parent about child-rearing practices generally, and sexual training specifically, Roberts presses for the value and utility of psychological training and understanding being promoted and encouraged by religious leaders and institutions. When the professional clergy take the lead in offering and encouraging such education, the entire community benefits. Clergy informed by the psychological community's deep understanding of these matters is crucial for an effective participation of the religious community in the healthy nurture of its children through the maturation process towards adulthood.

****

We have been tracing some of the main causes that contribute to the development of neuroses, and we can now summarize our findings by taking a cross-section glance at the neurotic personality. ... First, the standards by means of which the individual judges himself have become internalized in such a manner that they function, in part, automatically and unconsciously. ... Therefore, his own picture of what constitutes being "good" or "amounting to something" may be seriously out of line with his needs as a unique individual, and even out of line with what is indispensable to the psychological health of *any* child. Second, rejected impulses do not cease operation merely by being excluded from consciousness; but so long as the conscientious part of the self has the upper hand, these repressed impulses are compelled to engage in a sort of running warfare. ... Thirdly, there is the *ego*, which coincides with the individual's conscious picture of his own personality. If his conscientious standards function, for the most part, automatically and his repressed impulses drive him unconsciously, what power is left to the poor ego? ... We can describe a neurotic person, therefore, as one who is not free to be himself -- fully, naturally and simply. ... many neurotic structures can be explained as desperate attempts to hold the self together against the threat of complete disintegration.

What is heartening about Roberts' approach to instruct the clergy about psychological insights into the causes of neuroses is his matter-of-fact presumption that the clergy reading his book is receptive to this kind of instruction. Splendid! Roberts assumes that the reluctant will close the book and walk away but for the clergy who stay the course, they will be the benefactors. Of course, Roberts points out, the deep-seated origins of neuroses are in the unconscious. A child caught in the untenable situation of being torn between what he thinks his parents or society expects of him and what he expects of himself will inevitably generate stress and tension which must be dealt with in some fashion, and, says Roberts, often that method is repression and subsequently neurosis rising from the unconscious caverns of the mind. The loss of personal freedom occurs and the individual becomes the victim of the dictates of his unconscious repressions. In the midst of this stress, the individual becomes a prime candidate for the benefits of psychotherapy and it lies often with the clergy to identify this situation first and to take action.

****

Without entering into theological questions at the moment, it should be obvious from such a summary that these psychotherapeutic aims are compatible with the aims of sound religion. It is also well to note one of the reasons why neurotic disorders and interest in religion are sometimes found together. The person who can "adjust" comfortably to a thin, externalized existence will not feel the need for a deeper orientation, and he is not likely to get sick. ... Psychotherapists have long recognized that a neurosis can be a blessing in disguise; for it can prevent a person from settling back into a narrow, obtuse, humdrum organization of his life, and compel him, the course of seeking to get rid of his unhappiness, to "break open" into a more complete employment of his own vitality and insight.

Roberts is a theologian first and last but one who is aware of and sensitive to the contributions psychotherapy is in a position to offer in the exercise and practice of ministry. He is particularly keen to identify points of "convergence" between psychotherapeutic practice and pastoral ministry, and the psychology and theology that lie behind both fields of study. What is so very striking and beneficial here is Roberts' quick recognition that there is often, not always, a direct link between neurotic disorders and religious beliefs and practices, what in some circles is called the "psychiatric fallout of religion." Often, says he, religion becomes the escape mechanism for not dealing with serious emotional issues and problems, what, we should be reminded, Karl Marx referred to as the "opiate of the people," namely, a mechanism for numbing the mind to avoid discomfort. Neuroses can, says psychotherapy, be a blessing in that it, too, functions as a mechanism for numbing the sensibilities to the otherwise unbearable situations of emotional disturbance.

****

Often people for whom religion has been a matter of intense, shattering personal experience, instead of a matter of conventional observance, have been "neurotic" in the sense that they have been driven to seek deeper orientations than those provided by the "closed" society in which they lived. This does not mean that all the religious solutions they have reached have been equally valid. When religious fantasies are used to consolidate a neurosis they can produce "remedies' worse than the disease they are supposed to cure. Nevertheless, it is also true that fruitful struggle to cope with and to overcome inner conflict may drive a man into the deepest levels of religious awareness and understanding.

Quick to elaborate upon the "dangers" of the convergence of neuroses and religious beliefs, Roberts cautions the clergy reader about efforts to deepen the "faith experience" within the life of a person suffering from debilitating neurosis, for in the doing of that there is the greater danger of exacerbating the individual's problem. These deep plunges into faith and neurosis have historically been the things of which mystics and religious fanatics have been made. Not always, but commonly, this journey leads to greater problems than the initial mental disturbance. It has been half-facetiously suggested that if Prozac had been around during the Middle Ages, we would have no saints at all!

****

CHAPTER III HOW THERAPY WORKS, AND WHY

Why does psychotherapy work? The simplest answer is that it provides a situation in which a person can be completely honest with himself and with a fellow human being. Conversely, it provides a situation in which he can discover how much he has deceived himself hitherto; the manner in which his ideal picture of himself, his unrecognized needs, and his special way of trying to make the universe conform to his private demands, have caused him to distort reality. ... In the literature concerning mental illness, the materials which furnish an account of neurotic and psychotic disorders are much more clear-cut and definite than those which deal with the techniques of healing. ... A general account of "our inner conflicts' covers tendencies and traits which, in various ways, are operative in everyone. But the healing process, if it is to be effective, must be "tailor-made" to fit each individual.

Keeping in mind that Carl Rogers, at this juncture in time, was just finalizing his "client-centered therapy" model for clergy and other mental health workers, Roberts is very eager to present psychotherapy as a viable modality of international nurture between clergy and their constituency. Also and necessarily, he is forced to simplify the nature of psychotherapeutic counseling, both in terms of the "how" of it and the "why" of it. To speak about depth psychology in simple terms is a challenge to anyone but he seems to be up to the task. He points out, for instance, that the characteristics of mental illness -- neurosis, psychosis, conflict, stress, etc. -- are fairly standardized within the profession in terms of definition and description. Today we have the DSM series (Diagnostic and Statistical Manual) produced by the American Psychological Association. In those days, there was nothing nearly so sophisticated and standardized. Yet, within the profession, there was a consensus more or less about the definitions and descriptions of psychiatric symptoms. However, as he emphasizes, the treatment process and optional modalities of care were extremely disparate. More on this phenomenon later.

****

Granted adequate psychiatric training and experience, here are some of the skills which vary with the personality of the therapist: ability to form an accurate over-all impression of the individual he is working with; ability to move from a general knowledge of the dynamics of normal and abnormal psychology to an illuminating application in the particular case; ability to penetrate behind the appearances, the tone of voice, the incidental gesture, the seemingly trivial details, to what is going on in the other person; ability to grasp intuitively (though on the basis of hard-won, text-book knowledge) how apparently unrelated items fall together into a pattern; ability to interpret dreams; ability to anticipate crises and turning points. Most of all, the therapist's effectiveness depends upon his ability to detect his own limitations -- lack of sympathetic insight, inability to be sufficiently objective, involuntary ways of "using" the patient to fulfill his own needs.

Having set the stage for a recitation of the various and multiple skill-sets required within the profession of psychotherapeutic practice, Rogers then proceeds to itemize them with little or no elaboration. The list is telling in terms of both his understanding of the range of the professional tools available to psychotherapists and the scope of treatment modalities implied in these tools. Following this impressive roster of skill-sets required in the profession, he concludes by emphasizing the importance of the therapist being willing to recognize and own his skill limitations, implying that this is not a bad thing for clergy to acknowledge for themselves as well.

****

In ordinary life, the person who faces serious emotional problems is usually isolated, no matter how many relatives and acquaintances he has, in the sense that he knows no one to whom he would dare communicate the nature of his problems. Therapy not only puts an end to such isolation; it offers the kind of reassurance which enables a person to move forward into painful and frightening forms of self-understanding he would not otherwise have the strength to face. In a word, therapy offers a human relationship in which the false-front is no longer necessary. Therefore it makes it possible to become aware of how false the front is and of what it is concealing. ... Psychological conflicts arise in connection with dynamic, emotional relationships with other persons. Therefore, the most direct way of removing them involves replacing condemnatory, confining and artificial relationships with a form of human fellowship which embodies the opposite characteristics.

That therapy provides an arena of confidentiality and trust is for Roberts a central function. It should be pointed out that since his day many empirical studies have been done on clergy stress and burnout, suggesting that the absence of a "safe haven" for debriefing for the pastor constitutes a primary cause of emotional breakdowns among the clergy. Therapy, in whatever form, must first and foremost provide this two-fold function of confidentiality and trust. Later, Harry Stack Sullivan, the father of modern American social psychiatry, will emphasize the centrality of "interpersonal relations" as the key ingredient which is absent or flawed in all mental illness and emotional dysfunction. Roberts is eager to emphasize this to the clergy as well. The problem, the big problem, for many clergy is that their faith-based theological orientation often precludes a "non-judgmental" assessment of an individual and, therefore, an inability to create an atmosphere of trust.

****

In any case, a human relationship in which one can be oneself, without fear of rejection or exploitation, is like an oasis in a desert for countless people. That fact must stand as a commentary upon our prevailing patters of family life, friendship, economic success and church membership. Since acceptance of the patient is the foundation of therapy, the misunderstandings which have arisen concerning it must be discussed. "Acceptance" does not mean that one fools himself into thinking that the patient is more lovable, harmless or noble than he is. It does not mean that value-judgments concerning the constructive or destructive consequences of a given action or character-structure must be suspended. It does not mean that the therapist must eradicate his own likes and dislikes. It does mean, however, that a no condemnatory attitude is genuinely adopted, not merely "put on," because it facilitates the task.

Anticipating Carl Rogers and client-centered therapy, Roberts waxes eloquent when speaking of an "oasis in a desert" for individuals, all too many in the modern world, who are in need of a safe haven of refuge infused with trust and confidentiality. That today for many, if not most, modern peoples such a place is difficult if not impossible to find, and such a relationship eludes most of us and certainly the clergy who must, at all cost, protect themselves from even appearing to be in need of such a place and such a relationship.

****

Freud embodied the principle we have just described when he encouraged his patients to tell him everything that came into their heads, excluding nothing. The method of free-association, where one lets the mind run without reins, is a useful technique in this connection. ... Another major method for gaining access to such material is, of course, the interpretation of dreams. Discussion of this topic lies beyond the scope of a brief sketch. We cannot here attempt to adjudicate the dispute between Freud and Jung. The former developed an elaborate and ingenious theory to show that dreams speak a highly condensed, emotional language but that even in sleep the "censor" which guards consciousness operates in such a way that the dream material has to disguise its full import. Jung assumes that dreams can mean exactly what they say, when they are properly understood. Despite these theoretical differences, many patients discover for themselves that a widening of what they are able to "take in" when they are fully awake goes hand in hand with an increasing ability to grasp what their dreams are saying.

Without prejudicing his own psychological orientation and throughout the book always giving fair attention to competing systems of thought, Roberts often refers, if not defers, to Freud and the well-established psychoanalytic tradition when speaking of psychotherapeutic practice. This "oasis" he has been speaking of with such passion, he says, was embodied fully in the work of Freud. Whether using free association or dream analysis, Freud created an atmosphere of acceptance and confidentiality, infused with a deep and abiding sense of trust between patient and doctor, client and therapist. This atmosphere of acceptance and confidentiality can prove of great benefit in the pastoral counseling environment, as well.

****

As we have seen, the therapist has standards of value by means of which he differentiates between illness and health, conflict and integration, creativity and sterility, growth and rigidity. They may not be formulated with conceptual finality; but they enter into his entire procedure, as flexible rules-of-thumb. However, it is an essential part of his view of human nature to recognize that the best results can be promoted only by helping the patient to develop his own standards of value, instead of imposing those of any one else upon him.

When suggesting psychotherapeutic practice to the average clergyperson, Roberts is keen to go slowly, because the very nature of pastoral ministry is fraught with the notion that to identify what is "right" and what is "correct" and what is "biblical" is implicit in the profession and, therefore, works counter to the notion of a non-judgmental environment of acceptance and affirmation of the client/patient's own worldview and ethos. This is one of the greatest difficulties and, we might even suggest, impediments to clergy engaging in psychotherapeutic counseling. How can a clergyperson hold on to his own religious beliefs about moral behavior while allowing the client to hold forth in a worldview and ethos far removed from his own? Therein lies the challenge and, from the perspective of many practicing psychologists, the impossibility of a fair and reasonable use of effective psychotherapy by such clergy.

****

CHAPTER IV THE DEVELOPMENT OF PERSONAL BELIEF

We now turn ... to a discussion of the bearing of psychotherapy upon Christian views of man.... Religion incorporates our most passionate hopes and fears, our deepest sense of solidarity with other human beings and with cosmic power, our most intimate commitments, and our most crucial beliefs concerning the value of life. ... Let us acknowledge, then, that feelings and unconscious motives, as well as intellectual processes, play a part in the formulation of religious beliefs, and that this is not necessarily to their discredit. Our statement applies just as inescapably to negative as to positive attitudes as much as to the atheist as to the man who believes in God. Hence, it is not intended to settle questions of truth and falsity. It is intended, rather, to widen the context in which we approach such questions, and to counteract the illusion that we can afford to regard ourselves as pure thinking machines.

Roberts now turns to the primary focus of his book, namely, the relationship between psychotherapy and theology, particularly a Christian view of the human person, what is called in traditionalist's language, a theological anthropology, but in this context what might be called a theological psychology. Acknowledging that feelings and unconscious motives are a part of religious faith may sound mundane and naïve to psychologists today but when said for the clergy to hear, it was, at the time, a bold statement. Such insight does not require proof but serves to broaden the context of discussion between psychologists and clergy when dealing with religious attitudes and behavior.

****

In this connection the discoveries of psychotherapy are relevant to a distinction which has always been important to religion itself, the distinction between genuine faith and pseudo-faith. These discoveries enable us to see more clearly how willingness to accept truth, as contrasted with the inclination to distort or evade it, depends upon inner security as well as intellectual acumen. Most religious traditions call attention to the difference between believing a doctrine only theoretically and believing it whole-heartedly. The former is likely to be sterile; the latter unites intellectual assent with warm feeling and eager action. The implications of this difference need to be examined thoroughly.

That psychotherapy can play a role in sorting out good faith from bad faith is a fact that Roberts is eager to emphasize to the clergy. Too often religious people are duped by their own failure to identify the difference and thus victimized by the confusion. Religious faith is not merely or solely a matter of an intellectual acceptance of a system of doctrines. Indeed, rational cognition is a part of a belief system but emotional response based on personality formation and development is likewise. Here, knowledge of the way the unconscious serves the ego is crucial for a reasonable understanding of how religious belief and behavior function. Psychologists understand this and clergy need to as well.

****

Estrangement between reason and emotion is often connected with the fact that we receive our beliefs at the hands of parents (and the institutions they represent) and the gradual process of being permitted to think and feel for ourselves may be blocked in various ways. Many of us reach maturity with social, moral and religious assumptions which we have either passively accepted or had forced down our throats, instead of having found an opportunity to work them out and verify them for ourselves. ...

Such beliefs can even be employed as a strait jacket to keep 'dangerous" reactions from expressing themselves.

His sensitivity to the maturation process of the human personality and the fundamental role parenting plays in that process suggests that Roberts has a genuine appreciation for the psychological dynamics operative in the exercise of both reason and emotion when it comes to religious matters. Failure to understand this reality is the cause of much misinterpretation of adult behavior by layman and clergy alike. When it comes particularly to religious beliefs and practices, children are most vulnerable to parental influence and, even in adulthood, continue to maintain a childlike understanding of faith and practice. Freud said that reasonably mature thinking adults are often well-rounded, except in the arena of religion where they have, regrettably, "remained in the nursery" even into adulthood. Childish beliefs are fine for children but not for adults.

****

No one can be religious, even though his religion may fall outside the confines of the churches, without finding some means of expressing his personal faith within a tradition and a community which implement it. While only a few men can be religious pioneers (prophets), every one can discover the applicability of a belief to his own life. The fact that the belief may be centuries old and commonly accepted among his associates need neither prevent him from making it his own nor compel him to do so. The path to maturity in religion is the same as the path to maturity generally. During childhood, it is natural that we should be dependent upon adults for guidance in matters of behavior and thinking. Granted a pair of healthy parents, the transition from dependence to independence takes place without undue stress and strain. The child is allowed to assume responsibility as he becomes able to shoulder it.

Whether Roberts is technically correct or not in observing that only in community can faith find expression, nevertheless, he believes it and that position serves well the Christian churches which are always and desperately seeking members to maintain themselves. Roberts emphasizes the communal nature of religious formation because, in his world, it is indispensable for the maturation and development of an adult-level religious self-understanding. He does not allow much room here for the individual seeker to find his own way into a mature religious understanding, preferring rather to emphasize the community as the source of strength and knowledge.

****

In large segments of Judaism, Catholicism and Protestantism, if the parents are "firm believers" then religion is the subject concerning which independent, critical thought is *least* encouraged. The child is given no grounds for believing that his religious tradition is something he can gradually make his own; he is expected to swallow it, as it is spooned into him, without asking questions. ... This authoritarian approach ignores the fact that the most effective way to deal with the doubts and temptations of later life is to begin as early as possible in nurturing those capacities for independent judgment, critical thought, and spiritual discernment...

Ironically though insightfully, the stronger the religious belief within a family the greater the limits on freedom of thought and expression. Families with little or no religious belief identify, therefore, create a free and easy atmosphere for personal exploration and experimentation, with fear, on the part of the child, of condemnation or correction. Furthermore, the strong religious family also unfortunately too often creates an environment where the maturation process in religious self-understanding is stifled or strangled, whereas in the less religious families there is room and opportunity for personal growth of the child towards a mature religious belief.

****

> Two opposite pathways are open to a child who grows up under such conditions. First, he may remain docile and subservient, and so long as he can avoid situations that compel him to question his inherited beliefs, he may get along indefinitely without much trouble. ... His religion is largely a matter of habit, an unthinking bit of filial piety. ... He derives no genuine strength from his faith, and when a crisis arises either he finds that faith empty or he clings to it blindly as a means of escaping the full impact of peril, misery, sickness or grief. ... In the second place, the child may rebel. The rebellion can take the form of open conflict with his parents, and it can include virtually everything. ... an especially deep-seated revulsion for the Church is instilled in adolescents because it is pervasively associated with oppressive restrictions. ... The worst tragedies of adolescence, including juvenile delinquency, are partly traceable to the fact that vitality, joy in living, longing for adventure, and maturing sexual desire can only express themselves, in many homes and community environments, through the negative pathway of rebellion.

Roberts is at his best here as a pastoral counselor and one who seems to understand human nature quite well even though he is not a trained psychologist or psychotherapist. “Two roads diverge in a yellow wood,” Frost once wrote, and this seems to characterize Roberts’ insights into the maturation process of children raised in a religiously stifling home environment. Either children “hunker down” and stay below the religiously scrutinizing radar and “go through the motions” of compliance to religious dictates of the family and faith tradition or, not uncommonly, they rare up and rebel boldly and aggressively and, therefore, not infrequently, overly react in the most negative of ways to all things religious. In both cases, the child suffers severely, as does the family.

****

> Against these extremes of rigid authoritarianism and spiritual rootlessness which can be found in American family life, we

should recognize that a child needs to grow up in an atmosphere where the behavior and inner content of his parents' lives are basically consistent with the ethical and religious principles they acknowledge. He should be permitted to formulate his own beliefs, within this context, as rapidly as his capacities for independent thought, moral judgment and religious decision mature.

The extremes are very common and constitute the basis for much of what is called, we have already mentioned, the psychiatric fallout of religion. In either direction, extremely religious or radically secular, the child finds himself either stifled or anchorless. There must be a happy medium in which a child senses perimeters for his thought, but freedom within those perimeters. Each faith tradition must determine for itself what those acceptable perimeters are. Whether Amish or Unitarian or somewhere in between, there is flexibility within very conservative traditions, and limits within very liberal traditions. To have them and know them is beneficial to the child growing up and to the family practicing their faith.

****

CHAPTER V THE IMAGE OF GOD

The Christian doctrine that man is created in the image of God means two things. First, that, like the rest of nature, man is dependent upon God for coming into existence and for the maintenance of existence. Second, that he possesses unique capacities which distinguish him from the rest of nature. ... The, with some assistance from Eve and the Serpent, man "fell," and the divine image -- his original nature -- was impaired. ...What Adam lost in the fall was his proper human nature. This "total corruption" of the image of God has not prevented men from being able to exercise their intelligence in connection with cultural pursuits.

In an attempt to help the non-theologian, even the non-Christian, understand where Christian clergy are coming from in terms of their "understanding" of human nature, Roberts thinks himself forced, more or less, to engage in a lite dose of catechism regarding the Christian doctrines of God and the fall. The complication is, however, that the Christian church itself has mixed ideas and confused notions about both doctrines -- the nature of God and whether or not there even was a fall that affects human behavior and spiritual destiny today. But, he tries.

****

Man cannot move a step toward self-knowledge except by employing endowments which he did not create, within the context of an origin he cannot fathom, directed toward a destiny he cannot descry. Nevertheless, he is a creature capable of creativeness, and his gifts are his to do with as he will. Persons, through decision, make history; nature, apart from persons, simply passes through change. Therefore, at the opposite extreme from trying to play God, man may come to regard himself as more impotent than he actually is. Ancient stories such as the Prometheus myth reflect the fact that man has viewed the autonomous exercise of his powers as dangerous. Yet failure to find outlets for his creativity is just as perilous as the irresponsible employment of it. In this connection, many versions of the doctrine need to be corrected or expanded in the light of psychotherapy.

Somewhere between playing God and feeling completely powerless, the mature individual finds himself situated. He has some freedom but not without limits; he has some power but is not all-powerful. In the midst of these conflictions, the individual in search of self-understanding must exercise what freedom he has and what power he can muster to address the verities of life. He may opt for a religious worldview and ethos or for a secular one, but to the extent that he is aware of himself making the choice, to that extent he is exercising a healthy response to life's reality.

****

The regrettable alienation of modern culture from Christianity must be understood, in part, as a reaction against ecclesiastical shackles which, if they had not been thrown off, really would have prevented man from carrying through important forms of progress, enlightenment and self-understanding. The failure of Christianity to furnish an organic center for culture has meant that many of these potentially creative powers have run riot. Modern society, armed with technology and dreaming of self-sufficiency, has been set adrift to fashion its own gods and ideologies. These dreams have indeed brought our civilization to the edge of the abyss. But part of the explanation lies in the fact that the Church, by labeling "sinful" human resources which are potentially creative, ha failed to provide a religious framework within which these potentialities could be expressed and guided; as a consequence of their repudiation they have been driven into revolt and aggressiveness.

Roberts has said what Freud had already done in his book entitled, *Civilization and Its Discontents,* namely, pointing out the conflicting relationship between religion and culture and especially Christianity and culture. That civilization (a term Freud uses for "culture" interchangeably) is often at odds with the individual's right, and freedom of expression is self-evident to psychologists as well as theologians. What is desired and desirable, says Roberts, is a creative dialectic between the individual and culture, the individual and religion, and culture and religion. To draw strength from the dynamism of such a tripartite relationship would benefit the individual, religion, and culture.

****

Man is in his own body and mind a compendium of every preceding "level" of evolution -- physical, chemical, biological and psychological. The resources he draws upon, in seeking to become at one with himself, are not merely "his"' they are rooted in the whole creation, which is grounded in God. Therefore man can become at one with himself only by finding his place in a harmony much wider than himself; but this harmony is not "pre-established"' he has a share in winning, in actualizing, it. He cannot fulfill his own nature unless his capacities gain free expression; but neither can he fulfill his own nature unless his freedom is brought into right relationship with God.

The complexities of the evolutionary process affecting the environment, both physical and emotional, must be acknowledged even if not (yet) completely understood. The requirement, however, is for the individual to feel empowered by the exercise of his freedom of expression but, argues Roberts, the theologian and Christian of faith, this freedom of expression must be within the context of a personal encounter with God, a point he is not willing to relinquish nor to allow of compromise. If man is to be free, he must be free within the context of a relationship with God and nothing short of that will do.

****

CHAPTER VI MORALISM

The concept of responsibility has been a source of endless difficulties in psychology, philosophy and theology. ... Nevertheless, psychotherapy has thrown light upon the problem by uncovering the manner in which we are determined by unconscious forces. Its findings point to a form of self-determinism. The self is not merely the passive resultant of inherited constitution plus environmental influences; it builds up an internal unity of its own which enters actively as well as passively into interplay with the surrounding world and other persons.

Existentialism was just coming into a place of real strength at the time of Roberts' writing. Sartre's opus, *L'Etre et le Neant* (1943), and translated into English as *Being and Nothingness* (1956), was riding high, and existentialism had even captured the imagination of Christian and Jewish theologians and philosophers. The central place of personal responsibility was now the focus of much attention and coupled with psychoanalysis's ability to plumb the depths of the unconscious, there was strong motivation to seek for a convergence or coagulation of existentialism, responsibility, and Christian theology. John Macquarrie was to bring the topic to full fruition in theological circles with his 1965 *Studies in Christian Existentialism,* but Roberts was addressing the pastor in the parish at this point in 1950. He did it convincingly and with deep and practical insight.

****

Because psychotherapy is committed to the increase of man's capacity to achieve responsibility, it must oppose those forms of psychology which, when taken seriously, spread the illusion that man is an automaton. Yet because it is determinist, it assumes that what is called "moral wrong," as well as mental and physical disease, must be regarded as the necessary consequence, in a given moment, of the interplay between a formed character-structure and an external situation. This does not mean that the distinction between what man can help and what he cannot help disappears entirely; but it does mean that some of our ideas concerning *how* man can alter conditions may have to be revised.

Roberts was not naïve in his assessment of some of the emerging "popular" schools of thought within depth psychology, which were bent upon reduction of individual freedom to mere determinism, but Freud and psychoanalysis were not part of that shallow movement. Freud, Jung, and Adler avoided that trap of popularism by staying true to the agenda they set in their own work. The danger, as Roberts points out, is that determinism reduced the moral imperative to a biological given, and this will not do, either for religion or culture. Good psychology can and does make a distinction between what is possible and what is required in human behavior, and religious leaders will do well to pay attention lest their pastoral counseling appear shallow and irrelevant.

****

In contrast with moralism's generalizations about free will, psychotherapy leads to the conclusion that human beings use whatever freedom they possess, but that they differ tremendously in the degree to which they have reached that internal harmony on which freedom is based ... Psychotherapy also stands in contrast to moralism insofar as the latter rests on an atomistic view of the self. Every therapist knows that the moral capacities and incapacities of the individual are so powerfully determined by his constitution and formed character-structure that often the only way to alter the effects of early conditioning involves his retracing the past, in feeling as well as in thought.

The value of psychotherapy in assessing the individual's exercise of freedom is held in high estimation by Roberts *vis a vis* the shallow moralism which discounts the complexities of the human personality and the role of the unconscious in decision-making matters. Moralism discounts the etiology of ethical decision-making components of human personality, and fails to take into account the maturation process of the individual from childhood to adulthood.

****

Psychotherapeutic findings can be used helpfully as one tries to confront the predicament of man in a communal, instead of a purely individual, context. The path of human development starts, inevitably, in a condition of undifferentiated dependence upon the group (the primitive "we"). Unless the process of development is blocked, the normal individual goes through a gradual consolidation of independence and self-consciousness, becoming a unique center of organized thought, feeling and initiative. Yet he reaches maturity, not by maintaining his isolation, but by being able to establish relations of mutual support and co-operation with the community (the adult "we"), without relinquishment of individual responsibility. The anxieties of our age have driven many men regressively away from individual freedom into primitive forms of group solidarity.

Freud, more so than any of the early psychotherapists, pointed decisively to the role of psychoanalysis in differentiating the complex components involved in the individual/communal relationship and dialectic. Adler came soon thereafter, and eventually Carl Rogers addressed the issue substantially, with Harry Stack Sullivan making the greatest contribution to the subject by emphasizing a social psychiatry built around the central issue of interpersonal relations as the arena for mental health and wholeness. The struggle for personal freedom has too often forced individuals into situations requiring a major effort of differentiation from the community, all the while needing communal interaction to maintain mental stability. The paradox and irony are palpable.

****

CHAPTER VII BONDAGE TO SIN

At certain points there is a remarkable parallel between the Pauline-Augustinian conception of original sin and the psycho-analytic conception of neurosis. Freud more than once called attention to the parallel. In both instances man finds himself in a condition of inner conflict, and filled with hatred, envy and mistrust toward his neighbors. In both instances it is the basic condition that is enslaving; particular "sins" or "symptoms" are peripheral effects deriving from this central cause, and particular "good deeds" make little dent upon the basic condition. In both instances the injurious influences of others are seen to be so interwoven with personal reactions that it is almost impossible to differentiate between them.

Always eager to identify points of continuity and convergence between the Christian religion and depth psychology, Roberts is quick to notice that the biblical and early Christian teachings regarding the doctrine of original sin were not unlike much of what Freud had to say about the functioning of the *libido* within the domain of the unconscious. Whether practicing clinicians in the fields of psychotherapy would agree with him or not was of no significance to his own assessment of these apparent parallels. He is aware, of course, that Freud had noticed the similarities at certain junctures himself and, thus, Roberts is not out of line in mentioning them. Roberts then proceeds to recite the three or four specific points of intersection, noting elsewhere, of course, that many Christian bodies do not accept the doctrine of original sin. This, of course, left Roberts and the psychologists with the problem of identifying the points of continuity and relevance of depth psychology to those Christians, known in theological circles as the Pelagians and Neo-Pelagians, i.e., Christians believing that infants are born without the scare of Adam's sin and are not, therefore, held responsible to God for their acts until "the age of discretion."

****

Despite the fact that it is deterministic, going hand-in-hand with belief in predestination, the Christian doctrine of original sin does not abrogate the conception of personal responsibility. On the contrary, it holds that men are "without excuse" because they possess the capacity to distinguish between good and evil. ... The motive behind the doctrine of sin, then, is not to drive in a sense of despair and insufficiency just because one enjoys seeing men wriggle in agony. The motive behind it is to reach full awareness of the depth of the human problem. It is folly to say that we should not feel guilty when we look back on our own lives, leaving nothing out. The sense of guilt is a sign that we have not become totally insensitive, hardened and irrecoverable.

Ironically, at least to the eye of the non-Christian, the individual is still responsible for his actions even though he may or may not have been cursed with the sin of Adam even before his birth! Because of our innate ability, our birthright, if you will, to distinguish between right and wrong and even though we are born in sin ourselves, we are responsible for choosing to remain in the state of sin or to turn to God for forgiveness. Guilt is, indeed, the driving force, as explained by Roberts, speaking on behalf of the entire Christian religion and calling upon depth psychologists to corroborate this assessment.

****

Psychotherapy can be regarded as documenting to the full, and widening our awareness of, what the human race is up against in attempting to reach inner freedom and society security. It offers clinical details on some matter of which the fathers of the Church were either completely ignorant or only vaguely aware in their description of human ills and perversities. ... If psychotherapy has widened our acquaintance with the ramifications of "sin," it has at the same time widened our conceptions of how this bondage can be overcome.

Roberts is now in full throttle calling upon psychotherapy, with a special affection for Freud and the psychoanalytic school, to corroborate and validate the fundamentals of the Christian doctrine of original sin and, by extension, the full range of theological anthropology as propounded by the Augustinian school of theology embraced by both the Roman Catholic Church through the commentaries of St. Thomas Aquinas and through Luther and Calvin for the Protestants.

****

Strictly speaking, sin is alienation from God and is therefore not a merely psychological category. Nevertheless, psychology can be used to advantage in attempting to reach a sound doctrine of sin, relieved of harmful encumbrances. Such a doctrine would include at least the following observations: (1) Evasion of responsibility aggravates a problem or delays its solution. (2) A full awareness of personal limitations, and contrition for those which are alterable, are preconditions of moral improvement. (3) The social ramifications of evil, which run far beyond what the individual can control or alter, violate our conceptions of what life could and should be like; therefore, even at those points where one has to "accept" them, the acceptance is not simple acceptance. (4) When sin is faced in a personal relationship of trust, a man may be enabled to "do something" (by a method which is the reverse of moralistic effort) about problems he was previously impotent to solve. In any interpretation of man there are, obviously, two possibilities of error. The first is to underestimate or fail to implement those resources of health and recovery which are actually available and the enhancement of which is desperately needed. ... Psychotherapy has made an important contribution towards increasing man's capacity to solve his own problems, both by deepening the diagnosis and by tapping hitherto latent resources. ... The second possibility of error, however, (especially from the theologian's standpoint) is one of exaggerating the extent to which man can solve the problem of evil "on his own."

Further validating his argument, Roberts identifies four crucial ingredients in the nature and composition of sin which are likewise identified and described in the clinical work of practicing psychotherapists. Having done so, he then emphasizes the two options left to the individual and society in determining our individual and corporate response to these characteristics, namely, we can either underestimate their meaning and relevance to modern life or we can overestimate them. Either way, the human predicament is precarious and it is left to both psychotherapists and theologians, working in consort, to retrieve man from such a destiny.

****

CHAPTER VIII STATIC VIEWS OF SALVATIONS

Theologians regard the possibility of bondage to sin as linked with God's purpose in granting men the gift of freedom. There is no way in which even God could create human beings capable of making moral decisions without running the risk that such freedom would be abused ... Theology also holds, of course, that God possesses inexhaustible resources for dealing with sin, and that the operation of these resources is discernible in two forms. The first is usually called divine "judgment:; it sets limits to the destructiveness of evil, mainly through the tendency of evil to destroy itself. ... God's second strategy in His struggle with man is the redemptive one of actually transmuting evil; both in the individual and in society, He converts anxiety into trust and selfishness into love.

According to the Christian doctrine of sin and grace, at least as expounded by the Augustinian variety of theology embraced by Roberts, God not only has created a world in which man is free to exercise his freedom and, thereby, engage in sin (having a propensity to do so owing to the fact of original sin in the first place), but also the exercise of freedom making him amenable to God's grace of forgiveness if man ceases from his sinful ways, not unlike therapy in the sense that help is on the way if the individual needing help is receptive.

****

Christians believe that this redemptive purpose has been revealed supremely in the life and sacrifice of Jesus Christ. ... For many Christians one of the most inspiring aspects of this belief has been the realization that a man does not have to undertake the hopeless task of making himself good, by sheer, moralistic will-power, before being able to come into the presence of God trustfully. For them the heart of the Gospel has been the message that God is willing to accept them as they are, if they will turn to Him in penitence and faith. (Is this an Oximoron? JHM)

To the non-Christian, the irony, even the oxymoron, of this kind of logic is astounding. The notion that God is willing to "accept them as they are," namely, sinful man, "if they will turn to Him in penitence and faith" seems profoundly contradictory to the clinical mind. If God is accepting of man as he is, then why is he then required to turn to God in penitence and faith? He is not accepted as he is but rather, if he will change, namely, if he will repent of his sinful ways and believe in God, and do as God would have him do, and remain faithful to the end, and not turn his back on God, THEN and only then will God accept and save him. Roberts suggests that the "static view of salvation" has missed entirely the point of what Carl Rogers will soon be calling "client-centered counseling," wherein the individual is accepted as he is but with conditions! This view has, at this point in his presentation, turned its back upon the fundamentals of psychotherapeutic practice and become the altar-calling preacher of the evangelical sort.

****

The consequences of a static view of salvation may be manifold ... The first consequence is hypocrisy. ... A second possible consequence is self-righteousness. ... A third possible consequence, however, is unresolved despair. A fourth possible consequence, though it may be an ingredient in any of the three already mentioned, is extreme self-repudiation.

Roberts, like most liberal theologians and Christian pastors, is no friend of static salvation, recognizing the destructive character of that worldview and ethos. Whether hypocrisy, self-righteousness, despair, or self-repudiation, the benefits of salvation defined in static terms is counterproductive to living wholly in the world. There must be another way of understanding the Christian doctrine of salvation which can integrate the insights of contemporary psychotherapy.

****

CHAPTER IX A DYNAMIC VIEW OF SALVATION

Over against the foregoing results, let us set a "dynamic" conception of salvation. Here the validity of an ethical or a religious ideal depends upon its power to *resolve* conflict. Insofar as a person finds organic harmony between his ideals and his unforced behavior, the resulting release and serenity provide a firm and stimulating basis for further development along the same lines. He becomes a "gracious" instead of a "moralistic" human being. So far as Christianity is concerned, this conception implies that its saving purpose is to give men a faith and a mode of life which will make them no longer ashamed of themselves. It cures guilt, not by putting forward ideas which assure men willy-nilly that they are "all right," but by releasing a power which removes the *causes* of guilt.

A non-static view of salvation draws upon the "dynamics" of wholeness and healing. The emphasis is not upon damnation but resolution of guilt and conflict in one's life, not unlike the mission of depth psychology. Not merely moralistic in its view of the world and his relationship to others, dynamic salvation emphasizes the integrality of the human person with himself and his community. To identify and then expunge the causes of guilt in one's life is the driving force here.

****

Christian salvation cannot be conceived in such a way that it incorporates what would make each man whole unless theology pays more attention than it has in the past to the widely divergent needs and capacities of different individuals. (1) For many persons in our competitive culture the chief problem is connected with their aggressive, egocentric fixation upon material possessions, social-standing and power, and with their starvation of those resources which make for sympathy, affection and friendship. (2) At the opposite pole, however, the chief problem can be connected with slavish dependence, lack of firmness, and a symbiotic living through others. This can take forms which look like laudable Christian meekness; but it is uniformly accompanied by unconscious self-seeking and hostility. ... (3) For some, the chief problem is connected with aloofness and with fear of being entangled in any sort of give-and-take relationship. (4) For others, a perpetual need for companionship indicates failure to achieve enough self-possession so that one can stand it to be alone.

Challenging Christian theology to engage in a broader view of the human predicament, Roberts calls upon pastors and teachers of the Christian faith to account for the broad complexities of the human person and his relationship to himself and his community. Problems of aggression, egocentrism, greed, and the quest for power drive individuals into a helpless state of stress and despair. On the other hand, others are in the grip of fear and loneliness, anxiety about relationships, failures in family life. Christian theologians can listen and learn a great deal from practitioners in depth psychology in assessing the human situation and, then, respond pastorally.

****

CHAPTER X PSYCHOLOGY AND THEOLOGY

If naturalistic humanism is right, man must look solely to himself for the furtherance of ethical principles and for communal endeavors worthy of his loyalty; and the sooner he finds this out, the better. On the other hand, if Christianity is right, then human beatitude is dependent upon an alignment between man's own sources and divine power; and the sooner we learn this, and come to terms with its implications, the better. In the last analysis, if a naturalistic theology is to be held against Christian belief in God, it should be based on religious commitment, not on the assumption that one can have insight into such questions best by abstracting himself, so far as possible, from religious concern. In the last analysis we cannot seek to interpret what psychological facts mean, in the sphere of religion, except by employing positive or negative theological convictions. If a religious experience actually is evoked by God, then it is difficult to see what can be gained by treating it as though it were not. And if God is unreal, then this consideration determines the true significance of the phenomena studied by the psychology of religion and provides the indispensable basis for their full explanation.

The time has come for Roberts to demonstrate the effectiveness of his appeal to theology and psychology to come together in a meaningful and beneficial manner for the modern person and society. Opening with a classic statement characterizing the opposing sides to be either "naturalistic humanism" and "Christianity," Roberts suggests that if the former is correct in its assessment of the human predicament as man solely responsible for himself in the world, or if the latter is correct in claiming that the human person is dependent upon a God of love and forgiveness, the sooner we decide and determine which is correct the better all around for everyone. "In the last analysis," argues Roberts, all of these questions must eventually and inevitably be answered within the context of religious concepts, because the only way to deal with the proposition that man is either in a world created by God or he is not is through an act of faith. If God is real, then the religious agenda must be honored. If God does not exist, then the humanistic world is what we have to deal with.

****

The foregoing warning against "psychologism" must be coupled, however, with a warning against "theologism." The task of formulating a theological interpretation of man must be tackled afresh in each generation, and what one attempts to say from a Christian perspective can hardly be related effectively to the thought of this generation if it ignores or fails to comprehend the recent contributions which have been made to a "science of man." The task of understanding and ministering to the world's needs is not served wisely by setting up some exclusively theological source of information, and then using it rigidly as a principle of selection in determining what one will welcome or what one will repudiate among the findings of recent psychology.

If we must avoid the "psychologism" of a humanistic worldview and ethos, i.e., a *weltanschuuang*, then we are equally bound to avoid the dangers of simplistic theologizing, a theological agenda that simply continues to recycle old answers to new problems, failing to take into account the deepening of human understanding presented to us through the research efforts of the behavioral and social sciences.

****

In this book I have attempted to show that some of the basic concepts of psychotherapy are correlative with the human side of events which Christian doctrine interprets. Insofar as I have succeeded it follows that the therapist's description of bondage to inner conflict should be incorporated in the doctrine of sin, and his description of healing (through the release of involuntary changes which occur in a personal relationship of trust and acceptance) should be incorporated in the doctrine of grace. It also follows that ultimately psychiatry cannot understand its own task aright except within the framework of a Christian view of man and God. But the full confirmation of such a standpoint will be reached, if it ever is, only as psychiatrists, and especially Christian psychiatrists, pay more attention than they have thus far to the full range of religious living and faith on the part of strong, healthy people; and it will be reached only as doctrinal theologians take a more direct part in revitalizing the healing ministry of the church.

Beginning with a generous affirmation of the contribution psychotherapy, in all of its various and even competing schools, can make for an understanding of the human situation and our modern predicament, Roberts is true to his faith and his vocation as a Christian theologian in saying that even the best psychology will not be able to complete its work without embracing the truth of the Christian view of man and his relationship to God. It is heartening, even if off-putting, to have a Christian theologian attempt a dialogue with clinical psychology, especially when that theologian is not reluctant to state his own position with respect to religious belief and his personal faith. His last, though somewhat be-limiting, appeal is for there to be something along the order of a Christian psychiatry, for it will be with these professionals, both trained in psychotherapy and as believing Christians, that psychology and theology can finally converge.

CHAPTER SIX

Gordon Allport and *The Individual and His Religion*

Though Roberts was responsible for bringing depth psychology and Christian theology into direct dialogue, the psychology of religion was not destined to morph into a sub-set of Christian thought. The pursuit of the role and application of the psychology of religion was from the beginning perceived to be more broadly cast. Later in the century, we will see the psychology of religion focus again upon specific religious traditions, with Bakan on Judaism and Roberts and Fromm on Christianity. But for now, it fell to Gordon Willard Allport (1897-1967) to refocus upon the interfacing of psychology and religion. The son of a country doctor from Montezuma, Indiana, and the product of an iconic exemplification of the Protestant religion and work ethic, Allport, along with his mother and their numerous children, assisted the father in a family-run hospital and clinic. Following his older brothers to Harvard University, Allport took his B.A., M.A., and Ph.D.(1922) and, winning a coveted traveling fellowship, spent two years studying at, first, the Gestalt School in Berlin, Germany, and another year at Cambridge University in England. First taking a teaching position in psychology at Harvard University, he then taught for four years at Dartmouth College before returning to spend the remainder of his academic career back at Harvard. Becoming the editor of the *Journal of Abnormal and Social Psychology,* Allport went on to be President of the American Psychological Association and President of the Society for the Psychological Study of Social Issues, dying in Cambridge, MA, at the age of seventy years old.

Allport's internationally acclaimed study of the nature of personal religion in the development of the individual, *The Individual and His Religion*, was published by Macmillan in 1950, and became a recognized classic in the study of the function of religious sentiment in the personality of the individual. Five years later, his *Becoming: Basic Considerations for a Psychology of Personality* (1955)would clench his reputation. Neither a Freudian nor a Jungian, but rather falling loosely into the social psychology school of the time, Allport did quote Jung in saying that, of his thousands of patients over the age of thirty-five with which he dealt, "all have been people whose problem in the last resort was that of finding a religious outlook on life (Jung,1933)." Allport's interest was the relationship between religious beliefs and practices -- ideology and behavior -- as relates to the maturation process of the personality, contending that religion in an individual's life can mature along with his or her personality if attended to properly. Yet, Allport never argued for the truthfulness of religion, merely its influence upon individual maturation, both for good and ill. "My effort," he wrote in the Preface of this little classic, "is directed solely to a portrayal of the place of subjective religion in the structure of personality whenever and wherever religion has such a place. My approach is psychological ... I make no assumptions and no denials regarding the claims of revealed religion" (1950:xi). Here was a recognized psychologist from an established school applying his science to the study of religious ideology and behavior. His work was internationally acclaimed and set the bar even higher for both disciplines in that, irrespective of the truthfulness of religious belief, there is indisputably a "relationship" between what one believes about the meaning and purpose of his or her individual life and the development and maturity of that individual's personality and well-being. Allport said of his work: "A man's religion is the audacious bid he makes to bind himself to creation and to the Creator. It is his ultimate attempt to enlarge and to complete his own personality by finding the supreme context in which he rightly belongs. In these pages, I have undertaken the task of discovering the place of religion in the life-economy of the individual, of seeking a psychological understanding of the nature and functioning of the religious sentiment, and tracing the full course of religious development in the normally mature and productive personality" (1950:9). This he did and, setting the bar higher than yet had been set, he challenged scholars and researchers in both camps, psychology and religion, to demonstrate the viability and efficacy of this interfacing agenda.

Selections from *The Individual and His Religion: A Psychological Interpretation,* by Gordon W. Allport, with commentary.

NOTE: In the following, the original text will be printed in *Arial Unicode MS* typestyle (as is this note itself to illustrate) as an easy and aesthetically pleasing way of identifying the primary source paragraphs. The author's commentary will be in *Times New Roman*. It is hoped that this differentiation between the "primary source" and the "commentary" made by use of differing typestyles will prove helpful and not disruptive to the reader. *I have also chosen to use a quadruple asterisk (****) to separate the primary text from the commentary.*

CHAPTER ONE ORIGINS OF THE RELIGIOUS QUEST

Among modern intellectuals -- especially in the universities -- the subject of religion seems to have gone into hiding. Is it because the educated portion of mankind is learning to live with less finality and is coming to distrust embracing formulae of all types? Or is it because in their zeal to liquidate pseudo-knowledge and to discover truth in a piece-meal fashion the universities have found it necessary quietly to adopt a thoroughgoing secularism? Whatever the reason may be, the persistence of religion in the modern world appears as an embarrassment to the scholars of today.

Though one of Harvard University's most distinguished psychologists, Allport seemed never to be completely comfortable with that community of scholars. One might suggest the answer lay in his continued attachment to his childhood religious upbringing in which such talk as he heard and found in Harvard would have been somewhat discounted. Nevertheless, Allport did become a major voice in psychological research, especially as regards behavior and attitudes of the young, and this book draws heavily from data base studies which he himself administered or was acquainted with as consulting psychologist. His opening salvo against the superficiality of intellectuals seems to be, if nothing else, an attempt to raise the comfort level of the non-scholarly readership among the clergy and lovers of religion. It seems to have worked, for the book proved to be a bestseller and eventually a classic, revered by religious leaders, more so than by psychologists.

****

This trend toward doubt, toward secularism, toward psychologism, does not in the slightest degree mean that religion is a thing of the past, or that it is on the way out. History shows that as fast as institutional religion decays it has a way of reviving. ... The argument of this chapter is that the subjective (personal) religious sentiments of mankind -- whatever the fate of institutional religion may be -- are very much alive and will perhaps always remain alive, for their roots are many and deep. ... Before we ask about the roots of religion in the life of the individual we do well to inquire whether there is a single basic form of experience that is inevitably a part of every religious sentiment.

Whether Allport's assessment of the apparent demise of religion and religious interests within the academy was correct or merely a politically correct thing to say to the clergy, he was astute in his assessment of the rise of secularism fostered by growing doubt as to the continued viability of religious truth in light of modern literary criticism. Secular societies' fascination with the coming and competing schools of depth psychology and psychotherapy fostered a kind of intellectual condescension towards all things religious and, unfortunately, bred a sort of naïve reductionism, what Allport calls "psychologism." Allport takes up the earlier position of William James in attempting to differentiate between "personal" and therefore subjective religious sentiments and "institutional" and therefore objective religious expression. He does it with refinement and quite convincingly. This position does beg the question of the "truthfulness" of religious belief, but neither James nor Allport were willing to go down that slippery road.

****

In denying that the religious pattern in the individual's life possesses a standard form, we are not thereby denying it a personal form. Quite the contrary, in any given individual there are characteristic feelings and recurrent concepts highly typical of his own mental life. He is likely to have a well-organized personal sentiment that can presumably, with intensive psychological study, be accurately construed and understood. Even though in their religious lives people are not consistent with one another, they are as a rule markedly consistent with themselves.

This is the core of James and Allport's argument for and defense of "personal" religious sentiments which express themselves both in beliefs and behavior. Granted the wide range of personality characteristics among all peoples, there is a tendency, at least among the healthy, to be consistently true to themselves, says Allport, even if compliance with institutional mandates is less common. There is a great deal of contradiction from the psychoanalytic schools of thought regarding Allport's contention that individuals maintain a verifiable "consistency" in their own beliefs and behavior, but that is another discussion not to be pursued here.

****

Just as there is no standard pattern of content in a subjective religious experience, so too there is no common point of origin. ... Though we fail to find psychological support for a single and specific religious instinct we do find a tendency to identify religious thought and feeling with the operation of some one single bodily or mental mechanism. ... To make a spectroscopic analysis is not easy, since the prisms of each personality are unique. In nearly all instances, however, we find that in the course of development the religion of the individual has been refracted by (1) his bodily needs, (2) his temperament and mental capacity, (3) his psychogenic interests and values, (4) his pursuit of rational explanation, and (5) his response to the surrounding culture.

Each of these formative factors requires separate comment, although it is only through their synthesis that they engender the religious sentiment.

Allport stays true to his contention, based, as he would argue, on data-base studies conducted by himself at Harvard and his colleagues elsewhere, that religious experience is a very individual and private matter without demonstrable continuities of origin or character. Yet, religion exists, and it exists in the lives of individuals, not just institutions. Therefore, he suggests, there are at least five identifiable components found in the emergence of religious sensibilities within the individual personality, and the coagulation, if you will, of these five components fosters the context within which religious sentiment emerges.

****

I have suggested that subjective religion is, in the first instance, the flower of desire. ... To illustrate the evolution of values and their final bearing upon subjective religion, let us take the central phenomenon of egoism. ... This psychogenic interest in the integrity of personality beginning with my own ego, and developing finally to embrace both an ethics and a theology, is only one illustration of the process I am depicting. ... Thus it comes about that under conditions of fear, illness, bereavement, guilt, deprivation, insecurity, the restoration of values through religion is commonly sought.

The etiology of religion is linked to the emergence of a sense of values within the individual personality, beginning, says Allport, with desire driven and guided by the ego as it appears in the maturation process of childhood. Under such motivation and oversight, the development value system adopted and adapted by the individual produces, under the driving force of religious sentiment and sensibilities, both an ethic (a formalized and systematized mechanism of moral assessment and behavior) and a theology (a systematic recitation of the why and how and where of the individual). It is the "life situation" of encounter with the "verities of life," such as fear and illness and guilt, which create an existential matrix for the fostering of these religious sensibilities.

****

Now the factors that we have been considering --- desire, temperament, values -- are relatively speaking the more emotional roots of the religious sentiment in the individual. It is unfortunate that limitations of vocabulary force psychological analysis to treat emotion and reason, affection and cognition, as if they were separate provinces of mental life. ... It follows that subjective religion, like all normal sentiments, must be viewed as an indistinguishable blend of emotion and reason, of feeling and meaning. When we study it we are dealing with neither rationality nor irrationality, but rather with a posture of the mind in which emotion and logical thinking fuse.

Unnecessarily critical of psychology's inability to differentiate effectively and with acute refinement distinctions between the various emotions and sensibilities of the human personality, Allport, nevertheless, is keen to attempt an exploration of the "subjective" character of religious sentiment by calling for a creative synthesis, or at least a positive balance, between reason and emotion as well as rationality and feeling. Allport is eager to emphasize that religious sentiment of the "personal" sort comprises a merging of both feeling and meaning, of reason and emotion, and though religious institutions may ignore or disregard the necessity of this merging of sentiments, the individual does not. To maintain psychological balance, Allport contends that an individual must be able, or at least attempt, to hold both reason and emotion together.

****

Most individuals, however, are not sufficiently contemplative nor sufficiently imitative to adopt in *toto* the explanation offered by any one master theologian. They may grasp parts of his system of thought, and sense the direction of the system as a whole. But they find that they require their own interpretations when they are in the grip of the engrossing pressures of their lives. ... The universe is simply incomprehensible. Fragments of it may be fairly well understood, but not the interrelation of these fragments, and certainly not the design of the whole. Every man wonders at times about the void which gave way to creation, and about the successive links that connect this original void to his own momentary state of wonder. To many men, religion is primarily a search for complete knowledge, for unfissioned truth.

In an attempt to validate the non-compliance of religious individuals to whole systems of theological thought, Allport points out quite astutely the uniqueness of the individual personality as needing room to find its own way amidst a plethora of theological systems which have been hammered out over the centuries, systems that are airtight in terms of logic but which, alas, often fall short of speaking to the full range of human needs and emotions within the individual believer. Thus, religious institutions, while promoting and propounding theological systems of thought, religious individuals must happily go along, taking what they need and finding what works in their emotional lives, leaving the rest behind. A sort of native logic seems to operate within the religious individual when it comes to taking what works and leaving what does not work.

****

CHAPTER TWO THE RELIGION OF YOUTH

Since religion, whatever else it may be, involves meaning and interpretation at every step, we must concede at the outset that religion of childhood is of a very special order, having little in common with the religion of adulthood. In infancy, of course, religion is lacking. Desires there are, and a rudimentary social responsiveness; but neither intelligence nor self-consciousness are sufficiently developed to sustain anything that might be called a sentiment, least of all such a highly complex mental organization as the religious sentiment. ... A characteristic of the child's early religious concepts is his *anthropomorphism.* How could it be otherwise, since within his world of experience powerful and loving agents are people. Furthermore, he is usually taught that God is, in fact, a male personage. With few exceptions, therefore, children visualize God as an old man, or as a rich man, superman, or king. And, frequently, though not as universally as Freud makes out, God possesses the attributes of the physical father.

The distinction between childhood religious sentiments and those of adults made by Allport allows the discussion to focus precisely upon the personal, subjective, and individual character of religious behavior. He was not the first but was one of the early best psychologists in making this distinction and demonstrating the importance of it in assessing religious beliefs and behaviors. That religion is fundamentally comprised of "meaning and interpretation" as an analytical observation sets the stage for a systematic analysis of childhood religious sentiments with special attention to the propensity to "make human," that is, to anthropomorphize religious beliefs and experiences. He easily and even casually defers to Freud's rather over-extended characterization of God as "super dad" but acknowledges and owns it as a fair and reasonable observation. He makes little of it, however, other than to point out the similarities between descriptions of God and descriptions of a child's image of his own father. Psychoanalysis had a field day with this idea while Allport simply had a nice afternoon's stroll through the city park!

****

The child's theology gradually begins to approximate that of his elders. And normally there is in the pre-puberty period an intense desire to identify with the in-group. Religious practices, if such occur in the family, are taken for granted; and the institutional membership of the parents is rarely questioned. ... Usually it is not until the stress of puberty that serious reverses occur in the evolution of the religious sentiment.

Compliance with religious norms of understanding and behavior constitutes the primary attitude of children. Whatever is good for mother and daddy is good for the child and this suits the child splendidly. Conflict over religion between parents and pre-pubescent children is rare if existent at all. The conflict comes later when the child as youthful inquisitor begins, often and even unwittingly, at the suggestion of the parents and their religious institution which "encourages" religious interests. The result is not always what was expected or desired of either parents or church.

****

Three forms of religious awakening are commonly distinguished, the first being the *definite crisis*, or conversion experience. Of a large group of contemporary college students who reported some form of religious awakening, 14 percent acknowledged conversion experiences. Fifteen per cent reported the second, or *emotional stimulus,* type of awakening, wherein the upheaval is slight or absent, but wherein, nonetheless, the subject is able to designate some single event which served as the effective stimulus to his religious re-orientation. Taking these two types together, we have 29 per cent who report that some traumatic or semi-traumatic event underlay their religious development. The remainder of our cases, 71 per cent, report a gradual awakening, with no specifiable occasion being decisive.

Allport is at his scholarly best when reciting and assessing data base studies which, at the time, were beginning to flood the psychological community. The refinement of research methodology was well on its way, and the studies produced during the 40s and 50s dealing with religious ideology and behavior are remarkably sophisticated. Allport here identified three fundamentally distinct forms of religious "awakenings," namely, the conversion experience (a small but volatile percentage), the event leading to religious awakening (only slightly larger but still really small), and thirdly the gradual awakening of the adolescent (a major portion of youth fall into this category). Allport was eager to study university student religious behavior and this study was a real beginning for his career in statistical analysis of data base studies of religious behavior among youth.

****

My we sum up by saying that (1) most students feel the need of including a religious sentiment somewhere within their maturing personalities; (2) for the most part they believe in a God, though their view is not usually of the traditional theistic variety; (3) a bare quarter are in essential matters orthodox and historically faithful to theological dogma; (4) the majority maintain some of the forms of traditional religious practices including prayer; (5) but the majority are clearly dissatisfied with institutional religion as it exists, so much so that 40 per cent of those who feel a religious need yet repudiate the church in which they were reared. If we take the entire student population who have had a religious upbringing, including those who feel no religious need and those who do, we find that 56 per cent reject the church in which they were trained.

What is profoundly helpful in establishing the psychology of religion as a discipline of its own within the academy was this use of statistical studies developed and administered by practicing psychologists and other behavioral and social scientists. There were a plethora of "surmises and speculations" regarding religious behavior but, as one critic is known to have flippantly observed, they were merely "speculations about an hypothesis." These data base studies were replete with empirical documentation and the interest in this type of psychological study began to have a major and positive influence on the rise of psychology as a free standing university curriculum and discipline. That the psychology of religion was right behind this burgeoning of growth was inevitable.

****

If youthful disaffection is so great how does it happen that institutional religion continues? Surely if half the student population in each generation desert the church of their ancestors, with few new student adherents being won, it ought not to take long for a vanishing point to be reached. The answer to this puzzle lies in two considerations. After the irreligious twenties, the period with which we are here dealing, many young people do in fact return willingly, and sometimes enthusiastically, to the institutional forms from which they rebelled. Secondly ... the vestiges of loyalty as reflected in nominal membership and at least occasional church attendance, linger on even among youth who have virtually lost their allegiance to church doctrine.

Of course, there were two major and radically distinct audiences watching with real interest these studies and the conclusions suggested by the statistical analysis. First, the institutional church had a vested interest and, second, the youth of America, too, had a vested but different interest. How does institutional religion continue to thrive when the youth are consistently turning away from organized expressions of their personal religious sensibilities? Youthful adolescence, with its propensity to rebel and protest, is inevitable and genuinely characteristic of each generation. However, when the rebellious stage is past and these youth begin their own families, they tend both to be re-attracted to "institutional" expressions of religion for their own children and, likewise, begin to relate to the sentimentality of their own childhood religious attachments which they wish to share with their own children. So, the cycle continues to repeat itself without a great deal of loss, ultimately, to organized religion and the institutional expressions of it in church and synagogue (and today the mosque).

****

There remains one aspect of the loss of the centric faith and the drift to non-theological liberalism to be considered. The shift is unquestionably due in part, though not entirely, to the ignorance of students today regarding the teachings of theology. The "queen of the sciences" has fallen from her throne. Were evidence needed we could point to the decline of doctrinal and Biblical teaching in church schools, to the lack of college courses dealing with the tents of faith, to the reports of many chaplains in the armed services who found only the densest of ignorance of historic doctrine. One may read student autobiographies dealing with personal religious history without finding the slightest comprehension of the theological position which they, more likely than not, are in the process of rejecting.

Nevertheless, there is a growing school of thought embodied in what is commonly called liberal or secular humanism, which is considered in many circles as a viable alternative to religious faith and practice. Allport is fully aware of the enduring and looming reality of secular humanism and attributes its rise in popularity, not just to the seeming absence of "theological" knowledge among the young but due much to it. That the Bible is seldom used as a model, and its symbols and stories are decreasing in familiarity among the youth, are certainly an exacerbating feature of this drift towards the secular. Even in cases where youth think of themselves and present themselves as "spiritual" or "religious," it is commonly in the total absence of any reference to institutional religious traditions and teachings and not unusually a presentation of beliefs precisely as contra the established forms of religious ideology.

****

CHAPTER THREE THE RELIGION OF MATURITY

A person of twenty, thirty, or even seventy, years of age does not necessarily have an adult personality. In fact, chronological age is a comparatively poor measure of mental and emotional maturity, likewise of religious maturity. In emerging from childhood one gives up the egocentrism of his thought and feeling only under pressure, and ordinarily environmental pressure does not force a maturity of religious outlook upon the individual as inexorably as it does other forms of maturity. For the individual's religion is usually regarded by others as his own business and, so far as others care, can easily remain egocentric, magical, and wish-fulfilling. Hence, in probably no region of personality do we find so many residues of childhood as in the religious attitudes of adults.

Freud had said it first, if not better, namely, that most adults still maintain their religious views which they had learned first from the nursery. Allport was quick to point out, not just from the psychoanalytic school but from data base studies, that Freud was correct. The reason that religion, more than any other component of the human personality, is so vulnerable to perpetual immaturity is precisely because an individual's religious beliefs are considered in western societies, at least, as strictly off limits to public scrutiny or social prying. Alas, each individual from adolescence onward is left to his own devices in the maturing process and where in all other aspects there are mechanisms in place to assure a more or less easy transition from childhood to adulthood, from immaturity to maturity, there is no established mechanism to assure that an individual's understanding of religion and his ability to articulate religious beliefs and practices will likewise mature along with his social and emotional development.

****

The attributes of a mature personality are three in number (as discussed at length in G. W. Allport, *Personality: A Psychological Interpretation,* NY: Henry Holt & Col., 1937, chapter 8). First, a variety of psychogenic interests is required which concern themselves with ideal objects and values beyond the range of viscerogenic desire. ... A second attribute is the ability to objectify oneself, to be reflective and insightful about one's own life. ... Finally, a mature personality always has some unifying philosophy of life, although not necessarily religious in type, nor articulated in words, nor entirely complete. ... I doubt that any scientifically supported criteria of maturity would differ substantially from these three.

It was Allport's study of the human personality which resulted in the 1937 book that established him as a major figure in American psychology. His work quickly settled itself into the best circles and on the most refined shelves of the leading universities and practicing psychologists in the country. His definition and explication of the components and characteristics of the human personality are now common, and his insights into this aspect of the human person contributed greatly to both his understanding of the religious sentiment and his acceptance in the field of the psychology of religion as a leading voice.

****

Most of the criticism of religion is directed to its immature forms. When immature it has not evolved beyond the level of impulsive self-gratification. Instead of dealing with psychogenic values it serves either a wish-fulfilling or soporific function for the self-centered interests. When immature it does not entail self-objectification, but remains unreflective, failing to provide a context of meaning in which the individual can locate himself, and with perspective judge the quality of his conduct. Finally, the immature sentiment is not really unifying in its effect upon the personality. Excluding, as it does, whole regions of experience, it is spasmodic, segmented, and even when fanatic in intensity, it is but partially integrative of the personality.

If Allport was criticized by his professional peers, and he was on occasion, it was precisely because he always came across as a bit defensive on the side of religion and religious sentiments. With William James, he was concerned with the "value and meaning" of the religious experience, with no real interest in whether the tenets of religion were actually true or not. That was irrelevant to the function of the religious person. With that posture towards the subject, much of what he had to say was as readily, if not more so, accepted by the religious establishment as by the psychological community. His description and criticism of "immature religious sentiment" is a case in point, arguing that most criticism of religion coming from the non-practicing set was addressed to the immature forms of religious sensibilities and that most critics have not taken the time to consider more mature forms of religious behavior for critical study.

****

The astonishing thing about the religious sentiment, and to a less degree about any sentiment, is that, although it entails many component attitudes and objects of interest, it represents nonetheless a stable unit of mental life. The component attitudes are variable but all contribute to a single well-patterned system. Shall we then define the mature religious sentiment as a *disposition, built up through experience, to respond favorably, and in certain habitual ways, to conceptual objects and principles that the individual regards as of ultimate importance in his own life, and as having to do with what he regards as permanent or central in the nature of things?* Thus defined, the religious sentiment allows wide variation both in the human race at large and during the course of any single individual's development.

Allport then sets out to argue for the systemic integrity of a mature form of religious sentiment, its behavior and its ideology. Mature religion, unlike the shallow disjointed and narcissistic forms of immature religion, constitutes a composite sentiment that has integrity and unity and functions positively for the believer. It addresses issues of finitude and destiny, answering questions about why things happen the way they do and for what purpose, and the future and purpose of human life. A mature address to mature questions is the character of mature religion, Allport argues.

****

The multiplicity of interests that fall within the religious sentiment I designate as "differentiations" of this sentiment. It is better to do this than to regard them as myriads of separate sentiments: toward the church, toward the divine, toward world brotherhood, toward good and evil. For it is evident that these components, though discriminable, are woven into a pattern. … those who have not developed a differentiated sentiment often show a kind of uncritical abandon. They may say, 'I don't know enough about it to be rational; I'm accepting my religion on purely emotional grounds," or, "I believe what I was taught, and that's good enough for me." There is here no reflective articulation of parts.

Allport is as hard on the practitioners of immature religion as any non-theist. The immature form of religion functions to both justify and maintain a level of shallowness within the adult mind, which borders on irresponsibility. Not only a failure to understand one's relationship to the world but a genuine disinclination to ask the propitious questions about where we came from, why are we here, and where are we going characterize the immature person, who uses religion solely as a comfort pillow when things become complicated, confusing, and baffling. Yet, there is still no interest in trying to become informed, but rather a ready willingness to "let go and let God" or, "I don't understand any of it but the pastor does," sort of mentality. This simply will not do, says Allport, because it does a disservice to religion and stifles the individual's potential for maturity and personal responsibility.

****

Immature religion, whether in adult or child, is largely concerned with magical thinking, self-justification, and creature comfort. Thus it betrays its sustaining motives still to be the drives and desires of the body. By contrast, mature religion is less of a servant, and more of a master, in the economy of the life. No longer goaded and steered exclusively by impulse, fear, wish, it tends rather to control and to direct these motives toward a goal that is no longer determined by mere self-interest.

Narcissistic and superstitious, this kind of shallow nursery-style religion for the adult is a great disservice to his capacity to delve deeper into the meaning, purpose, and direction in life. Rather than offer solace and security, it is fraught with danger, for when the real questions of life are presented to such an individual, the magical world of a superstitious religion fails to function and assistance is nowhere to be found within it. Mature religion, on the other hand, steps to the fore with answers well thought-out and developed over a period of personality development and the maturation process of adulthood. Criticism of mature religion has its place, says Allport, but to use the criticisms of immature religion to apply to mature religion will not do.

****

CHAPTER FOUR CONSCIENCE AND MENTAL HEALTH

Psychiatry and religion both see man as a far from perfect being. For centuries religion has endeavored to improve the situation. Psychiatry has only recently entered the list, and its youthful vigor raises new hope. ... Clearly we are undergoing a great ideational revolution. But the achievements of this revolution are not yet conclusively favorable. Mental disease has not diminished; rather it has increased, at least among the older third of the population. In the American states with the best hospital facilities, it is now estimated that one person in ten will receive institutional care for mental ailment some time during his life. We know too that in recent times social disorganization in the guise of war, mass persecutions, divorce, delinquency, show upward rather than downward trends. The suffering of individuals has not lessened, but has been bitterly aggravated. Hence, statistically viewed, the success of modern psychotherapy has been up to now not merely negligible but negative.

Allport's interplay between "old" religion and "new" psychiatry is more a literary device than a real address to their potential relationship, for the former is "faith-based" and the latter is "science-based." More than anyone, he shows that he is fully cognizant of the differences as well as their relevance to convergent possibilities. Of course, every concerted human effort,from the beginning of reflective self-consciousness, has sought to bring about a better world in which to live, whether it was religion and philosophy or engineering and agriculture. That psychiatry and its cognates of psychology and psychotherapy have joined the effort is simply another historic advancement in human effort at self-betterment. Allport is aware of that, of course. His suggestion that there is some correlation between the appearance of psychology and the rise of mental illness is, of course, ludicrous. That there has not been a decline in mental illness but a perceived increase, furthermore, cannot be attributed to the appearance of the science of psychology, but rather that science must be given credit for having identified the depth and breadth of mental illness within the human community. Psychology did not cause it. Psychology has identified it and has called it to our attention. Allport is less than generous in his assessment of his own profession, and one believes he is going "overboard" to hold the attention of religious practitioners as he approaches the core of his work.

****

The psychiatrist, although he is himself a physician, receives less support from other physicians than he is entitled to expect. Few medical men realize fully the truth that what the patient believes profoundly affects his health. Untrained in psychology, in psychiatry, in psychosomatic medicine, and bewildered by the irrational troubles of their patients, physicians often prefer to treat ailing organs rather than ailing persons. ... Psychotherapy, for all the progress it has made, is still a young art. Practitioners are few. The techniques of treatment are not yet well tested. A few devices, like sedation, shock, or surgery, are technically specialized. But for the most part psychotherapists employ implements borrowed from the clergy. The reason is simple enough: until recent times the church alone dealt with troubles of personality.

Allport is, however, quick to both defend and promote the work of psychiatrists, suggesting that they are on the bottom rung of the medical practice ladder. Medical professionals (at least at the time he was writing) receive little or no training in dealing with mental illness beyond the use of psychotropic medications for behavior modification. The psychogenic disorders found among the mentally ill fall outside the purview and training of traditional medicine. Psychotherapy, a specialization which focuses upon psychogenic rather than biogenic disorders, is practiced by trained professionals equipped to deal with emotional dysfunctions within the human personality and, suggests Allport, many of their methods and insights are derived from the practice of ministry, from the clergy themselves. The reason for this, explains Allport, is that the faith-community has been the first and quickest to identify and respond to mental disorders, leaving medicine to focus upon the biogenic maladies of the human body.

****

If the therapist's techniques are in the main so similar to the pastor's, why is the cure of souls gravitating more and more out of the hands of the church and into the hands of psychiatrists? There are several reasons. For one thing, people prefer to look for physical causes of their difficulties, and the psychiatrist, being a medical man, may find such a cause. If he does, then the patient is saved from the necessity of facing up to the realities of his inner life. A cause in the body is less disturbing than a cause in one's character. The pastor, he fears, will not sense the possible physical basis for his trouble, but may confuse mental, physical, and moral aspects in a manner that will be humiliating. The pastor, he fears, may at inappropriate moments preach or pray or pass moral judgment. Further, the vast prestige of modern science mantles the psychiatrist, and the patient approaches him with high hopes, thinking no doubt of the spectacular achievements of contemporary medicine.

There is a trend, then and now, Allport suggests, of modern society drifting towards the practitioners of psychotherapy and away from the clergy in the seeking of help with mental illness and emotional dysfunction issues. The influence of secular humanism has proven to be a major factor in this drift and has also served to launch the professional practice of counseling psychology and its various cognate professions into national prominence just as the clergy and the church are struggling to stay relevant and conspicuously beneficial to the general public as instruments of emotional nurture. The proximity of psychotherapy and its correlative professions of psychiatry and counseling are more aligned with medicine than with religion and this, says Allport, makes it more attractive as a venue for emotional health by disassociating the practice from the presumed judgmental nature of much of the counseling offered by religious practitioners.

****

Psychotherapy knows the healing power of love, but finds itself unable to do much about it. On the side of theory … it lacks an adequate concept of the nature of tenderness. On the side of practice, the psychotherapist finds himself unable to supply the love his patient needs, nor to receive the love the patient wants to give. The normal stage of "transference" in the course of treatment betrays this need, but it is a temporary step. Transference must be broken. … By contrast, religion -- especially the Christian religion -- offers an interpretation of life and a rule of life based wholly upon love. It calls attention again and again to this fundamental groundwork. On love for God and man "hang all the Law and the prophets." The emphasis is insistent. … Perhaps the very insistence of religion in this matter is in part responsible for the "tenderness tabu" that has descended upon psychology.

One of the ironies, Allport points out, of the practice of psychotherapy is its difficulty or inability to know what to do with what he calls the "healing power of love." Akin to medical practice in treating the symptom rather than the person, psychotherapy is at a disadvantage as he sees it when compared to pastoral ministry, for the former is bound to a biogenic model of health while the latter is aligned with a psychogenic or even a spiritual basis for health and well-being. Whereas psychoanalysis emphasizes the need to deal with transference of the patient-doctor relationship wherein that experience, which must inevitably be "broken," the pastor's role is to heal and nurture the individual's need for relationship built upon love and trust and tenderness. The very thing that is "forbidden" in psychology is the central ingredient in religious nurture, explains Allport.

****

Pastoral-psychiatric teamwork is a rapidly expanding conception. As with teams it is necessary for one member to be more flexible and adaptable than the other, in order that the relationship may run smoothly. It seems likely that the clergy and the theological schools for the present will have to be the suitor, the planner, the adaptor, until the team is strongly established. We note the vigorous disposition on the part of the clergy to include psychology in their program of training. Not yet do psychiatrists seem to sense their need for the inclusion of philosophy and theology in their preparation for practice.

The solution, not new but at the time Allport was writing it was considered a rather radical idea, is the partnering of the two types of emotional nurture. Ministry and medical practice might just find that they compliment rather than compete with each other. Medicine and counseling might just prove to be the right combination of psychogenic and biogenic insights into mental illness and health and wholeness needed to bring about a real breakthrough for western society suffering from stress and alienation. But, given the recalcitrance of medical training and medical practitioners, it has inevitably fallen to theological schools and ministry training courses to equip clergy with the insights and skills needed to make them professional peers with their medical counterparts. Someone has to relinquish the dominant role, suggests Allport, and the profession of ministry is more akin to that mindset than is the practice of medicine. But with clergy willing to take the training and find their place alongside if not just in the footsteps of medical practitioners, there is a good chance that the patient will be the long term beneficiary.

****

CHAPTER FIVE THE NATURE OF DOUBT

Doubt, like disbelief, is technically a secondary condition of mental life. It is an unstable or hesitant reaction, produced by the collision of evidence with prior belief, or of one belief with another. It is apparent that disbelief is relatively more final and single-minded than is doubt. Yet since doubt represents incipient disbelief, and since it springs from the same psychological sources, we shall be justified in treating these two states of mind together (doubt and disbelief). For convenience we shall direct our remarks to the topic of doubt.

Ever the psychologist, albeit one very sensitive to the emotional relevance of religious sentiment (whether religion is true or not is of no consequence to the individual's emotional well-being), Allport identifies the vulnerability of modern society and the contemporary individual when it comes to authoritative belief versus legitimate doubt and even unrequited disbelief. A healthy doubt is a good thing, Allport assures us (and twenty years later the leading liberal Protestant theologian, Paul Tillich, will write the definitive book on the topic entitled, *The Faith to Doubt*). Allport anticipates, unwittingly, Tillich's great contribution to this emotional nuancing of faith and certainty. Where there is doubt (and disbelief), there is room for inquiry and growth, whether it leads to faith or to a mature justification for not believing. Either way, says Allport, the individual benefits.

****

Religion, aiming to deal with the most inclusive of relationships --- aiming to bind fact, value, and ultimate reality --- is the most controversial, the most doubt-ridden, the most elusive of all the fields of mental activity. It would be so, even if the temper of the times did not at present intensify the situation. Having turned from religion to higher education, great masses of people regard the former as an obscurantism from which they must emerge. They have learned the first lesson taught by higher education which is to avoid being duped. The first lesson is all that many ever learn. It is not the function of the psychologist to pass on the legitimacy or illegitimacy of any doubt. His duty is merely to elucidate a process which he finds to be a universal and necessary part of mental life. He holds that if each person understood the doubting process, he would be in a better position to determine the cogency of his own grounds for belief or disbelief.

Religion's primary agenda of binding "fact, value, and reality" together in one believable package, says Allport, constitutes the most problematic situation confronting the individual in modern society. The rise of secular humanism, with its emphasis upon higher education and the dominance of the sciences in those primary fields of study such as medicine and psychology, has resulted in a tainting of religious belief with an aura of unreality or superficiality. Modern man needs science, says the new age, and modern science has displaced religion which attempted to answer fundamental questions of the meaning and purpose of life which now modern science has taken in hand to answer. Modern science, and particularly psychology, have created an environment in which each individual feels empowered to make his own judgments regarding the meaning and purpose of life without coaching from religious leaders and institutions. That is our current situation, says Allport.

****

The subtle relation between militant atheism and positive religion has sometimes been pointed out. "Atheism, rightly understood," writes Oswald Spengler (in his *Decline of the West*, trans. 1926) "is the necessary expression of a spirituality that has exhausted its religious possibilities ... It is entirely compatible with a living wistful desire for real religiousness -- therein resembling Romanticism, which likewise would recall that which has irrevocably gone." By reacting so violently against religion, an ardent atheist in reality betrays a deep interest in the religious mode of life. One of the commonest states of mind at the present time is "religious agnosticism" wherein individuals react against formal religion lest it impede the free exercise of their minds, but at the same time often maintain the highest standards of ethical conduct, and may vaguely relate these standards to the moments of reverence and wonder that they occasionally experience. The point to note is that in reacting against the intellectual slavery of an idea, the resulting negativism often pertains to specific content rather than to basic values.

Atheism, suggests Allport, has almost reached religious proportions in its perpetration, for its adherents have taken on an aura of certainty and aggressive denunciation characteristic of the religious fanatic. Furthermore, religious agnosticism has become a perceived panacea for individuals driven by a deep sense of moral behavior and ethical standards but not under the mandate of a religious ideology. The irony which Allport sees, is that these very individuals are themselves the embodiment of an ethical standard reflective of the religious ideology of which they purport to be antagonists.

****

CHAPTER SIX THE NATURE OF FAITH

Faith is basically man's belief in the validity and attainability of some goal (value). The goal is set by desires. Desires, however, are not merely pushes from behind (drive ridden). They include such complex, future-oriented states as longing for a better world, for one's own perfection, for a completely satisfying relation to the universe. So important is this forward thrust in all desires emanating from mature sentiments that I propose the term "intention" to depict the dynamic operation we are endeavoring to describe. Better than "desire" this term designates the presence of the rational and ideational component in all productive striving. Some sort of idea of the end is always bound into the act itself. It is this inseparability of the idea of the end from the course of the striving that we call faith.

With William James, Allport has no time or patience with those who would attempt a dialogue between religion and psychology based on the quest for "truth," a truth which they say has no real relevance for the emotional well-being of the individual. Whether religion is true or not is of no importance. What is important, they say, is that one has "faith" to believe in the religious community's ideology. The desire for a better world is the driving force behind religious faith, a longing for peace and security, a searching for stability in an unstable world, the desire for meaningful relationships in a world fraught with danger and fear and anger and hostility. If religious faith offers this, then religious faith has demonstrated its value for the human community.

****

We must never lose sight of the individual differences that characterize the operation of the religious sentiment. It is from this point of view, I think, that prayer, ritual, and dogma can best be approached. All are means of focusing the religious intention during a definite period of time. Prayer takes many forms. At one extreme it is self-reflective, analytical, hardly distinguishable from strenuous intellectual efforts to relate scattered fragments of life.

Not group-think or mass-appeal but individual nurture is the driving force for religious sentiment, says Allport, and this is the correct arena to assess its value and merit to the individual in society. Prayer, ritual, and dogma focus the individual's attention upon the desired effects of religious faith. Whether celebrated collectively or in solitude, these are the instruments which foster religious consciousness, and it is the individual who benefits from their utility. These items should constitute the focus of psychological research into religious belief and practice. It is here where the psychology of religion can make its greatest contribution to an understanding of the relationship between theology and psychology, between faith and emotional well-being.

****

Where does revealed religion enter into the individual's struggle for validation? It unquestionably assists him if he is persuaded that God of His free generosity has chosen to give dependable, if partial, knowledge of Himself through the devices of the intelligible universe that affect our senses, including, for example, those divinely ordained symbols employed in the sacraments which are sensible signs of what is hidden in Him. It helps to assume that God chooses to declare Himself to us in our own language. Faith, based on this premise, is enjoined by the historic church, and is for millions the decisive consideration. But it is well to note that the church allows also supporting means of faith, including the rational arguments of theology, and the avenue of mystical contemplation or immediate experience. It shows psychological wisdom in multiplying the avenues through which various individuals may achieve the heightened degree of confidence in the validity of their own beliefs.

In concluding his inquiry into the nature of the individual and his religious sensibilities, Allport makes his strongest case for the legitimacy of the faith experience. Never wishing to approach the issue of truth itself, Allport, with William James, is very content with believing in the value and efficacy of religious faith in so far as it services the needs of the individual with confidence and certitude when facing the future. If it helps, it is good. No clearer instance of the "pragmatic school of thought" as perpetrated by Dewey can be found in religious discussions than is found in James and Allport. If it works, its good. That settles the question regarding the efficacy of faith.

A man's religion is the audacious bid he makes to bind himself to creation and to the Creator. It is his ultimate attempt to enlarge and to complete his own personality by finding the supreme context in which he rightly belongs. (Gordon Allport, 1950).

CHAPTER SEVEN

Eric Fromm and *Psychoanalysis and Religion*

Eric Fromm (1900-1980), a German psychoanalyst and the only child of Orthodox Jewish parents, was educated at the University of Frankfurt am Main in jurisprudence before transferring to the University of Heidelberg where he studied sociology under Max Weber's younger brother, Alfred, as well as psychiatry under Karl Jaspers. Taking his Ph.D. in sociology from Heidelberg in 1922, he went on to become a psychoanalyst at the Frieda Reichmann's Psychoanalytic Sanatorium in Heidelberg, after which he joined the Frankfurt Institute for Social Research where he completed his training and residency. Fleeing Nazi Germany in the 1930s, he went to Geneva and subsequently to New York, where he taught at the New School for Social Research and then at Columbia University. It was here that he became a life-long colleague and confidant of Karen Horney whose book, *Self Analysis* (1942), reflects their close association in life and thought. Working in the development of the New York Branch of the Washington School of Psychiatry after leaving Columbia, Fromm became a co-founder, along with Harry Stack Sullivan, of the William Alanson White Institute of Psychiatry, Psychoanalysis, and Psychology. He later moved to Mexico City and taught on the National Autonomous University faculty in the medical school before returning to teach psychology at Michigan State University and, subsequently, at New York University. He died in his home in Switzerland at the age of eighty years old, all the while maintaining an active clinical practice.

Whereas Allport, as a social psychologist whose international notoriety was established by his *The Individual and His Religion*, brought the study of the psychology of religion to focus upon the value and function of religious ideology for the individual, whether religion was true or not, Fromm, as a psychoanalyst, chose to emphasize the efficacy of psychoanalytic insights into the human condition which religion serves. Religion is not in danger of scientific scrutiny, nor is psychoanalysis treading on forbidden ground. Rather, whereas religion addresses a fundamental need found in the human condition, psychoanalysis provides a scientific mechanism to understand, assess, and facilitate an address to that human situation, a condition which is fraught with fear, anxiety, and uncertainty about the verities of life and our future in the world. "Psychoanalysis assesses the persistent tension between traditional religion and the underlying philosophy of psychoanalysis," explains Fromm, "which many believe regards the satisfaction of instinctive and material wishes as the sole aim of life." Fromm argues that "psychoanalysis is neither the enemy of religion nor its ally but rather is concerned with the human reality behind theological doctrines and with the realization of the human values underlying all great religious teachings" (Fromm 1950). Though his 1956 classic, *The Art of Loving*, is considered his greatest work, catapulting him into international notoriety as a psychoanalytically insightful social critique, it was his inquiry into the nature and function of religious beliefs and practices and their relationship to the healthy, inquisitive, and scientifically astute human mind, namely, *Psychoanalysis and Religion* (1950), which proved to be just that approach to the psychology of religion which made it equally and legitimately the domain of both psychologists and theologians alike.

Selections from *Psychoanalysis and Religion,* by Erich Fromm, with commentary.

NOTE: In the following, the original text will be printed in *Arial Unicode MS* typestyle (as is this note itself to illustrate) as an easy and aesthetically pleasing way of identifying the primary source paragraphs. The author's commentary will be in *Times New Roman.* It is hoped that this differentiation between the "primary source" and the "commentary" made by use of differing typestyles will prove helpful and not disruptive to the reader. *I have also chosen to use a quadruple asterisk (****) to separate the primary text from the commentary.*

CHAPTER ONE THE PROBLEM

Never before has man come so close to the fulfillment of his most cherished hopes as today. Our scientific discoveries and technical achievements enable us to visualize the day when the table will be set for all who want to eat, a day when the human race will form a unified community and no longer live as separate entitled. .... Man has crated a new world with its own laws and destiny. Looking at his creation, he can say, truly, it is good. But looking at himself what can he say? Has he come closer to the realization of another dream of mankind, that of the perfection of *man?* Of man loving his neighbor, doing justice, speaking truth, and realizing that which he potentially is, an image of God?

Fromm is both psychologist and pastor, both psychoanalyst and philosopher of culture. Eager to applaud the improvement in the quality of life of the human community from subsistence living in primeval days to the luxury of modern technological living, Fromm simultaneously alerts us to that which is most strikingly missing in our emotional lives. Our psychological well-being is far from what it should be if it is to keep pace with the comfort of our physical lives. Our inner peace and our interpersonal relations are in dire need of improvement, and where is that to come from but within ourselves and, says Fromm, both religion and psychology can help.

****

While we have created wonderful things we have failed to make of ourselves beings for whom this tremendous effort would seem worthwhile. Ours is a life not of brotherliness, happiness, contentment but of spiritual chaos and bewilderment dangerously close to a state of madness -- not the hysterical kind of madness which existed in the Middle Ages but a madness akin to schizophrenia in which the contact with inner reality is lost and thought is split from affect. ... Man has ceased to believe that the power of reason can establish the validity of norms and ideas for human conduct. This change in the intellectual and emotional climate has had a profound impact on the development of psychology as a science.

Fromm expounds on what our human potential is and, in contrast, what the realities of modern life really are. We are not eager to build community, to nurture relationships, to serve the common good. We are driven to seek after selfish interests benefiting only ourselves even at the expense of the community around us. These situations, suggests Fromm, have themselves been the caldron within which the science of psychology has happily emerged. These human conditions have made a special place for this science, a science constructed to specifically address these desperate times in which we live.

****

Academic psychology, trying to imitate the natural sciences and laboratory methods of weighing and counting, dealt with everything except the soul. It tried to understand those aspects of man which can be examined in the laboratory and claimed that conscience, value judgments, the knowledge of good and evil are metaphysical concepts, outside the problems of psychology; it was more often concerned with insignificant problems which fitted an alleged scientific method than with devising new methods to study the significant problems of man. Psychology thus became a science lacking its main subject matter, the soul; it was concerned with mechanisms, reaction formations, instincts, but not with the most specifically human phenomena: love, reason, conscience, values. Because the word *soul* has associations which include these higher human powers I use it here and throughout these chapters rather than the words "psyche" or "mind."

However, the very science precipitated by this social malaise which has the capacity to address our deepest needs as individuals and as a society of people has chosen, alas, to emulate the physical and natural sciences. Psychology has attempted to present itself as a science using the same domain assumptions and operating under the mandated methodologies of the deductive sciences and, therefore, has overlooked the very thing that it is uniquely crafted to address, namely, the condition of the human "soul," the "inner being of the human person." Fromm is eager to validate his use of the term "soul," a term Freud avoided like the plague, but one with which Jung was quite comfortable. "Soul,"" for Fromm, simply means the inner self of the individual, his mind and psyche, but the term "soul" itself conveys a special resonance for Fromm and provides a linguistic cross-over term with religion.

****

Then came Freud, the last great representative of the rationalism of the enlightenment, the first to demonstrate its limitations. He dared to interrupt the songs of triumph of mere intellect. He showed that reason is the most valuable and the most specifically human power of man and yet is subject to the distorting effect of passions, and that only the understanding of man's passions can free his reason to function properly. He demonstrated the power as well as the weaknesses of human reason and made "the truth shall make you free" the guiding principle of a new therapy.

Though Freud was disinclined to use cross-over language, abjuring any need or value in conversing with religion and its leaders and promoters, nevertheless, Freud was the one, says Fromm, who ventured into the troubled waters of rationalism and its shortcomings. Man is more than thought, says Freud, he is more than reason and logic and system and process. Man has an inner self, a self composed not only of rational thought but of irrationality itself deposited conveniently in his unconscious which, contrary to the ideas and wishes of the complete Lockean rationalist, does not stay quiet but intrudes into the inner workings of human behavior. This should be and is the agenda set for a psychology, a depth psychology, worthy of the name. Fromm concurs and then demonstrates how it might, indeed, interact with religious ideology and religious behavior to our advantage.

****

Freud's method, psychoanalysis, made possible the most minute and intimate study of the soul. The "laboratory" of the analyst has no gadgets. He cannot weight or count his findings, but he gains insight through dreams, fantasies, and associations into the hidden desires and anxieties of his patients. In his "laboratory," relying only on observation, reason, and his own experience as a human being, he discovers that mental sickness cannot be understood apart from moral problems; that his patient is sick because he has neglected his soul's demands. The analyst is not a theologian or a philosopher and does not claim competence in those fields, but as a physician of the soul he is concerned with the very same problems as philosophy and theology: the soul of man and its cure.

Fromm's work, like Freud's, had to do precisely with the human soul, with the inner being of the individual. No lab jacket encumbers the psychoanalyst, nor test tubes nor Bunson burners. Rather, it is the inner workings of the human mind which must be plumbed, and through the use of dream analysis and free association and a plethora of other techniques the therapist, the psychoanalyst, is able to plumb the depths of the mind. Neurosurgery, however, can only intrude into the physical brain, leaving the human mind untouched. It is "soul work," an agenda designed to assist the modern person who has neglected the care and nurture of his inner being, his inner self, his soul, says Fromm. It is here where modern psychology and ancient theology converge, on the topic and treatment of the human soul.

****

If we thus define the function of the psychoanalyst we find that at present two professional groups are concerned with the soul: the priests and the psychoanalysts. What is their mutual relationship? Is the psychoanalyst trying to occupy the priest's domain and is opposition between them unavoidable? Or, are they allies who work for the same ends and who should supplement and interpenetrate each other's field both theoretically and practically?

Bolder, if not outright braver, than most professional practitioners in depth psychology, Fromm is confident in identifying the points of continuity between the clergy and the psychotherapist. Contending that both are in the business of ministering to the individual's well-being by seeing after the affairs of the "soul" of modern man and his society, Fromm wishes to advance the rather radical notion that both the clergy and the therapist are allies and compatriots in the treatment of the inner man. To be sure, this is the strongest claim from the psychology side of things that we have found, though theologians and pastoral counselors like David Roberts have been suggesting it all along. The radical difference here is that one of the leading psychoanalysts of the day is saying it also.

****

I want to show that to set up alternatives of either irreconcilable opposition or identify of interest is fallacious; a thorough and dispassionate discussion can demonstrate that the relation between religion and psychoanalysis is too complex to be forced into either one of these simple and convenient attitudes. I want to show in these pages that it is not true that we have to give up the concern for the soul if we do not accept the tenets of religion. The psychoanalyst is in a position to study the human reality behind religion as well as behind nonreligious symbol systems. He finds that the question is not whether man returns to religion and believes in God but whether he lives love and thinks truth. If he does so the symbol systems he uses are of secondary importance. If he does not they are of no importance.

Fromm is not naïve and is not suggesting nor is he presuming a "commonality" of perspective and motivation, of intentionality and sameness. There is no possibility and there would be no benefit, says Fromm, if both clergy and psychologists, both religion and the practice of psychotherapy, were to presume a commonality which failed to differentiate their differences, differences in theory and practice, in ideology and intentionality. No, they are not the same, but psychology needs not discount the clergy because psychology cannot embrace religious ideologies and practices nor should the clergy discount psychotherapy because the science of psychology is unwillingness to embrace a theological worldview. Both professions have a mission to nurture the soul of modern persons and society, and this they share as a common goal. It is that which lies behind religious beliefs and practices, the love of truth and the will to love others, which should be and is the focus of psychoanalysis. To know the why and the how of religious belief, rather than the ideological system, constitutes the depth psychologist's agenda.

****

CHAPTER TWO FREUD AND JUNG

Freud dealt with the problem of religion and psychoanalysis in one of his most profound and brilliant books, *THE Future of an Illusion,* Jung, who was the first psychoanalyst to understand that myth and religious ideas are expressions of profound insights, has dealt with the same topic in the Terry Lectures of 1937, published under the title *Psychology and Religion.* If I now attempt to give a brief summary of the position of both psychoanalysts it is with a threefold purpose: (1) To indicate where the discussion of the problem stands now and to locate the point from which I want to proceed. (2) To lay the groundwork for the following chapters by discussing some of the fundamental concepts used by Freud and Jung. (3) A correction of the widely held view that Freud is "against" and Jung "for" religion will permit us to see the fallacy of such oversimplifying statements in this complex field and to discuss the ambiguities in the meanings of "religion" and "psychoanalysis."

Fromm is sufficiently established as a world figure in depth psychology to feel confident in his assessment of the works of both Freud and Jung. Being himself a neo-Freudian, we can anticipate Freud coming out somewhat better than Jung, but Fromm is critical of both as well as complimentary of significant aspects of both of their systems of social and individual analysis. His purpose is to state what the present situation is, to sort out the fundamental concepts of each, and to propose a synthesis of the best of their systems, while dispelling many of the false notions regarding their schools of thought. The balance and fairness of the treatment of each is very inviting.

****

For Freud, religion has its origin in man's helplessness in confronting the forces of nature outside and the instinctive forces within himself. Religion arises at an early stage of human development when man cannot yet use his reason to deal with these outer and inner forces and must repress them or manage them with the help of other affective forces. So instead of coping with these forces by means of reason he copes with them by "counter-affects," by other emotional forces, the functions of which are to suppress and control that which he is powerless to cope with rationally.

Freud, explains Fromm, understood religion to be a coping mechanism for individuals who have failed, or who wish not to grow up, to mature, and to embrace the verities of life without a crutch. Religion is that crutch, it stands in for the individual who chooses immaturity and infantile fixations rather than the necessity of being "condemned to freedom," the requirement in a world to assume responsibility for one's self devoid of a Father God . This, for Freud, is the meaning and function of religion and the explanation of its origins. Admittedly, says Freud, for many people, religion is as good as a neurosis in allowing them to cope with the uncertainties of life.

****

Freud's analysis of the psychological roots of religion attempts to show *why* people formulated the idea of a god. But it claims to do more than to get at these psychological roots. It claims that the unreality of the theistic concept is demonstrated by exposing it as an illusion based on man's wishes. Freud goes beyond attempting to prove that religion is an *illusion.* He says religion is a *danger* because it tends to sanctify bad human institutions with which it has allied itself throughout its history; further, by teaching people to believe in an illusion and by prohibiting critical thinking religion is responsible for the impoverishment of intelligence.

Freud, explains Fromm, not only explains the "origin" of religious ideology but also demonstrates how it functions as an "illusion" to protect the immature individual from the uncertainties of life. The reason Freud "attacks" religion is not to be vindictive or small-minded, but rather, as a psychotherapist eager to foster maturity among adults, he wishes to demonstrate how religion, like neurosis, protects the individual's immaturity at the peril of his own opportunity for growth and emotional development. It stifles critical thinking by substituting infantile and adolescent answers concocted by religious leaders eager to perpetuate their institutions of control.

****

The dangers which Freud sees in religion make it apparent that his own ideals and values are the very things he considers to be threatened by religion: reason, reduction of human suffering, and morality. But we do not have to rely on inferences from Freud's criticism of religion; he has expressed very explicitly what are the norms and ideals he believes in: brotherly love, truth, and freedom. Reason and freedom are interdependent according to Freud.

Fromm explains that Freud sees religion as serving to block rational thought among the adults of modern society to the peril of that society itself. It is, in a word, immoral what religion does to people, and therein lies the irony. Religion claiming to promote morality when all the while it perpetuates an immaturity of mind devoid of rationality and, thus, promoting immorality by promoting infantile projections into adulthood. A mature individual believes in love, truth, and freedom but all three, suggests Freud, are denied by religion and stifled in their development.

****

Man must educate himself to face reality (says Freud). If he knows that he has nothing to rely on except his own powers, he will learn to use them properly. Only the free man who has emancipated himself from authority -- authority that threatens and protects -- can make us of his power of reason and grasp the world and his role in it objectively, without illusion but also with the ability to develop and to make use of the capacities inherent in him. Only if we grow up and cease to be children dependent on and afraid of authority can we dare to think for ourselves; but the reverse is also true. Only if we dare to think can we emancipate ourselves from domination by authority.

Only when the individual realizes that he is condemned to freedom will he grow into a mature state of mind wherein he assumes responsibility of what he does and why he does it. To "let go and let God" is the worst form of infantile behavior by adults for it suggests that they have relinquished all responsibility for doing the right thing because it is the right thing to do. They do what they do because they believe (and are taught) that it is the will of God, not because it is right to do it. This kind of religiously motivated authority structure is the prime creator of guilt in the human psyche and it is guilt that is the oil for the machinery of religious institutions, explains Freud.

****

It is significant in this context to note that Freud states that the feeling of powerlessness is the opposite of religious feeling. In view of the fact that many theologians -- and, as we shall see later, Jung too to a certain extent -- consider the feeling of dependence and powerlessness to he core of religious experience, Freud's statement is very important. It is expressive, even though only by implication, of his own concept of religious experience, namely, that of independence and the awareness of one's powers. I shall attempt to show later on that this difference constitutes one of the critical problems in the psychology of religion.

Freud and the theologians agree on one major point, ironically, and that is that powerlessness is the core of religious feeling. For Freud, this is the very thing that keeps individuals from maturing into adulthood with its accompanying reason and responsibility, and for theologians, it is the very thing that assures a feeling of dependence of the believer upon God. Whether these feelings of powerlessness and helplessness are good or bad will be addressed by Fromm later.

****

Jung's use of the concept of truth is not tenable. He states that "truth is a fact and not a judgment," that "an elephant is true because it exists." but he forgets that truth always and necessarily refers to a judgment and not a description of a phenomenon which we perceive with our senses and which we denote with a word symbol. Jung then states that an idea is "psychologically true in as much as it exists." But an idea "exists" regardless of whether it is a delusion or whether it corresponds to fact. The existence of an idea does not make it "true" in any sense. Even the practicing psychiatrist could not work were he not concerned with the truth of an idea, that is, with its relation to the phenomena it tends to portray.

Fromm is not sympathetic to Jung's underlying domain assumptions, particularly his notion of the relativity of the concepts of truth and fact. Jung is too much on the side of William James and Allport who wish, in the world of religious belief at least, to think that a thing is "true" if it is believed to be true by the believer. Whether or not a thing is true is irrelevant in the world of religious belief, for all that is important is that the believer believes a thing to be true. This is bad science and worse philosophy, but constitutes the very logic that has kept religion in business for centuries. To have leading psychologists support such an irrational concept, says Fromm, is ultimately disastrous to the individual, society, and the professions of science as well.

****

After discussing his methodological premises, Jung presents his views on the central problem: What is religion? What is the nature of religious experience? His definition is one which he shares with many theologians. It can be summarized briefly in the statement that the essence of religious experience is the submission to powers higher than ourselves. .... Having defined religious experience as being seized by a power outside of ourselves, Jung proceeds to interpret the concept of the unconscious as being a religious one. According to him, the unconscious cannot be merely a part of the individual mind but is a power beyond our control intruding upon our minds.

Fromm dismisses Jung's bad science and poor methodology for analyzing religious ideology and behavior and turns to Jung's descriptions of what he understands religion to actually be and how it functions within the individual and society. That Jung and theologians are all on the same page seems troubling to Fromm for there is a tacit and implied consensus of agreement about religion which makes psychoanalytic assessment of religious ideology and behavior problematic. However, Jung seems (at least it appears to be so) to employ a trick here in dealing with clergy for, though they agree that religion is "submitting to a higher power," whereas theologians assume we all agree that this means God Himself (!), Jung actually means the "unconscious" and all that that implies. Since the unconscious of each individual is more than that individual, it must mean that the unconscious is a source and power "higher" than the mere individual, something shared by all past, present, and conceivably in the future. Here, Jung's integrity is questioned by Fromm in terms of an honest redefining of a term mutually agreed upon but now changed in meaning to suit Jung.

****

It is a necessary consequence of his definition of religion and of the unconscious that Jung arrives at the conclusion that, in view of the nature of the unconscious mind, the influence of the unconscious upon us "is a basic religious phenomenon." It follows that religious dogma and the dream are both religious phenomena because they both are expressions of our being seized by a power outside ourselves.

Jung actually presses the point by arguing that since the unconscious constitutes a source of power higher than any individual, and this function is, indeed, a religious phenomenon, then they both, religion and the unconscious, function the same and are, therefore, essentially the same thing. He then presses on with the analogy that religious ideology and the dream are both manifestations of religious phenomena because they both speak on behalf of a source of power above and beyond any individual. This, Fromm can hardly abide, and it might be said that as Jung moved further and further into this line of "reasoning," he lost credibility among most practicing psychoanalysts and psychotherapists of his day (with the exception of Americans who seemed to resonate with this line of thought). Subsequently, it was the clergy moreso than any other profession that took up Jung's cause and has continued to promote it without the general support of the profession of psychiatry and its cognates in the various counseling fields of depth psychology.

****

Does our examination of Freud's and Jung's attitudes towards religion bear out the popularly held opinion that Freud is a foe and Jung a friend of religion? A brief comparison of their views shows that this assumption is a misleading oversimplification. Freud holds that the aim of human development is the achievement of these ideals: knowledge (reason, truth, logos), brotherly love, reduction of suffering, independence, and responsibility. .... For Jung, religious experience is characterized by a specific kind of emotional experience: surrender to a higher power, whether this higher power is called God or the unconscious. ... Freud opposes religion in the name of ethics -- an attitude which can be termed "religious." On the other hand, Jung reduces religion to a psychological phenomenon and at the same time elevates the unconscious to a religious phenomenon.

Whereas Freud dismisses religion as a stifling of human maturity, offering the individual a childish way out of all responsibility by calling upon the individual to continue to revel in the infantile dependence upon an all-power Father God, Jung, on the other hand, has chosen to essentially equate religion with the unconscious and, therefore, appear to argue in favor of religion as in no way different from the unconscious. Both reduce religion to something less than religious people seem to think that it is -- Freud reduces it to an illusion and Jung to the unconscious. Fromm is eager to move deeper into a possible relationship in which religion is allowed to remain what it claims to be while psychology is permitted to identify those motivating factors "behind religion," which involve the nurture of the human soul, our inner being.

****

CHAPTER THREE AN ANALYSIS OF SOME TYPES OF RELIGIOUS EXPERIENCE

Any discussion of religion is handicapped by a serious terminological difficulty. While we know that there were and are many religions outside of monotheism, we nevertheless associate the concept religion with a system centered around God and supernatural forces; we tend to consider monotheistic religion as a frame of reference for the understanding and evaluation of all other religions. ... For lack of such a word I shall use the term religion in these chapters, but I want to make it clear at the outset that I understand by religion *any system of thought and action shared by a group which gives the individual a frame of orientation and an object of devotion.*

Of course, Fromm must offer his own working definition of religion. Indisputably, Freud and Jung both dealt with religion in terms of a monotheistic construct and both, though Freud was Jewish, dealt specifically with the kind of religion practiced among European Christians. Fromm is much more cosmopolitan in his treatment of religion and in his definition of it. He wishes to broaden the concept and the experience well beyond western monotheism (interesting that neither Freud nor Jung have anything to say about Islam, a religion with 1.5 billion adherents!). Fromm's definition sounds remarkably akin to a political ideology with the striking caveat in his definition of the expression "object of devotion." Yet and still, one can venerate and even offer a kind of devotion to Mao's *Little Red Book* or Marx's *Das Kapital* or Hitler's *Mein Kampf.*

****

Self-awareness, reason, and imagination have disrupted the 'harmony' which characterizes animal existence. Their emergence has made man into an anomaly, into the freak of the universe. He is part of nature, subject to her physical laws and unable to change them, yet he transcends the rest of nature. He is set apart while being a part; he is homeless, yet chained to the home shares with all creatures. Cast into this world at an accidental place and time, he is forced out of it, again accidentally. Being aware of himself, he realizes his powerlessness and the limitations of his existence. He visualizes his own end: death. Never is he free from the dichotomy of his existence: he cannot rid himself of his mind, even if he should want to; he cannot rid himself of his body as long as he is alive -- and his body makes him want to be alive.

Fromm waxes eloquent in his assessment of the predicament of modern man and the "uniqueness" of his situation. Not that he readily acknowledges that we, too, are members of the animal kingdom but are, in a sense, profoundly different because we are troubled by our own duplicity -- our reflective self-awareness has put us in a situation where we know that we know and what we know is our finitude. Our mind is our blessing and our curse; we can think, and what we think about is often our own demise. This makes us susceptible to ponderings related to the experiences and issues addressed historically by religion -- where did we come from, where are we going, what is our purpose -- and, now, the modern science of psychotherapy offers assistance.

****

The disharmony of man's existence generates needs which far transcend those of his animal origin. These needs result in an imperative drive to restore a unity and equilibrium between himself and the rest of nature. He makes the attempt to restore this unity and equilibrium in the first place in thought by constructing an all-inclusive mental picture of the world which serves as a frame of reference from which he can derive an answer to the question of where he stands and what he out to do. … He has to strive for the experience of unity and oneness in all spheres of his being in order to find a new equilibrium. Hence any satisfying system of orientation implies not only intellectual elements but elements of feeling and sense to be realized in action in all fields of human endeavor. Devotion to an aim, or an idea, or a power transcending man such as God, is an expression of this need for completeness in the process of living.

Animals do not need religion, to put it simplistically, for they are not in the grip of the human dilemma. The disharmony Fromm speaks of is a uniquely human phenomenon. Devotion, reverence, dedication to a mission, and purpose in life all constitute propensities within the human being, we might say the human "soul." These things make their appearance in religion with its superstitions and magic, pretending answers to the unfathomable problems and challenges of life in a pre-scientific world. With the coming of modern science, however, these propensities have not yet disappeared, those motivating factors of intentionality behind religion are, indeed, still very much present. Here, psychology has a real opening to offer a deeper understanding of those factors which have produced religion by providing an in-depth look at the human person, the inner self, the very soul of the individual.

****

Man is not free to choose between having or not having 'ideals,' but he is free to choose between different kinds of ideals, between being devoted to worship of power and destruction and being devoted to reason and love. All men are 'idealists' and are striving for something beyond the attainment of physical satisfaction. They differ in the kinds of ideals they believe in. The very best but also the most satanic manifestations of man's mind are expressions not of his flesh but of his 'idealism,' of his spirit. Therefore a relativistic view which claims that to have some ideal or some religious feeling is valuable in itself is dangerous and erroneous.

Sounding very much like the existentialist Jean-Paul Sartre, Fromm is eager to remind us that we are not at liberty, like all other animals, to pay no attention to our situation because we are self-reflective, and knowledge of our predicament is ever with us. Finitude is around every corner and we know what death means and that it awaits us all. Furthermore, we are both *homo symbolicum* and *homo herneneuticus*, namely, we are both the symbolizing and interpreting creatures of our world. We live in a world of humanly created ideas and ideals, of goals and ambitions. But the ownership and management of these ideals is the bane and burden of the human community and the individual. We are, indeed, responsible for what we think and what we do with what we think.

****

What I have said about man's idealism holds true equally for his religious need. There is no one without a religious need, a need to have a frame of orientation and an object of devotion; but this statement does not tell us anything about a specific context in which this religious need is manifest. Man may worship animals, trees, idols of gold or stone, an invisible god, a saintly man or diabolic leaders; he may worship his ancestors, his nation, his class or party, money or success; his religion may be conducive to the development destructiveness or of love, of domination or of brotherliness; it may further his power of reason or paralyze it; he may be aware of his system as being a religious one, different from those of the secular realm, or he may think that he has no religion and interpret his devotion to certain allegedly secular aims like power, money, or success as nothing but his concern for the practical and expedient. The question is not *religion or not* but *which kind of religion*, whether it is one furthering man's development, the unfolding of his specifically human powers, or one paralyzing them.

Fromm is comfortable speaking of "religious needs," and by this he means the desire to have answers to the verities of life. He does not suggest that we need a personal god, but he does suggest that we all are susceptible to the need for ideological moorings, for a base for our ideas and ideals. Whether that is in the form of a personal Father God or a more ideological form is left to the individual within his own cultural setting. We all are in such need and this need can be filled in a variety of both good and bad ways. It is left to the individual, within the context of his cultural confinements, to make the choice of what form these religious needs are met. Fromm's work is easier than Freud's, for Fromm is trying to "work with" the whole concept of "religious needs" (defined, of course, in new and more broadly conceived ways), whereas Freud is simply eager to dispense with the whole concept and address the adult issue of maturity and responsibility.

****

The thesis that the need for a frame of orientation and an object of devotion is rooted in the conditions of man's existence seems to be amply verified by the fact of the universal occurrence of religion in history. This point has been made and elaborated by theologians, psychologists, and anthropologists. ... Adherents of tradition religion have often indulged in a fallacious bit of reasoning. Stating out with so broad a definition of religion as to include every possible religious phenomenon, their concept has remained associated with monotheistic religion, and thus they proceed to look upon all no monotheistic forms as precursors of or deviations from the "true" religion and they end demonstrating that the belief in God in the sense of the Western religious tradition is inherent in man's equipment.

Few would disagree with Fromm's contention here that a "frame of orientation" and an "object of devotion" constitutes a unique characteristic of the human person and society. Even the most outspoken atheists will agree to this, but where the rub comes is in presuming that this means necessarily a "religious need" unless we are permitted, with Fromm, to so define the meaning of that expression to free us from an absolute attachment to a transcendent being of power and might. Devotion is not inevitably tied to a transcendent god, for the experience of awe, wonder, and mystery is just as strong within the hearts and minds of non-theists as with theists. Believers in God do not have the advantage when it comes to sensibilities regarding the awe, wonder, and mystery. That is for anyone and everyone, argues Fromm.

****

It was Freud who saw the connection between neurosis and religion; but while he interpreted religion as a collective childhood neurosis of mankind, the statement can also be reversed. We can interpret *neurosis as a private form of religion,* more specifically, as a regression to primitive forms of religion conflicting with officially recognized patterns of religious thought. One can look at a neurosis from two aspects. One can focus on the neurotic phenomena themselves, the symptoms and other specific difficulties in living which the neurosis produces. The other aspect is not concerned with the positive as it were, with the neurosis, but with the negative, the failure of the neurotic individual to accomplish the fundamental aims of human existence, independence and the ability to be productive, to love, to think.

Fromm is a good psychoanalyst and would not disagree with Freud in saying that religion and neuroses share the same etiology and function. But, in the spirit of dialogue, Fromm would have us consider the possibility that neurosis itself might constitute a primitive form of personal religion, given the fact that it often manifests itself with a specific orientation and a focus of devotion.

****

There is one important difference between a religious cult and neurosis which makes the cult vastly superior to the neurosis as far as the satisfaction gained is concerned. If we imagine that the patient with his neurotic fixation to his father lived in a culture where ancestor worship is generally practiced as a cult, he could share his feelings with his fellow men rather than feel himself isolated. And it is the feeling of isolation, of being shut-out, which is the painful sting of every neurosis. Even the most irrational orientation if it is shared by a considerable body of men gives the individual the feeling of oneness with others, a certain amount of security and stability which the neurotic person lacks. There is nothing inhuman, evil, or irrational which does not give some comfort provided it is shared by a group.

However and notwithstanding the similarities of neurosis and religion, the profound difference in the two, Fromm points out, is that whereas the former is fraught with loneliness and isolation, alienation and dysfunction, the latter is characterized conversely as an arena of collegiality and camaraderie, of friendship and shared orientation towards a corporate goal. The sharing of a thing is a component of being human, and it is in this sharing, for good or ill, that has maintained the human community in perpetuity, through good times and bad. Religion, as defined by Fromm, functions in this capacity and the motivations and intentionalities "behind" such religion constitutes the psychological depth of the human soul.

****

Can we trust religion to be the representative of religious needs or must we not separate these needs from organized, traditional religion in order to prevent the collapse of our moral structure? In considering an answer to this question we must remember that no intelligent discussion of the problem is possible as long as we deal with religion in general instead of differentiating between various types of religion and religious experience. ... I shall therefore deal with only one distinction, but one which in my opinion is the most important, and which cuts across non-theistic and theistic religions: that between *authoritarian* and *humanistic* religions.

Fromm will not let us get by with simply embracing or dismissing "religion in the abstract." Though he goes into great detail about a variety of religious traditions and their beliefs and practices, for our purposes in understanding the contribution he has made to the emergence of the discipline of the psychology of religion, we will look at his two fundamentally divided categories of religion, namely, the authoritarian and the humanistic religions.

****

What is the principle of authoritarian religion? The definition of religion given in the Oxford Dictionary, while attempting to define religion as such, is a rather accurate definition of authoritarian religion. It reads: "Religion is recognition on the part of man of some higher unseen power as having control of his destiny, and as being entitled to obedience, reverence, and worship." ... The essential element in authoritarian religion and in the authoritarian religious experience is the surrender to a power transcending man. The main virtue of this type of religion is obedience, its cardinal sin is disobedience. Just as the deity is conceived as omnipotent or omniscient, man is conceived as being powerless and insignificant. Only as he can gain grace or help from the deity by complete surrender can he feel strength. Submission to a powerful authority is one of the avenues by which man escapes from his feeling of aloneness and limitation.

Without question, this is the fundamental type of religious ideology which Freud and the whole psychoanalytic school of depth psychology has chosen to be the object of its attack. Fromm and virtually all recognized psychotherapists would agree. Submission to a power source constitutes the worst type of religious oppression.

****

Humanistic religion, on the contrary, is centered around man and his strength. Man must develop his power of reason in order to understand himself, his relationship to his fellow men and his position in the universe. He must recognize the truth, both with regard to his limitations and his potentialities. He must develop his powers of love for others as well as for himself and experience the solidarity of all living beings. He must have principles and norms to guide him in this aim. Religious experience in this kind of religion is the experience of oneness with the All, based on one's relatedness to the world as it is grasped with thought and with love. Man's aim in humanistic religion is to achieve the greatest strength, not the greatest powerlessness; virtue is self-realization, not obedience.

On the other hand, Fromm is eager to point out that humanistic religion is quite different. This kind of religion is based upon the nurturing and fostering of humanitarian goals and interests, in responsibility and sharing, in compassion and justice. However, there is a dark side to this orientation, for man just chose to engage in a sort of transference of his best goals and ambitions onto the object of devotion itself. God is the embodiment of all that is good and man can "participate" in that goodness by obedience to Him. Herein lies the problem of endorsement and credibility.

****

While in humanistic religion God is the image of man's higher self, a symbol of what man potentially is or ought to become, in authoritarian religion God becomes the sole possessor of what was originally man's: of his reason and his love. The more perfect God becomes, the more imperfect becomes man. He *projects* the best he has onto God and thus impoverishes himself. Now God has all love, all wisdom, all justice -- and man is deprived of these qualities, he is empty and poor. He had begun with the feeling of smallness, but he now has become completely powerless and without strength; all his powers have been projected onto God.

Fromm is remarkably attuned to theological formulations because what he has proposed is precisely what the theological world presumes to be the case. Either one is confronted with a God who is not pleased with our sinful humanity, or a God who demands that the individual conform to His example. Humanistic religion espouses a God of benevolence and compassion and, thus, man is obliged to become what God expects, whereas authoritarian religion espouses a God who is demanding of obedience and, if obeyed, offers protection and solace. Either way, a God-dependency is implied.

*****

Analysis of religion must not stop at uncovering those psychological processes within man which underlie his religious experience; it must proceed to discover the conditions which make for the development of authoritarian and humanistic character structures, respectively, from which different kinds of religious experience stem.

Fromm is very astute in realizing, as Freud did in his own way (though Jung seemed somewhat to be lacking in this perception), that the psychological motivations "behind" religious ideology is the work of psychologists where theologians are held responsible for holding the party line when it comes to obedience and the reality of God and His demands upon believers.

*****

The ambiguity of thinking, the dichotomy between reason and a rationalizing intellect, is the expression of a basic dichotomy in man, the coextensive need for bondage and freedom. The unfolding and full emergence of reason is dependent on the attainment of full freedom and independence. Until this is accomplished man will tend to accept for truth that which the majority of his group want to be true; his judgment is determined by need for contact with the herd and by fear of being isolated from it. A few individuals can stand this isolation and say the truth in spite of the danger of losing touch. They are the true heroes of the human race but for whom we should still be living in caves.

There is a Jewish tradition found within Hasidic mystical philosophy that says that in each generation there is a small cadre of individuals who carry the world on their shoulder owing to the depths of their spirituality. They are called the *lamid vav*. It is here that Fromm should be well informed from the Jewish tradition about the presence of individuals in the world who carry it forward. These are the true heroes of the world though only God knows who they are. Neither they nor their neighbors realize or recognize that they are of the *lamid vav*.

****

The minute study of the process of rationalization is perhaps the most significant contribution of psychoanalysis to human progress. It has opened up a new dimension of the truth, it has shown that the fact that someone sincerely believes in a statement is not enough to determine his sincerity, that only by understanding the unconscious processes going on in him can we know whether he rationalizes or whether he speaks the truth. Psychoanalysis of thought processes is not only concerned with those rationalizing thoughts which tend to distort or hide the true motivation but also with such thoughts which are untrue in another sense, that of not having the weight and significance which is attributed to them by those who profess them.

It is, says Fromm, psychoanalysis rather than theology that is credited with having made the deepest study of human consciousness. It is not enough for a person to say what they believe or even to demonstrate their commitment to that belief. It is the truth of a belief that ultimately must determine its viability. Rationalization of belief is not the same thing as demonstrating rationally that a thing merits belief. Herein lies the difference between "blind faith" and a truthful understanding of our place in the universe.

****

CHAPTER FOUR THE PSYCHOANALYST AS "PHYSICIAN OF THE SOUL"

The difference between that psychoanalysis which aims primarily at *social adjustment* and psychoanalysis which aims at the *"cure of the soul"* is what is important. In the beginning of its development psychoanalysis was a branch of medicine and its aim was to cure sickness. The patients coming to the psychoanalyst suffered from symptoms which interfered with their functioning in everyday life; such symptoms were expressed in ritualistic compulsions, obsessional thoughts, phobias, paranoid thought systems, and so on. The only difference between these patients and those who went to a regular physician was that the causes of their symptoms were to be found not in the body but in the psyche, and the therapy was therefore concerned not with somatic but with psychic phenomena. But the aim of the psychoanalytic therapy was not different from the therapeutic aim in medicine: the removal of the symptom. If the patient was freed from psychogenic vomiting or coughing, from his compulsive acts or obsessive thoughts, he was considered cured.

Fromm now takes on his own profession, making a radical distinction between those psychoanalysts who are concerned "only" with social adjustment and those, it might be said of his own camp, who are concerned with a broader definition of what he understands to be their responsibility, namely, dealing with the "cure of souls." Though this is very religious language, used for example in the Episcopal Church in reference to each parish in any diocese as a "cure of souls," Fromm is intent upon using it because it places front and center the issue of the human "soul" as the fundamental agenda for psychotherapy as well as the focus of religious ideology and religious institutions.

****

Many people who came to psychoanalysts were not sick in the traditional sense of the word and had none of the overt symptoms mentioned above. They were not insane either. They often were not considered sick by their relatives and friends, and yet they suffered from "difficulties in living" -- to use Harry Stack Sullivan's formulation of the psychiatric problem -- which led them to seek help from a psychoanalyst. ... What was new was the fact that Freud and his school offered for the first time a comprehensive theory of character, an explanation for the difficulties in living in so far as these are rooted in the character structure, and a hope for change. Thus, psychoanalysis shifted its emphasis more and more from therapy of the neurotic *symptoms* to therapy of difficulties in living rooted in the neurotic *character*.

It was left to psychoanalysis to recognize that there are individuals in modern western society who are in need of therapy, who, however, are not suffering from any identifiable psychiatric disorder. They are adrift in a sea of confusion about the meaning and purpose of life, what their mission should be, how they should live out their lives. Psychoanalytic practitioners found themselves dealing with healthy individuals who were in a malaised confusion about the meaning and purpose of their lives. It was an issue of character rather than psychiatric symptoms.

*****

We see that it is not easy to determine what we consider to be the sickness and what we consider to be the cure. The solution depends on what one considers to be the aim of psychoanalysis. We find that according to one conception *adjustment* is the aim of analytic cure. By adjustment is meant a person's ability to act like the majority of people in his culture. In this view those existing patterns of behavior which society and the culture approve provide the criteria for mental health. These criteria are not critically examined from the standpoint of universal human norms but rather express a social relativism which takes this "rightness" for granted and considers behavior deviant from them to be wrong, hence unhealthy. Therapy aiming at nothing but social adjustment can only reduce the excessive suffering of the neurotic to the average level of suffering inherent in conformity to these patterns.

Psychoanalysis that aims at only curing the symptoms of a patient is a therapeutic practice without a defined mission. Curing symptoms is hardly worth the effort and certainly beneath the integrity of psychiatric practice. What is needed "beyond adjustment therapy" is a rediscovery of the place of the soul in the human person's *repertoire* of self-definitions of the meaning and purpose of life. Psychoanalysis is in a position to address the demands of a soul that has lost its way, an address to the inner being of the individual wherein a self-understanding of the meaning and purpose of life can be found and cultivated.

****

It is the tragedy of all great religions that they violate and pervert the very principles of freedom as soon as they become mass organizations governed by a religious bureaucracy. The religious organization and the men who represent it take over to some extent the place of family, tribe, and state. They keep man in bondage instead of leaving him free. It is no longer God who is worshiped but the group that claims to speak in his name. This has happened in all religions. There is hardly a situation in which the phenomenon of love and of its many distortions can be studied as intimately and accurately as in the analytic interview. There is no more convincing proof that the injunction "Love they neighbor as thyself" is the most important norm of living and that its violation is the basic cause of unhappiness and mental illness than the evidence gathered by the psychoanalyst. Whatever complaints the neurotic patient may have, whatever symptoms he may present are rooted in his inability to love, if we mean by love a capacity for the experience of concern, responsibility, respect, and understanding of another person and the intense desire for that other person's growth. *Analytic therapy is essentially an attempt to help the patient gain or regain his capacity for love.* If its aim is not fulfilled nothing but surface changes can be accomplished.

Fromm shows his full colors in this observation about the meaning and purpose of psychoanalysis. It is singularly the responsibility of the profession to cultivate within each individual that primordial sense of love for others and service to humankind. In modern western society, the individual has been reduced to a money-making machine which must not permit his need for love or his desire to extend love impede the social expectations that he will be "productive," namely, be a money-making machine that puts his own personal needs for soul nurture to the back of his emotional agenda. It is perceived as a sign of weakness to indicate a need for love or even a desire to extend love to others. This must not happen in western society if an individual is to be successful.

****

The problem of guilt plays no less a role in psychoanalytic procedure than it does in religion. Sometimes it is presented by the patient as one of his main symptoms. He feels guilty for not loving his parents as he should, for failing to do his work satisfactorily, for having hurt somebody's feelings The feeling of guilt has overpowered some patients' minds and they react with a sense of inferiority, of depravity, and often with a conscious or unconscious desire for punishment. It is usually not difficult to discover that this all-pervasive guilt reaction stems from an authoritarian orientation. They would give a more correct expression to their feeling if instead of saying that they feel guilty they said that they are afraid -- afraid of punishment or, more often, of not being loved any more by those authorities whom they have disobeyed.

It is said that guilt is the gift that keeps on giving. Fromm, in the company of all of the previous psychotherapists we have been considering in this enquiry, is quick to point out the ever present reality of guilt within the matrix of human experience. There is good and healthy guilt, the kind that prods one to do his rightful duty, and there is the bad and unhealthy guilt, the kind that destroys an individual's self-worth, his ability to recognize his strengths and gifts, the kind that eats him from the inside out and, therefore, says Fromm, deprives him of his own soul. Religious institutions have, moreso than any other social arena other than the family itself, been the beneficiaries of both fostering and feeding guilt feelings within the human community and, not surprisingly, offering to assist the individual in removing the feeling of guilt if he conforms to their demands and expectations. Using guilt to grow the church is an age-old phenomenon, and it continues today, explains Fromm.

****

One aspect of religious experience is the wondering, the marveling, the becoming aware of life and one's own existence, and of the puzzling problem of one's relatedness to the world. Existence, one's own existence and that of one's fellow men, is not taken for granted but is felt as a problem, is not an answer but a question. Socrates' statement that wonder is the beginning of all wisdom is true not only for wisdom but for the religious experience. One who has never been bewildered, who has never looked upon life and his own existence as phenomena which require answers and yet, paradoxically, for which the only answers are new questions, can hardly understand what religious experience is.

That motivation behind religious experience, explains Fromm, is the wonder in life, what some have called being grasped by the awe, wonder, and mystery of living in the world. The answers come in the form of more questions about life's meaning -- who we are, where we came from, what is our destiny. Whether these emotions, which underlie religious experience, are answered with a belief in a transcendent being or in fostering an ever-deepening sense of awe, wonder, and mystery is left to the individual and the cultural and social framework within which these experiences occur.

****

Another quality of religious experience is what Paul Tillich (the Christian theologian) has called the "ultimate concern." It is not passionate concern with the fulfillment of our desires but the concern connected with the attitude of wonder I have been discussing: an ultimate concern with the meaning of life, with the self-realization of man, with the fulfillment of the task which life sets us. This ultimate concern gives all desires and aims, inasmuch as they do not contribute to the welfare of the soul and the realization of the self, a secondary importance; in fact, they are made unimportant by comparison with the object of this ultimate concern.

Citing the Christian theologian Paul Tillich, Fromm points out that beyond the experience of awe, wonder, and mystery (which often produces a sense of "religious" awareness), there is an overriding encounter existentially in the lives of each individual with what is called here the "ultimate concern" of life, that around which everything else, all experience, as wonder, all value and sense of duty centers its time and attention. This ultimate concern takes precedence over all other values and provides a sense of orientation, an anchor, a mooring for one's life. This, Tillich and others, call religious experience, whereas humanists and those outside western culture may prefer to merely think of it as the deep experience of being human. Tillich argues that this experience, common to every self-reflective person, precludes the possibility of anyone actually being an atheist because everyone has this experience of ultimate concern which, for him, simply means an encounter with God. Fromm and psychotherapy would beg to differ. The individual's experience, to be sure, is real. The explanation as to the source of the experience is where the difference comes in to play.

****

It is this process of breaking through the confines of one's organized self -- the ego-- and of getting in touch with the excluded and disassociated part of oneself, the unconscious, which is closely related to the religious experience of breaking down individuation and feeling one with the All. The concept of the unconscious however, as I use it here, is neither quite that of Freud nor that of Jung. In Freud's thinking the unconscious is essentially that in us which is bad, the repressed, that which is incompatible with the demands of our culture and of our higher self. In Jung's system the unconscious becomes a source of revelation, a symbol for that which in religious language is God himself. In his view the fact that we are subject to the dictates of our unconscious is in itself a religious phenomenon. I believe that both these concepts of the unconscious are one-sided distortions of the truth. Our unconscious -- that is, that part of our self which is excluded from the organized ego which we identify with our self -- contains both the lowest and the highest, the worst and the best.

Fromm takes a moment here to remind us that Jung has chosen to call the unconscious which every individual experiences in the dream state is synonymous with religion, and that connecting with one's unconscious is another way of connecting with religious experience. Jung uses dreams and their interpretation as a "theological hermeneutic" to enter into an individual's religious worldview through dream analysis. Only Jung has pressed the relationship of an individual's unconscious state to be synonymous with religious experience, and Fromm is opposed to this comparison.

****

CHAPTER FIVE IS PSYCHOANALYSIS A THREAT TO RELIGION?

The attitude common to the teachings of the founders of all great Eastern and Western religions is one in which the supreme aim of living is a concern with man's soul and the unfolding of his powers of love and reason. Psychoanalysis, far from being a threat to this aim, can on the contrary contribute a great deal to its realization. Nor can this aspect be threatened by any other science. It is not conceivable that any discovery made by the natural sciences could become a threat to religious feeling. On the contrary, an increased awareness of the nature of the universe in which we live can only help man to become more self-reliant and more humble. As for the social sciences, their growing understanding of man's nature and of the laws governing his existence contributes to the development of a religious attitude rather than threatens it.

In his concluding chapter on the relationship between psychology and religion, a relationship which centers around the nurture of the soul, Fromm is eager to emphasize that this soul in question is for the purpose of uncovering man's access to and utilization of the power of love and reason. Where religion and psychology converge is not over whether there is a God in the universe, but what is the meaning and purpose of love and reason, and in this recognition the presumed conflict between reason and faith, science and religion fades away. The answers, whether they exist or not, regarding such presumed conflicts --reason versus faith, science versus religion -- fall now outside our shared quest for the soul as a source of our strength and the basis for our confidence in the future.

****

The threat to the religious attitude lies not in science but in the predominant practices of daily life. Here man has ceased to seek in himself the supreme purpose of living and has made himself an instrument serving the economic machine his own hands have built. He is concerned with efficiency and success rather than with his happiness and the growth of his soul. More specifically the orientation which most endangers the religious attitude is what I have called the "marketing orientation" of modern man.

It is living in the modern commercialized materialistic world that constitutes the threat to man's soul, not religion, not science, not faith, not reason. The modern world (and we have caused it or at least brought it upon ourselves) functions now through economic motivations and political aspirations to reduce the individual to a consuming instrument of the state rather than a free and independent individual seeking to live a life of meaning and purpose of service to love and justice.

****

If man's highest value is success, if love, truth, justice, tenderness, mercy are of no use to him, he may *profess* these ideals but he does not *strive* for them. He may think that he worships the god of love but he actually worships an idol which is the idealization of his real goals, those rooted in the marketing orientation. Those who are concerned only with survival of religion and of the churches may accept the situation. Man will seek the haven of the church and of religion because his inner emptiness impels him to seek for some shelter. But professing religion does not mean being religious. Those, however, who are concerned with religious experience, whether they are religionists or not, will not delight in seeing the churches crowded and in conversions. They will be the most severe critics of our secular practices and recognize that man's alienation from himself, his indifference to himself and to others, which have their roots in our whole secular culture are the real threats to a religious attitude, not psychology or any other science.

Fromm is at his homiletical best here in preaching to modern man about the meaning and purpose of life. He suggests that many seek the church, seek out religious institutions and organizations, precisely because they are without religion, because their lives of empty consumerism are devoid of meaning and to hide from their own meager motivations to get more and have more and consume more; the individual seeks religious affiliations to validate and vindicate the shallowness of their chosen way of living in the world. While professing to be religious, they live lives of meaninglessness yet judging others who do not embrace a religious creed even if those others are living lives of meaning and purpose and direction. It is the deep experience of awe, wonder, and mystery, of the ultimate concern of life that brings meaning to people whether they call it religious or not. Living a fulfilling life is found in the experience of living it, not in professing some religious creed which is self-vindicating and self-validating.

****

"Do you believe in the existence of God?" has been made the crucial question of religionists and the denial of God has been the position chosen by those fighting the church. It is easy to see that many who profess the belief in God are in their human attitude idol worshipers or men without faith, while some of the most ardent "atheists," devoting their lives to the betterment of mankind, to deeds of brotherliness and love, have exhibited faith and a profoundly religious attitude. Centering the religious discussion on the acceptance or denial of the symbol God blocks the understanding of the religious problem as a human problem and prevents the development of that human attitude which can be called religious in a humanistic sense.

It is not what one professes to believe or not believe that determines whether or not they have chosen to seek the path in life that naturally nourishes the soul. The determination of such a choice is based upon whether the values are real or sham, whether the individual has encountered and continues to embrace the deep experience of awe, wonder, mystery, and the most meaningful concerns of living in a troubled world. Deciding whether one is religious or not based upon his profession of belief in God or not is to avoid the question of life, it becomes an escape mechanism from the real questions of, "Is one seeking love and justice in the world, or not?"

****

While it is not possible for man to make valid statements about the positive, about God, it is possible to make such statements about the negative, about idols. Is it not time to cease to argue about God and instead to unite in the unmasking of contemporary forms of idolatry? Today it is ... the deification of the state and of power in authoritarian countries and the deification of the machine and of success in our own culture which threaten the most precious spiritual possessions of man. Whether we are religionists or not, whether we believe in the necessity for a new religion or in a religion of no religion or in the continuation of the Judeo-Christian tradition, in as much as we are concerned with the essence and not with the shell, with the experience and not with the word, with man and not with the church, we can unite in form negation of idolatry and find perhaps more of a common faith in this negation than in any affirmative statements about God. Certainly, we shall find more of humility and of brotherly love.

Love and justice in the world will be found by those who seek to nurture the soul more so than by those who think the answers to the meaning and purpose in life is found in determining who believes in God and who does not. Not the institutional church but the core experience of awe, wonder, and mystery constitutes the essence of what is called a religious experience (with or without a proclamation of belief in a transcendent being of power and might). To encourage this experience is to nurture the soul in our individual and corporate goal of seeking love and humility, justice and kindness in our shared world. This is what Fromm understands to be the point of convergence between those who use religious language and those who practice psychotherapy. People of faith and people of science may never agree over the "question of God," but they can certainly share a mutual quest for the nurture of the human soul by fostering the deep experiences of awe, wonder, and mystery which lie beneath the religious quest.

****

CHAPTER EIGHT

Otto Rank and *Psychology and the Soul*

The dominance of the psychoanalytic school established by Sigmund Freud was shaken by the loss of several great practitioners as well as due to its inordinately imperialistic claim to exclusivity in psychotherapeutic theory and practice. As Alfred Adler and Carl Jung fell by the wayside, owing to professional censorship from Freud and his society of practitioners, so, likewise, did Otto Rank (1884-1939) likewise fall from favor. This fall, however, was profoundly surprising, as Rank was perceived by the inner circle to be Freud's heir apparent and certainly his right-hand man. Rank, an Austrian-born psychoanalyst and a medical graduate of the University of Vienna, chose, rather than to focus upon the more commonly accepted clinical application of psychoanalytic practice, to address issues implicit in mythology, literature, religion, and the arts, a decision which seemed to have pleased Freud initially a great deal.

Rank's first major work, which merited Freud's acclamation, was his *Art and Artist* (1907), employing Freud's theory of dream mechanisms to explain the mental processes operative within the artist's mind. Rank was, actually, a founding member of the International Psychoanalytical Association and its secretary for a number of years. However, after a falling out with Freud over Rank's unwillingness to continue to tout the Oedipus Complex as the center-piece of his own emerging psychoanalytic theory of human motivation as reflected in Rank's 1924 book, *The Trauma of Birth*, Freud removed him from both the editorship of the *Internationale Zeitschrift fur Psychoanalyse* and membership in the IPA. Consequently, Rank left Vienna with his wife and daughter and moved his prestigious psychoanalytic practice to Paris, where he remained busy as both a practitioner and research/writer for much of the remainder of his life, moving finally to New York City where he died in 1939, just five weeks after the death of Freud.

The courage to break from Freud was epic on Rank's part, having been designated publicly by Freud as his successor to the leadership of the psychoanalytic movement within psychiatry. But for Rank to address the taboo topic of "the soul" was nothing short of monumental. Yet, Rank's interest on the relationship between the discipline of psychology and the human experience of what he calls "the soul" was pivotal in his own development. The human will to live forever against death, the conflict between the individual and social consciousness which has produced both "consolation and inspiration" is what Rank came to call the "immortal soul," and he chose unabashedly to introduce the concept within the developing discipline of the psychology of religion. "Dealing with life, experience, growth, the soul, and man's need to believe in immortality, this volume (says the publisher) provides a penetrating study of man's spiritual development through the ages, of man's efforts to sustain himself spiritually in the face of knowledge and doubt, and of his destructive and creative strivings to come to terms with death" (1950:ix). The book's central thesis is that intellectual psychology cannot give the human person the immortal soul he desires, and that the consolation of attempting to rationalize spiritual matters out of existence, which too many psychologists have offered their followers, is futile. We must face reality, says Rank, no matter how painful it may be. Courage, to be sure, was the force behind Rank's challenge to psychology to confront honestly and boldly the reality of the soul and, also, for theologians, without pride or condescension, to realize the profound insight psychology offers to an understanding of the driving forces within the human spirit. Beyond Allport, who wanted us to accept the function of religion, whether true or not, Rank wants us to accept the truth of the human quest for immortality against the inevitabilities of death and the key role that religion plays in that quest.

Selections from *Psychology and the Soul,* by Otto Rank, with commentary.

NOTE: In the following, the original text will be printed in *Arial Unicode MS* typestyle (as is this note itself to illustrate) as an easy and aesthetically pleasing way of identifying the primary source paragraphs. The author's commentary will be in *Times New Roman*. It is hoped that this differentiation between the "primary source" and the "commentary" made by use of differing typestyles will prove helpful and not disruptive to the reader. *I have also chosen to use a quadruple asterisk (****) to separate the primary text from the commentary.*

CHAPTER ONE UNDERSTANDING ONESELF AND OTHERS

Pre-scientific and nonscientific psychology has always been the true psychological discipline and the source of all psychologies, including those that study the soul scientifically. Scientific psychology which seems to know very little about the soul claims to seek the truth about it, but rejects the contributions of ancient beliefs, religion, and myths to its interpretation. It performs experiments which seem always to prove that the soul does not exist, and it lets the more tolerant science of ethnology perform what constructive research it can. Psychoanalysis claims this neglected area of psychology as its own, but it brings in its materialistic psychology to "explain" the soul, instead of first trying to relate its mental concepts to the spiritual sources which generated them.

All of Freud's early followers were medical men, with the exception of Otto Rank, who took his degree in Germanic Studies from the University of Vienna, concentrating his attention and energies in the fields of art, literature, and particularly mythology. Later, of course, Erich Fromm, a sociologist, joins the distinguished array of Freudians and eventually becomes numbered among the neo-Freudians. This early work of Rank pleased Freud but latter proved Rank's undoing, as there is a decidedly anti-scientific tone to Rank's work and a prejudice in favor of ethnological studies of primitive art, ritual, and symbol. Rank, like Fromm, was fascinated with the concept of the "soul" in western society and was convinced that the scientific study of man had overlooked, even ignored, the reality of such. While hoping that psychology would re-address the omission, Rank and Fromm both became convinced that scientific, laboratory-based clinical psychology ignored the reality of the soul and it was left then to depth psychology to address the omission.

****

Our present task, therefore, is not to apply psychoanalysis or any other modern psychology to this problem, but to investigate the principles which govern the soul concept as the source and object of psychological study. Our approach necessarily will be genetic and not historical. This orientation brings us to the fundamental question of all psychology as science, which asks whether mental discipline is a proper concern for natural science or for philosophy, whether it is physics or metaphysics in the Aristotelian sense, and whether it is objective or subjective as natural science uses these terms.

The first agenda, explains Rank, is not to apply psychoanalysis to the concept of the soul in western thought but rather to pursue the principles which operate in the human psyche relative to the reality of the soul. This, argues Rank (but with little support from the Freudians with, however and not surprisingly, a great deal of support from the Jungians, and this to Freud's own chagrin) is the task which lay before depth psychologists and the agenda was not historical but biogenic. Rank then proceeds to argue for the philosophical orientation of depth psychology as the hermeneutical tool to investigate the characteristics of the soul rather than scientific psychology and its clinical laboratory basis for research.

****

As a synthesis of the conscious and unconscious, Freud's psychoanalysis has both its strong and weak points. Freud wanted to carry a realistic psychology of self-awareness beyond consciousness, and to transform the mystical unconscious into an object of self-observation and objective investigation. He did succeed in expanding both psychology and the domain of consciousness, but since he explained the unconscious as realistically as sensory psychology had explained conscious phenomena, he excluded all its purely spiritual content. To be sure, he recognized spiritual content when he recognized the unconscious, but in explaining the unconscious materialistically he rejected the soul, because consciousness obviously involves something more than data about the outer world. He tried to explain the added elements by referring to the unconscious, while conceiving of the unconscious itself as a sediment of reality.

Like Fromm, Rank is keen to stay in favor with Freud and he does so through most of his career, failing at the end to maintain orthodoxy. Rank was not pleased with Freud's insistence that the study of the unconscious could be an objective discipline whereas Rank pushed for a subjective, even mystical, enquiry. Objective assessment of the unconscious, argues Rank, caused Freud to dismiss its "spiritual" characteristics. Though Freud, drawing from his Hasidic tradition in Jewish mysticism, was not averse to the spiritual components of his assessment analysis, yet, suggests Rank, Freud was forced to reject the concept of the soul in his materialistic analysis of the unconscious. Treating the soul as a composite of sedimentary materials from the unconscious was far from addressing the issue Rank raised as to the reality and the centrality of the soul itself.

****

Psychoanalysis itself is a lively subject for psychological research, for it combines the objective and the subjective, the technical and the purely theoretical, the natural scientific and the social scientific aspects of psychology in a way never before achieved. However, this seems to make psychoanalysis the final chapter and not just a new trend in the history of psychology. For in psychoanalysis, as in the violent controversies over its significance and province, we encounter the old fundamental problem of whether it is physics or metaphysics, medical or philosophical, or psychological or spiritual. Now it is obviously all of these, as every real psychology always was, is, and presumably will be. Just the peculiar combination of such contradictory elements composes this doctrine of psychoanalysis which began as a technique for influencing others and ended as a new metaphysics of the soul, and embodied in its own unsolved problems those of all psychology.

Rank argues persuasively that psychoanalysis (and by extension all forms of depth psychology and its cognates in psychotherapy) consists equally of both objective and subjective materials. Of course, all of this rides on the back of the argument that there is more to psychology than objective analysis of material data gleaned from analysis. Psychoanalysis, argues Rank, consists of both objectivity and subjectivity, philosophy as well as biology, and metaphysics as well as physics, in the components needed for it to do its work. This particular therapeutic modality of treatment, plumbing the unconscious through dream analysis and free association, constitutes the major contribution which depth psychology has brought to the study of the soul itself.

****

CHAPTER TWO RELIGION AND BELIEF IN THE SOUL

In 1914, I made a study of the psychoanalytic attempt to understand primitive spiritual belief in relation to the psychoanalytic view of primitive peoples. ... I conceived of primitive belief in a body-soul as an expression of man's deeply rooted belief in immortality. The body-soul was originally thought of as a second, purely material self like the physical self which it survived, and the fact that primitive man first localized it in his shadow or mirror-image suggests that the loss of his own individuality seemed to him almost more inconceivable than unbearable. At the earliest stage of his so-called spiritual belief in the soul, man seemed to deny rather than fear his own death, for his idea of an immortal body-soul comprised a denial of death which canceled all possible threats to his perpetuity.

Rank, more so than any other of the early psychoanalysts beside Jung, became fascinated with the study of primitive peoples, their mythologies and their ideological understandings and behavioral manifestations of the relationship they experienced between the individual and his environment and society's relationship to its own destiny. The mind-body problem of modern philosophical enquiry was early manifest, says Rank, as a body-soul problem dealing with early man's sense of his finitude and his quest for eternal life as the denial of personal death. Thanatology, of course, becomes a topic of great interest to Freud and many of his followers later on but Rank was the first to sense its significance in the psychoanalytic tradition.

****

Thus the facts of death and of the individual's denial of death brought the idea of the soul into being; and, at a time when life was beginning to acquire a spiritual character, the problems of death and of its denial through belief were imbedded in an immortal body-soul which simulated and survived the ego as its Double. The problem of death seemed to face primitive man less in the form of anxiety, which he could deny, than in the death of others, which at first he did not have to ascribe to himself. When he finally did refer this experience of others to himself he took his first step towards an intuitive psychology of understanding others. Such a psychology is obviously contrary to its logical and scientific counterpart, which invites one to use one's own experience to understand others.

Rank argues persuasively, drawing from a wide range of ethnographic information gleaned by early anthropologists trained by Franz Boas at Columbia University, that early man's belief in the soul was linked to his encounter with, fear of, and the denial of personal death, expressing itself among the Neanderthals in the ritualistic burial of the dead where instruments of value to the living were included with the corpse. The death of others first gripped the Paleolithic person's imagination and fostered fear within his psyche only after he was able to move beyond denial of his own personal finitude. This shift from self to others constitutes the matrix for the emergence of the soul within early man.

****

Perhaps it is the application of our subjective psychology of dreams to the spiritual life of primitive man which has led so many ethnologists of our time to assume that the dream roles of the dead induced primitive man to believe in a soul independent of his body. But dreams were real to primitive man, and they presented him with the souls of other persons both living and death rather than with his own. Dreams even "delude" us in the same way since they exhibit dead or absent persons far more often than our own selves. I regard primitive man's reference of such dreams to himself as a second, conflictive stage in the evolution of spiritual belief which followed an initial "narcissistic" stage; so that just as his shadow or mirror-image allowed him to believe in his own body-soul, his realistic dreams induced him to accept the survival of the souls of others.

Dream analysis by untutored psychologists devoid of insights into the true nature of primitive man's experience of self and others has led them down the mistaken path of assuming that early man differentiated his soul from his body. Dreams were not fantasies to early man, argues Rank, but manifestations of the real world. These dreams constituted the basis for early man's confidence in the existence and the survival of the soul, his own and those of his peers.

****

The basic problem of primitive man was not the future but the present, and not the riddle of birth but that of death. The naive, narcissistic belief in a body-soul which perpetuated man's own bodily self beyond sleep and death, is obviously related to this latter problem. The second, totemistic stage could only support a belief in an immortal soul because it had to give up this naive narcissism in order to assure man a form of soul transmigration like that of natural reproduction. The third, or matriarchal, stage finally accepted human sexual processes for what they were, because current spiritual belief was concretized in the wife or mother. Woman owed her original social esteem to her totemistic role of soul-bearer. But since primitive man allowed the spirit of his ancestor to enter the embryo in order to save his own soul, he traded a part of his belief in individual immortality for one in collective immortality.

Early man had two enduring and pressing concerns, namely, the existential moment of life lived here and now and the phenomenon of death, what happens to me and my peers when life is taken away. Simple, straightforward reality and personal anxiety addressed the body-soul duplicity of life. Man lives through his sleeping and encounters reality through his dreaming, and both sleeping and dreaming are components of the body-soul duplicity. The belief that the totem itself is the carrier of the person and the clan gave individuals confidence to live in a world fraught with danger. The individual, in sharing this corporate experience and belief, relinquished somewhat his reliance upon himself and placed his ultimate confidence in the group, the clan, society itself, which endures collectively through time forever. The individual may die; the clan lives on.

****

Although there is a direct path from totemistic belief to Christianity, we should not overlook the changes undergone by social institutions of various peoples from totemism to Roman civilization. The transition from post-totemistic matriarchy to patriarchy of the Roman state was completely revolutionary in nature, so that with hits exaltation of the mother, its debasement of the father, and its spiritualization of the son, Christianity represents a quite new adaptation of old ideas to the changed shape of things. In its doctrine of the Trinity, which symbolized the identity of the Holy Ghost with the Father and son, Christianity attempted a new synthesis which transcended totemism, mother-divinity, and patriarchy. For the first time, the son received the spiritual role which the mother had held under matriarchy and the father had held under the family-state. This final stage made possible the emergence of the *individual*. Whom our modern democratic commonwealth recognizes as the product of matriarchy and paternal rule. This is the irreligious era of the rule of the child, which we shall discuss elsewhere.

Rank, sometimes too esoteric for the average reader, traces what he perceives to be the totemic tradition primitive man to the Roman Empire through Judaism to the Trinitarian Doctrine of the Christian faith. Whether his ethnographic sources are today considered reliable or not (and for the most part they are not), he weaves a convincing story from the materials he has gleaned from the literature to make his point that the final stage in this long process has been the emergence of the self-consciously constructed idea of the "individual" person. The emergence of this dominant individualism is the birth of the secular era in human history.

****

Christianity's new version of religious belief in the soul inheres in the fact that, in man's undying struggle to save his own soul, Christian belief saved all our souls from annihilation and from the loss of their esoteric meaning which had been threatened by the intensified efforts of legal and social institutions to make the soul materialistic and concrete. The success of such efforts would have meant the loss of belief in immortality, without which life would have had no purpose and value; otherwise man would not have fought and sacrificed for this belief as he has done now for centuries. Yet the soul is always in just as great danger from the inflated, introspective knowledge of self which modern psychology has established as a science of understanding the "causal" motives of thinking, feeling, and action.

Rank credits Christianity with the role of saving the soul in western modern society. The soul has been saved from social institutions and from materialistic degradation. Without the soul, there would be no belief in immortality and Christianity can not survive without the belief in the immortality of the individual's soul. Without immortality, said the bishops, there is no morality! Without a belief in the soul, the individual has no reason to live, to work, to strive, to move forward towards an immortal existence. However, modern day psychology has created a scientific understanding of the meaning and nature of the soul which has reduced it to mere thinking, feeling, and action, to mere conscious activities devoid of a sense of the soul's eternal value and worth. Herein lies the conundrum of modern scientific psychology -- it has re-discovered the soul merely to now reduce it to psychogenic function without eternal efficacy.

****

In a materialistic age which suffered from self-awareness and threatened to forfeit its belief not only in immortality but also in religion, as the exoteric representative of such belief, psychoanalysis signified a new attempt to save the spiritual in man. The most remarkable feature of this attempt was the fact of its occurrence within the mentality of our time, for it not only provided an exoteric symbolization and social concretion for the soul concept of earlier epochs, but it also tried to establish this concept in the manner of a natural science. Yet this kind of realistic psychology could only means the death of the soul, whose origin, being, and worth inhered necessarily in the abstract, the ineffable, and the esoteric. The initial appeal of psychoanalysis to man may be explained by its attempt to prove that his lost soul existed again; but man's final resistance to it is explained by its attempt to develop such proof by a scientific method.

However, suggests Rank, psychoanalysis has come on the scene to correct the shortcomings of scientific psychology and to remove the Christian imprint upon a belief in the soul dependent upon a

God complex. Psychoanalysis has reaffirmed the reality of the human soul and its potential for the nurture of life here and now in a world freed from the confinements of religious ideology. The human soul has been scientifically rather than religiously re-discovered.

****

CHAPTER THREE PSYCHOLOGY AND THE SEXUAL ERA

Our outline of the development of the soul concept from primitive belief in immortality suggests that sexuality was more restricted in primitive life than in antiquity or modern times. Even primitives, whom ethnologists regard as nonreligious, maintained firm social organizations and close regulation of sex. If cultures as primitive as these involved sexual restrictions, it is no wonder that the hypothesis of original promiscuity has not been substantiated by recorded history. This hypothesis characterized the evolutionary thought of our preceding century and its comparison of man with animals. But a closer study of the animal world, and of higher apes in particular, shows that many animals are monogamous, or that they are at least more restrictive in sexual relations than the term promiscuity would connote. And the hypothesis of primitive promiscuity can scarcely rest on any wish to restore this appealing state of affairs, because historical tradition shows no evidence of such a fantasy. Even contemporary experience can teach us that promiscuity yields no greater individual happiness than did the rigid sexual tabus of primitive cultures.

Out of step with the fantasies of modern thinking in believing that primitive peoples were rather restrictive in their sexual life and expression, Rank contended that contemporary sexual expressiveness is most decidedly a recent phenomenon in the history of the human animal. Close regulation of sexual behavior not only characterizes primitive societies today as empirically demonstrated in countless ethnographic studies, but Rank believed that such restrictiveness characterized early man as well. Freud's presumption of an early lifestyle of sexual promiscuity, upon which much of his early sexual theories was based as incorrect as indicated by a plethora of modern ethnographic studies of traditional societies' sexual mores.

****

On the basis of my own studies I am inclined to believe that human sex life did not develop from a primal state of promiscuity into one of restraint, but from a sexual life which was restricted biologically by rutting, and psychologically by spiritual belief, into a greater sexual freedom for the individual. At a certain stage of human evolution there occurred what one may call the discovery of sexuality. The ensuing "sexual era" succeeded a more primitive one that had been dominated by the stress of living and the threat of death. ... This primitive era had been characterized by a naive belief in immortality of the self, from which a dawning sense of death had produced the compensatory idea of an immortal body-soul preserved as the ego's double. What I have called the discovery of sexuality followed a painful relinquishment of individual immortality, which was precipitated by the further recognition of death inherent in man's unwilling acceptance of sexuality as a means of conquering death through procreative survival.

Rank argues that freedom of sexual expression, which so characterizes modern society and is so cherished by contemporary communities, is the result of a rise in western secularization and a valuation of the soul of humankind previously stifled by religious ideologies. A religious fascination with immortality and the differentiation between the body and soul, the former being finite and the later being immortal, has fallen from respectability under scientific scrutiny in modern times. Sexual drive is not the solution to finitude, in spite of early man's presumption to the contrary.

****

Jewish-Christian doctrine turned the complete identification of sex and reproduction into a religious dogma which modern science has interpreted causally. We find that causal interpretation expanded in the faulty psychoanalytic conclusion that sex plays the primary psychological role because of its biological primacy. Yet the place of sex in human history follows neither from its original biological role in reproduction nor from its ultimate psychological role in love, but from its spiritual role which substituted procreative for individual immortality. In antiquity the role of sexuality culminated in religious mysteries and cosmic sexual myths in which the soul and sexuality had much the same meaning. Christianity separated the soul from sexuality again, because by that time the sensual significance of sex had come to outweigh its biological and spiritual aspects.

The shift from the primacy of sexual expression from biological needs to psychological needs is credited, or blamed, on the demands of monotheistic religious ideology but, argues Rank, sexual motives are most clearly derived from spiritual needs expressive of man's desire for immortality. The separation of the soul from the body brought about a plethora of rules and regulations regarding sexual conduct based upon the desire of man to live forever in the expressive form of a quest for immortality. In doing so, sexuality took precedence over the centrality of the soul.

****

Belief in individual immortality is so much a part of the self that, although religious, sexual, and social organizations provide collective substitutes for individual immortality, the individual constantly seeks to perpetuate his ego and his self in individual works. ... We should consider the individual's uncompromising tendencies towards immortality in his dreams, his living, and his works, all as phenomena of will. I think it is important to bring out the fundamental opposition between the individual will, which seeks to perpetuate itself, and the collective soul, which is immortal, and to show that both are in great degree united in sexuality.

The human drive for personal immortality is, yet, a force to be contended with in modern society, for the appeal is to religion, which offers life eternal, and sexuality, which implies it as well. Sex, suggests Rank, is the convergent point of individual aspirations for immortality and society's quest for eternal existence. Rank has bested Freud by taking infantile sexuality and religion as illusion in Freudian psychoanalytic theory to a whole new level with both religion and sexuality converging upon man's quest for immortality. Even Freud did not go that far.

****

CHAPTER FOUR INDIVIDUALISM AND COLLECTIVISM

Social organization originally involved not a restriction of the individual, but a protection and extension of his ego through spiritual belief. Natural binding forces for society were fashioned from this communal ego interest. Tabus were not external prohibitions, but tributes which the individual willingly paid, not so much for the common good as for his self-protection which rested on that good. Morals and law were still embodied in community interest which was in effect a collectivized self-interest. The factors inherent in the original tribunal units came to serve the new ideology only through an acceptance of the individual's survival in his own children, which characterized the sexual era. By granting him the right to possess his wife and child, and by obliging him not to threaten the spiritual economy of others in the family group, society gave the individual a legal and moral assurance of the immortality embodied in his offspring.

Rank has contended all along that the human animal discovered the group before he discovered himself, and, therefore, the community took precedence over the well-being of the individual. Social rules and guidelines emerged for the survival of the group at the ready-and-willing expense of the individual's personal needs and desires. Moral law itself emerged as a mechanism to insure the strength and survival of the community, even when the individual was forced to be sacrificed. Immortality for the group took the form of immortality promised to the individual who was granted the right to a family, which was to be protected by the group itself. Here Rank separates from Freud considerably by arguing for the primacy and the historic precedence of the family over individual sexual drives which would be at the expense of the community's own well-being.

****

Up to the nineteenth century when it emerged as a natural science, psychology really represented the soul and various aspects of spiritual belief. Knowledge of the soul, which religious dogma had regarded as unattainable by man, was definitely not of psychological concern. The existence of the soul, which involves the question of belief in immortality, was either assumed or denied, the one or the other alternative being as indemonstrable as the existence or non-existence of God. The real threat to the soul lay not with the atheistic natural scientists, but with the individualistic soul-seekers who felt that they had to win their immortality independently of collectivistic spiritual ideology and beyond procreative sexual ideology, and whose need for personal immortality could be satisfied neither by the family or religion, nor by the state or people, which stood for both.

Primitive psychology, that is, pre-scientific psychology based on mythology and magic, sagas and legends of human history, addressed itself primarily to the existence and needs of the soul within the human person, including his spiritual needs and beliefs, as well as those of his community. The passion for immortality and the belief systems developed and espoused by society needed to feed that passion took no notice of the rise of scientific psychology, a psychology which provided a mechanism for the pursuit of the human soul in the absence of a belief in a Father God. These non-believers in God but seekers after the well-being of the human soul, explained Rank, did not constitute the great danger to religious institutions but rather the individualism which the "soul-seekers" represented, whether they were religious or not. The push for personal immortality took priority over communal concerns.

****

Just as the conflict between temporal and external beliefs and values ruled the Middle Ages, that between religion and science characterizes modern times. Until now the Church has been the victor in all these struggles because it offered the individual something which science both denied and lacked. All these bitter conflicts are really centered on one question: Is the individual immortal, and, therefore, is there a soul? Fleeting, worldly existence was less at stake than was the eternal bliss that religion promised, science denied, and psychological knowledge doubted. It is from this doubt that we suffer, and not from knowledge against which one can set belief, for belief cannot prevail against doubt. So man has tried to set up a new God to combat the Devil, a deity born of ancient spiritual belief but fathered by scientific intellectualism. This new god was Truth.

The primacy of the question of the human person's finitude is, says Rank, the fundamental question facing both religion and science. The answer to this question, which is not readily coming from either camp, is the answer which will settle the question as to the primacy of religion or science. Both religious ideologies and scientific methodologies have sought to answer the question of man's immortality, and each has done so by laying claim to the truth as the mechanism for providing eternal life to every individual who believes. Both science and religion have failed miserably in providing a believable answer to the question, because both have attempted an answer without including the centrality of the human soul as the starting point for enquiry and discussion.

****

Since progressive self-awareness had undermined belief in the soul, self-knowledge, which was the unwonted by-product of the growth of individualism, became all important, so that the necessity of tormenting self-awareness became the virtue of therapeutic self-knowledge, whose results were esteemed as "truth." However, since our intellectual processes are tied in with our wishes and passions and are determined by them, truth became a subjective or intellectualized individual religion which could be used to sustain man's ancient spiritual beliefs. And, in place of knowledge under collective belief (what *everyone* believes constitutes truth), individualism says, "What *I* believe is true." Religion's "I believe, therefore I am" (immortal) developed from philosophy's "I doubt, therefore I am" (aware of myself and therefore moral) into Cartesian psychology's "I think, therefore I am." With the help of psychology the ego tried thereafter to define its own truth. This was a final intellectual attempt to rescue the soul, but one which actually concealed the soul so cleverly behind an abstract concept of truth that it took all the forces of symbolism to incorporate the old spiritual belief into a cult of truth. Truth, which one cannot give upon and live, is the soul.

It is first and last the quest for soul which is the driving force behind religion and psychology, behind rationalism and scientific enquiry. And in both instances, they have failed because each endeavor has been built upon an objectification of the human agenda and has left the spiritual reality of life out of the picture.

****

The character of psychoanalysis as a psychological savior of the soul is best depicted by its two quite different off-shoots: Jung's collective psychology and Adler's individual psychology. Each of these theories develops unilaterally only one of the otherwise integrated aspects of psychoanalytic doctrine, and neglects Freud's characteristic natural science ideology of sex. For Adler, with whom the rational methods of psychoanalytic interpretation became hypertrophied, there remains absolutely no unconscious or soul. Jang's collective unconscious strands much closer to the soul than did Freud's individualistically conceived unconscious, which remained individualistic even when formulated as the "Id." If Adler's individual psychology was too rational in the sense of conscious interpretation of the ego, Jung's collective psychology was too irrational. The former was too psychological; the latter, too religious, as Freud's doctrine was too biological.

Rank is not reluctant to credit both Jung and Adler with propositions for the defining of depth psychology wherein the discipline is seen as the proper mechanism for the salvaging of the task of the soul quest in modern times. And yet, Alder failed because he was too rational when it came to the relationship between ego and soul, and Jung was too irrational for the same reason. Freud, concludes Rank, failed because he was too biological in his explanation of the function of the ego, discounting the spiritual dimension altogether.

****

CHAPTER FIVE DREAM AND REALITY

Man has long been intrigued by such phenomena as dreams, but he has not really learned much worth knowing about dreams *as such* because of his greater concern with what they *mean*, if anything. Primitive man believed that dreams had a special, divine significance; and whether they were responsible for animism, or *vice versa*, animistic man regarded them as evidence of his soul and its immortality. These two affirmative beliefs, on the one hand, and modern science's anti-spiritual denial that dreams are meaningful, on the other, serve to show how attitudes towards spiritual belief have variously conditioned the interpretation of dreams from time to time.

The quest for the "meaning" of dreams has been the greatest deterrent in understanding them, says Rank. From our earliest self-reflective consciousness, the human animal has dreamed and reflected upon those dreams, changing his understanding of what they were and what they might mean with every passing era of human development. And the driving concern behind all attempts to "understand" the "meaning" of dreams has to do with the human animal's desire for immortality and the relationship of his soul to his own finitude. Attitudes towards immortality and the soul, our spiritual self-understanding, have determined our interpretation of the meaning of dreams.

****

We now come to the psychological era, in which the dream acquired a "wish fulfilling" function not by virtue of its content, as Freud would say, but by virtue of the dream itself, irrespective even of its Freudian "latent" content, which is not spiritual but merely psychological. The dream itself did not concern wishes that could be fulfilled, but spiritual ones that could not be fulfilled. It showed man the soul that was independent of his body, and it was the dream as such and not its particular content that did this.

With the coming of modern psychological science and the emergence of Freudian psychoanalysis, the human community has moved to a higher level of reflective understanding of our relationship to finitude and the spiritual significance of the soul, our inner being. The unconscious, plumbed through dream analysis and free association, has demonstrated a separateness from consciousness the way the body is separate from the soul. They are connected, body and soul, but separate, and psychoanalysis is the mechanism for explaining how and why they are separate and how they may be merged again to the advantage of the individual and society as a whole.

****

By scientific criteria, the Freudian *Interpretation of Dreams* signifies a marked advance in the realm of subjective psychology, because it made the dreamer both the subject and object of psychological observation. The "observer" was excluded and, as Freud noted in his preface, the inner life of the person investigated was exposed to the scrutiny of outsiders to a degree yet unheard of in natural science. This remarkable attitude on Freud's part should have been able to disarm almost any critic, because it made Freud appear not to be placing any personal interest in an analysis of the father of psychoanalysis above the facts.

The genius of Freud is never denied by Rank and he extols the wisdom of Freud's psychoanalytic approach to dream analysis in his remarks regarding Freud's great classic, *Interpretation of Dreams.* It constituted a bench mark in the advancement of depth psychology, for it provided both an objective and subjective mechanism for interpretation relative to the individual's unconscious mind and his ego state of reflective self-awareness. These two worlds -- conscious and unconscious -- we now know are linked, thanks to the insights of psychoanalysis.

****

CHAPTER SIX SOUL AND WILL

It was the will to live, and not death anxiety, which produced belief in immortality, and it is the will which creates the dream. The dream seems to prove freedom of will to us as completely as it did to primitive man who translated his dream into reality. While the soul and body had originally been united in one being, primitive man began to interpret this freedom of the will as freedom of the soul from the body. But in his dream life his own soul's freedom of will was opposed by that of other souls which seemed to appear in his dream as uninvited visitors. Early met physicists explained the dream on the basis of a temporary withdrawal of the will during sleep. Freud, who regarded willing as the driving power of the dream, denied this freedom because he needed neither the soul nor willing to demonstrate the causal determination of psychic events. But the will problem cannot be solved by the dream or by an particular spiritual phenomenon, since it represents a phenomenon already affected by spiritual belief and interpreted in relation to it. Spiritual belief itself proves to be an expression of the will to live.

Rank is eager to demonstrate the origins of the mind/body split, or what he calls the soul and the body differentiation. It was man's "will to live" which created his desire for immortality, rather than his fear of death, and his will also, then, created the dream which became the mechanism for primitive man to experience and explore the meaning of freedom. Early man, and subsequently contemporary primitive peoples, have divided the soul from the body as they have separated the dream from the reality of daily living. Man's soul, in this worldview, is free so long as it is exempt from the encounter with the physical world. Spirituality is synonymous with freedom and this occurs in the dream and in man's expectation and imagination of immortality.

****

From a pure ego psychology, which for myself had finally crystallized into willing as the crucial personality problem, I have been led to a will-god without considering ethnological materials or theological points of view at all. Yet I can understand this elevation of the ego religiously only to the extent of its alliance with negative will or with self-resignation and humiliation. The new attitude which manifested itself as "religious" was that which came to use such irreligious spiritual creations as the will-god to justify individual willing. *Only with this moral tendency to justify does naïve projection of life power into spiritual immortality acquire that ethical stamp which we associate with religion.*

Rank is so convinced of his interpretation of primordial and primitive experiences that he has actually chosen to discount the utility of ethnographic evidence to validate his theory that the "will to live" is the fundamental problem of modern individuals and society. Religion evolves when the will-to-live ethos produces a spirituality of immortal existence. Here is the beginning of the religion problem as it affects the individual's personality development, choosing rather a religious worldview and ethos rather than one of freedom and independence wherein no promise of immortality exists.

****

Reverent humility before exalted beings was just a result of this reevaluation of will, from which arose the concepts of guilt and sin. We should like to try to understand spiritually this ancient and fundamental problem of religion, this moral attitude toward the will and its interpretation as evil, which we encounter in the concepts of guilt and sin as personal offenses. In the later traditions of the sexual era, which regard woman as the chief evil and sexuality as the "cause" of morality, we discover only ancient spiritual belief recast into the new ideology of procreative immortality. That is to say, the curse of sexuality follows from its destruction of man's belief in individual immortality. We may also recall that, as long as its necessity was denied, natural death, which was the first evil known to man, was believed to follow from his own transgressions.

Sin and guilt, the gifts of religion that keep on giving, have their etiology from the reverential demeanor produced by man's will to live in a world which wills him to die. Man's will to live is perceived and presented as sin, as the manifestation of evil brought about by the individual's own personal desire for immortality. Man is again blamed for his own predicament in the world. Man's spirituality is lost when he relinquishes his belief in the immortality of the soul in deference to his preference for the enduring life of the community which ultimately is manifested in sexual expression. Man's individual death, in this context, then became the first manifestation and encounter with evil. Man brought it on himself by desiring immortality and relinquishing the spiritual quest for the soul.

****

CHAPTER VII NATURE AND SPIRIT

Man seems now to have entered a new phase of his mental evolution, which is expressed in both physics and psychology. In other words, the modern physicist seems nature just as the modern psychologist sees man. Until recently both were ensnared in a natural science ideology whose amenability I recognized in the psychic sphere, just as certain physicists began to doubt its strict applicability to nature. On the basis of the same ideology which became so fateful for physics, Freud had fallen into the error of trying to discover behind mental phenomena a reality "free of consciousness," and of believing that he had found it in the "unconscious." He regarded his interpretations of the mental world as facts and as images of reality, just as the physicist had regarded his interpretation of the world as reality itself. But with this attempt to comprehend mental phenomena objectively, it became completely obvious that such comprehension could be mediated only by consciousness, irrespective of the subjectivity or objectivity of the observations made.

During the time of Rank, not unlike present-day psychology, there was a growing rift within the discipline between those who were laboratory-based scientists seeking the objectification of behavioral causality while others with a softer view of their discipline were seeking to grasp the "meaning" of life and the "will to live." The division centered around the distinctions between behaviorism and humanism, between reducing psychological study to biogenic traces of behavior components in human action and the study of the psychogenic traces linking action to intentionality. Rank believed even Freud had succumbed to the behavioristic tendency by attributing objectivity to his concept of the unconscious. It could not be done, Rank concluded.

****

The attempts of psychoanalysis and its various schools to achieve an individual psychology always ended in "the statistical average," as Freud's normal psychology, Adler's social psychology, and Jung's collective psychology all betray. For the individual simply lies beyond lawfulness, and cannot be fully comprehended or explained by the causality either of natural or social science. In my opinion, the only rewarding approach lies in a will psychology which includes both ways of considering the individual, yet does not attempt to understand him principally or solely on the basis of himself alone. For in the realm of psychology, too, a correct formulation of the problem seems to me more important than any attempts to solve it, which attempts may become necessary or possible only because of its faulty formulation.

The pitfall of objectifying human behavior was the sociological propensity to reduce all human activity to a normative average, telling us "generally" about human behavior and nothing specific about the individual. Rank became a champion of what he called "will psychology," a difficult thing to say or understand. Others began to prefer to call it the "will to live," patterning it after the Freudian's "will to pleasure," the Adlerian's "will to power," and the Franklian's "will to meaning." The "will to live," however, was truly adopted from Albert Schweitzer's "reverence for life," in which Schweitzer first used the term and concept of "will to live." Nevertheless, this Rank believed to be the context within which a convergence of biogenic objectivity and psychogenic subjectivity would be possible.

****

As I established many years ago, Freud's psychoanalysis tried to synthesize this antithesis of theory and practice, but miscarried in its completely unsystematic mixture of the two points of view. His psychic causality is purely historical, in that it tries to explain the present completely in terms of the past; while, at the same time, this causal understanding is obliged to function as the therapeutically effective agent, by effecting a different manner of reacting to the present and future. However, my analysis of the "analytic situation" has shown that the therapeutic agent is simply *present experience,* and not a historical understanding in which the "therapeutic" effect seems to consist of the displacement of certain actual impulses *from* present experience.

In the quest to find and study the "soul of man," Rank was keen on this convergence idea in which theory and practice, ideology and behavior, might be more carefully analyzed in relationship to man's both objective and subjective pursuit of soul.

****

Freud's causally explained displacement into the past implies something that is practically therapeutic instead of genetically causal. That is, because we believe we can understand the present better through the past, and because we can use the past to vindicate the present, we often regard the past as causally effective when in fact it is not. This "causal" explanation may have therapeutic effects, because it serves to justify the present by implying that neurotic reactions are more infantile, for example. Regarding the theoretical aspects of this view, Adler, Jung, and others raise the objection that such a reconstruction of the past as psychoanalysis seeks through a causal understanding of the present, must remain impossible or at least unapproachable as long as one does not apply finalistic points of view.

Rank joined Jung, Adler, and a few other carefully selected neo-Freudians in disassociating himself from the psychoanalytic use of the "past" as a presumed "therapeutic" treatment for the present. Dredging up incidences (actual and imagined) from one's past is used in psychoanalysis to interpret and adjust the present life situation of the patient, even in cases where the actual or imagined past event was in reality irrelevant to the development of the neurosis of the patient. Freud believed that so long as the patient believed it was true and relevant, the therapy was effective. Freud had many detractors from this simplistic and reductionistic approach to recollections of past experience remembered by the mental illness patient.

****

While the religious man projects his will power and his conscious moral attitude onto God, before whom he humbles himself while remaining haughty and powerful in other respects, modern man recognizes God in himself, and feels himself small and vain in comparison. He can rule nature but he cannot know it. That is, he can force his will causally, but this will itself remains as inexplicable and incalculable as natural events themselves finally are. It is characteristic that psychology along with physics should be in the midst of a similarly humbling self-awareness. Only this "feeling of inferiority" from which we all suffer is no "neurotic complex" such as Adler intended to cure by pedagogical measures; it is much more the developmental negativism of the religious man, who no longer can have any illusions about his unimportance.

Rank is neither sympathetic nor unsympathetic to either theists or non-theists. His interest in those individuals is to the social mechanisms committed to the nurturing of the human soul. Theists rely upon a God to whom they are submissive and obedient even in the face of their own hypocrisy of saying what they believe, on the one hand, and doing otherwise. Non-theists, on the other hand, rely upon themselves in the absence of a Father God, presuming that their needs can be met without outside assistance. It is the religious phenomenon that drives the individual, not to neurosis as Freud presumed, or to inferiority as Adler proposed, but to the realization that in the absence of immortality the individual is left to nurture his own soul with the realization of his insignificance in a world fraught with danger and inevitable suffering, grief, and death.

****

Psychoanalysis is to be regarded as therapy in the most completely illusion-promoting sense of the word; for its psychology is based on the relation of the *I* and the *Thou,* whether one interprets this relation religiously as does Jung, socially as does Adler, or as infantile in the Freudian sense. It does not recognize the individual as such, but as a being whose will is "causally" explained by sexual libido, and whose consciousness is finally determined by the unconscious. Theoretically, Freud has tried to explain the entire individual causally, whereas individuality itself means extra-causality. But in therapy the will becomes of subtle importance, not only in the seemingly weak-willed neurotic, of whose performance the analyst has such a low opinion, and whose will expression the analyst interprets as "resistance"' for the *therapist's will itself* seems to be described as something almost godlike in its potency.

Rank is shockingly candid in his understanding of psychoanalysis as an "illusion-promotion" mechanism for individual therapy, for it fosters a sense of interpersonal relationships regardless of whether one is religious or not. Neither Jung nor Adler nor Freud could avoid the inevitability of promoting an illusionary therapeutic relationship of the individual to his world.

****

I have tried to conceive of psychology as a creative expression of freedom of will in the spiritual sense, since I have shown repeatedly how it grew out of spiritual belief, and how it seeks to preserve the ideology of immortality, while no longer believing in the soul to which it owes its existence. ... Psychology has to do only with interpretations of spiritual phenomena in and of themselves, and as they refer to the individual self, whether they are already objectified or are still subjective. However, interpretation itself is nothing but an intellectualized will phenomenon, and while it may therefore be a matter of interpretation of the external world, of other humans, or of one's own self, there always lies in this kind of understanding an actual "handling" in the real sense of the word, a taking possession of a thing, a violation, a creation in the sense of one's own ego and in the likeness of one's self. The creative person fashions the world according to his conscious, willing ego; the neurotic type interprets it psychologically according to his moralistic, guilt ego; and the psychotic identified himself with it in the sense of his magic, spiritual ego.

A psychology which has been spawned by spiritual belief in the immortality of the soul is no longer possible, since the coming of modern western science. Primitive and primeval man had the luxury of a pre-scientific worldview and ethos which nurtured a psychology of spiritual depth. Now it is different, and western society is stuck with the practicalities of a psychology that has interpreted the world scientifically and has relinquished a hold on the human soul and its immortal aspirations. It is now left to modern man to use his creative skills of interpretation to "will a world" in which his conscious ego can function and thrive. Only the neurotic and the religious can now rely upon a magical spiritualized ego to foster this illusion of immortality.

****

Thus psychology is at no time an interpretation of facts such as one finds in physics and biology, but an interpretation of the attitudes of the individual self, which we project on others through the medium of so-called objective psychology. Psychology is interpretation of self in others, just as physics is interpretation of self in nature. In this sense, psychology is self-affirmation or self-assertion, and psychology as self-knowledge is self-deception or belief, for man's psychological creed is immortality.

Psychology as interpretation is Rank's great contribution to this field of study. It is not an interpretation of facts as in the hard and physical sciences but rather an interpretation of the individual's self-understanding. It is a hermeneutic of meaning, as explained by Heidegger and employed by Viktor Frankl in his logo therapy, a therapeutic modality of treatment that resonates very effectively with Rankian psychology. This, then, is modern psychology, and it works well in this modality.

****

CHAPTER NINE

David Bakan and *Sigmund Freud and the Jewish Mystical Tradition*

Near the end of the decade of the 1950s which, as we have noted, include blockbuster studies in the psychology of religion by Roberts, Allport, Fromm, and Rank, David Bakan (1921-2004), an adventurous psychologist who had taken his Ph.D. (1948) at Ohio State University and fresh to the University of Chicago (1961-1968) by way of the University of Missouri (1949-1961), came onto the scene with a radical application of etiological sleuthing applied to Sigmund Freud. A prolific writer and one whose courage matched that of Otto Rank's in daring to revisit the ideological infrastructure of Freud's psychoanalytic theories themselves, Bakan wrote the book for psychologists that equaled the insightfulness of Roberts' work written for Christian clergy. Ending his long and distinguished career at York University in Toronto, where he died in 2004, Bakan had been an executive member of the American Psychological Association and on the Advisory Board of the Canadian Council on Children and Youth. One of his international distinctions was becoming the founding editor of the *Canadian Journal of Community Mental Health.*

Bakan's *Sigmund Freud and the Jewish Mystical Tradition,* published in 1958 by D.Van Nostrand Company of Princeton, New Jersey, was destined, from day one, to become a controversial classic in the field of the history of psychoanalysis and a pillar of support for the psychology of religion. Bakan goes on to have a distinguished career as a scholar and teacher at York University in Canada, but this book, which came out upon his arrival at the University of Chicago, established him as a pivotal player in this emerging discipline. In the second edition, published by Schocken Books of New York, the publisher points out that Bakan chose to accept Freud's own distinction between being a Jew and his acceptance of Jewish doctrine and, by using this distinction as a hermeneutical tool, "demonstrates what power Jewish mystical doctrine retained in the formation of Freud's technical genius" (1958:ix). This had not been attempted, even hinted at, prior to Bakan, and the boldness of the venture elevated the psychology of religion as a field of study to that of a national agenda. "By sharpening the reader's perspective about the ways in which Freud was, and was not, Jewish," says Schocken, Bakan presented a book that spoke to all people in the modern world, an inquiry into the nature of the relationship between the etiology of faith and the development of the human personality. It set the stage for the next fifty years of research in the psychology of religion as regards the relationship between religious ideology and religious behavior.

Selections from *Sigmund Freud and the Jewish Mystical Tradition* by David Bakan with commentary.

NOTE: In the following, the original text will be printed in *Arial Unicode MS* typestyle (as is this note itself to illustrate) as an easy and aesthetically pleasing way of identifying the primary source paragraphs. The author's commentary will be in *Times New Roman*. It is hoped that this differentiation between the "primary source" and the "commentary" made by use of differing typestyles will prove helpful and not disruptive to the reader. *I have also chosen to use a quadruple asterisk (****) to separate the primary text from the commentary.*

PREFACE

The purpose of this essay is to explore an hypothesis concerning the intellectual antecedents of Freudian psychoanalysis. ... The hypothesis of this essay is that a full appreciation of the development of psychoanalysis is essentially incomplete unless it be viewed against the history of Judaism, and particularly against the history of Jewish mystical thought. This does not mean that we will be able to read psychoanalytic propositions directly out of Jewish mystical expressions. Our point is rather that Freud's repeated affirmation of his Jewish identity had greater significance for the development of psychoanalysis than is usually recognized.

Like David Roberts' earlier book, *Psychotherapy and a Christian*

View of Man, Bakan's book constituted a profoundly original first in the exploration of the relationship between psychology and religion. Whereas Roberts was focused upon a Christian doctrine of man, Bakan was concerned with the relationship, long believed to exist but no one had dared venture into these problematic waters, between Freud and the mystical tradition of his own faith community, Judaism. Needless to say, it caused a stir, not just within Judaism but also within psychoanalytic circles as well. Bakan never intended to present a scenario allowing for the mere connecting of dots to prove the "relationship." Rather, he proposed that the *zeitgeist* (spirit of the time) and the *weltanschuuang* (worldview and ethos) of Freud's own personal life necessitated both an exploration into and a demonstration of the connection. This he did, say some; this he attempted to do, say others. Whether successful or not, the demonstration of the insightfulness of this methodological approach to the history of ideas set a new and higher standard for the psychology of religion.

****

As we hope we will make clear in the course of this essay, Jewish mysticism played a special role in connection with Jewish contact with the Western world. ... Our attempt to understand Freud in terms of Jewish history should not be taken as indicating that we believe Freud to have been a secret scholar of Jewish lore. ... When the lore of Jewish mysticism is set down in books, it often comes in the form of little nuggets. ... In attempting to understand the development of psychoanalysis as an expression of Jewish mysticism, it has been our endeavor to emphasize the word *mysticism* as much as the word *Jewish.* ... We have sought to make the essay comprehensible to persons who are well versed neither in psychoanalysis nor in Jewish history.

Bakan never implied that Freud was either devious or unconsciously aware of the impact that his exposure to the Jewish mystical tradition, particularly of the Hasidic school nurtured by the Kabbalistic tradition and the textual tradition of the *Zohar* had upon him. That Freud was subject to the profound influence of mystical Judaism from his own childhood, his long family tradition, and the social milieu in which he grew up is presented in a most outstandingly obvious fashion by Bakan with such documented power and force as to be incontrovertible.

****

PART ONE THE BACKGROUND OF FREUD'S DEVELOPMENT OF PSYCHOANALYSIS

Freud once indicated that there have been three major blows to man's narcissism. Copernicus delivered the cosmological blow; Darwin delivered the biological blow; and psychoanalysis (Freud) delivered the psychological blow. ... The psychoanalytic movement seemingly originated as an effort on the part of a physician to cure certain ailments that were resistant to other forms of treatment; and it was in this guide that it first presented itself to the world. Yet, shortly after this introduction, it reached out to touch, infiltrate, and encompass practically every other form of intellectual endeavor. The major question of this essay: *Against what backdrop of the history of ideas shall we place these momentous contributions of Freud?*

Never one to be shy about the assessment of his own contribution to western intellectual history, Freud placed himself and psychoanalysis on a par with Copernicus' physics and Darwin's biology. He never doubted the profound discovery he had made in psychoanalysis. More than just a physician, from the beginning Freud set out to make a great discovery and demonstrate the profundity of that discovery in the treatment of mental illness. What relationship his insights as a physician had to his maturational experience as a Viennese Jew influenced by the mystical tradition of the Baal Shem Tov was Bakan's agenda.

****

If the scientific background with which Freud was intimately acquainted does not provide us with any cogent clue to the question of the origins of psychoanalysis, what other hypotheses might be advanced? ... The first is that *the idiosyncrasies of Freud's personal life were such that they formed him into a very special kind of being who could make the kinds of discoveries which he did.* ... The second of these "personal" hypotheses is what may be called the *"flash" or "revelation" hypothesis.* ...The third is the *hypothesis of genius. ... The last of our hypotheses of a personal nature regards psychoanalysis as the result of a germinal idea or a germinal observation dropped on the soil of an extremely rich mind. ...*

Four different explanations as to how Freud did it, how he made this "discovery" of the relationship between the unconscious and human behavior as seen and interpreted through dream analysis and free association early on emerged within the medical and scientific community, each attempting to identify that major ingredient which set Freud on the path to discovery. Bakan identifies, explores, and then dismisses each of these as fundamentally irrelevant to Freud's genius. Rather, Bakan sets out to demonstrate that the life situation and the historical circumstances of Freud prove pivotal -- a 19th century psychiatrist and Jew living in Vienna!

****

Freud's statement that these communications had "lain dormant," etc., can only be interpreted as the ascription to them of an importance which had been displaced from something else. An hypothesis concerning the latter is the subject of this essay. Freud's lack of clarity concerning the sources of his ideas recurs on several occasions which we shall enumerate below. This characteristic forces us to the conclusion that the origins of his psychoanalytic thought are related to repressed or at least suppressed material.

Of course, there were many Jewish physicians in the 19th century living in Austria. What made Freud different was his willingness to go where others had feared to venture. And, though he was reluctant even to explore the origins of these insights derived from his Jewish milieu, he was proud to be a Jew and did not shrink from drawing illustrative materials from the mystical sources of the Jewish faith. That there was a direct connection between his "discovery" and his "faith," even Freud was not in a position to discuss or explore. That it existed, nevertheless, was Bakan's point.

****

A system of thought such as was developed by Freud, made up of so many different propositions, so consistent in its mood, containing so many far-reaching implications, and with subject matter so diverse, could only be the result of a culture; and by a culture we mean the achievement of at least several generations, involving relatively large numbers of people, whose life experiences pool themselves into a characteristic entity, a socially carried and organized personality. Psychoanalysis is at least a theory of development, a theory of neurosis, a theory of healing, a theory of culture, a theory of the role of sexuality, an armamentarium of devices for interpretation of human imaginative productions, a pattern of interpersonal relationship, and a philosophy of religion.

In the history of ideas, there has not been a more disparately composed theoretical system than psychoanalysis, argues Bakan. It gleaned its insights from high and low, far and near, shallow and deep. It took a culture of history and ideas, not just an individual's own personal insights, even if a genius, to compose such a system of thought.

****

The thesis of this essay is that the contributions of Freud are to be understood largely as a contemporary version of, and a contemporary contribution to, the history of Jewish mysticism. Freud, consciously or unconsciously, secularized Jewish mysticism; and psychoanalysis can intelligently be viewed as such a secularization. As we hope will become clear in the remainder of this essay, Freud was engaged in the issues set by this history. Considerable illumination of the nature of psychoanalysis may be arrived at by tying it into this context. By separating the supernatural elements in mysticism from its other content, Freud succeeded in making a major contribution to science. We believe that this pattern, from mysticism to science, is one of the more important historical characteristics in the development of general science.

Bakan is at his boldest when he argues that the fundamental contribution of Freud is not just to the psychological traditions of psychotherapy but to the history of the Jewish mystical tradition itself. That is not to say that he discounts in any way, far from it, the central importance of psychoanalytic theory in deep psychology. That genius and contribution is established and is incontrovertible. What Bakan intends in this psychological study is to show that Freud has made a major, if not *the* major, contribution to the history of Jewish thought in drawing, wittingly or not, from the great mystical tradition of the Jewish faith.

****

Freud had a most excellent reason for not specifying this (Jewish) tradition -- if, indeed, he was conscious of its role in his thought. The reason is actually an eminently simple one: anti-Semitism, in which Jewish literature was a primary object of attack, was so widespread and so intense at the time that to indicate the Jewish sources of his ideas would have dangerously exposed an intrinsically controversial theory to an unnecessary and possibly fatal opposition. ... It is difficult, in the perspective of modern America, where the Jews are under less oppression than ever before in their history, to fully appreciate the intensity and reality of anti-Semitism at that time. The events which were taking place in Vienna can best be understood from the fact that they led eventually to the complete annihilation of 6,000,000 Jews, whose lives were systematically extinguished in places such as Bergen-Belsen, Auschwitz, Dachau, and Buchenwald. It was this massacre-in-preparation which provided the social and political background in which psychoanalysis was being developed.

Bakan is never certain to what extent, if at all, that Freud was self-consciously aware of his reliance upon the insights of the Jewish mystical tradition in the development of his psychoanalytic world. That Freud chose not to credit that tradition, if he even recognized his reliance upon, is, according to Bakan, fully understandable given the *zeitgeist* of Vienna. The rampant anti-Semitism of Europe at the time was palpable and Freud, as a physician, had to provide for his family and struggled, as do all beginning physicians and, at the time, particularly Jewish physicians, to make a living. To have identified the mystical sources within the Jewish tradition of his proposal for a psychotherapeutic treatment perceived by his Gentile colleagues as rather adventurous if not out right careless would have been a disaster.

****

Freud would have had good reason to deliberately conceal his sources if he were conscious that psychoanalysis was a development in the tradition of Jewish mysticism. ... We believe that Freud often wrote with obscurity, that he was motivated, consciously or unconsciously, to hide the deeper portions of his thought, and that these deeper portions were Kabbalistic in their source and content. The Kabbalistic tradition itself has secrecy as part of its nature and deals with secret matters. The Kabbalistic tradition has it that the secret teachings are to be transmitted orally to one person at a time, and even then only to selected minds and by hints. This is indeed what Freud was doing in the actual practice of psychoanalysis, and this aspect of the Kabbalistic tradition is still maintained in the education of the modern psychoanalyst. He must receive the tradition orally (in the training analysis). As the modern practicing psychoanalyst is quick to tell anyone, psychoanalysis is not to be learned from books!

Whether merely stylistic in nature or intentionally motivated, Freud's propensity for obscurity is most evident, and the closer he gets to the genius of his insights the greater the contrast between his insightfulness on the one hand and his reluctance to identify the context for his brilliance on the other. This is truly in keeping with the Kabbalistic tradition of Jewish mysticism -- hiding the source, and obscuring the origin of wisdom and insight is part of the tradition, indeed, is the distinguishing characteristic of Hasidic mystical thought. Freud's training of physicians who desired to become psychoanalysts required a one-on-one instruction, not the reading of papers and books, for those came as strictly supplements. For Freud, as with the mystics of old, the instruction in the mysteries required verbal instruction from the master, not textual exploration.

****

Freud was eminently aware that the material he was writing would arouse resistance on the basis of its content alone, as well as because he was Jewish. The resistance would probably have redoubled had he indicated the Jewish sources of his thought. ... The ability of the Jew to withstand opposition has historically been based on the Jewish community rather than in individual heroes. ... If we are skeptical of his explanation as to why it was not "entirely a matter of chance that the first advocate of psychoanalysis was a Jew," an "explanation of the explanation" readily presents itself. On the one hand, if he wanted to suggest that psychoanalysis is related to the Jewish tradition, he here indicated it clearly. On the other hand, for him to say it in its bare clarity, without qualification, would invite even greater resist Nance than that which is the subject of his paper, "The Resistances to Psychoanalysis."

Freud knew he had an uphill battle with his professional colleagues in Vienna and those who were not Jews would be even more difficult to persuade as to the viability of his psychoanalytic methodology. Nevertheless, given the Jewish tradition of oppression and Freud's resilience in the face of it, Freud pressed on with his work. Only once did he venture close to a public affirmation of the proximity of Jewish mysticism to psychoanalysis, but beyond that one occasion, he used subtlety and innuendo, insinuation and suggestion to hint at the relationship.

****

Thus far we have indicted that the question of the "origins" of psychoanalysis is an open one, that the usual hypotheses for explaining its origins are unsatisfactory, that great writers engage in dissimulation-in-writing when they are under conditions of persecution, that there was persecution of Jews at the time Freud was writing, that he was capable of dissimulation, and that he specifically talked of dissimulating-in-writing. These considerations are background material for our attempt to demonstrate that psychoanalysis is to be understood as developing in the tradition of Jewish mysticism.

Bakan is adamant in his contention that psychoanalysis fits nicely and easily into the Jewish mystical tradition and, though Freud never directly indicated that Hasidism was the origin of his psychoanalytic theories, the similarities are too great to overlook or discount. Therefore, according to Bakan, a study of Freud is a study in Jewish thought; a study of psychoanalysis is an investigation into the mystical tradition of Judaism. There can be no question of it, due to the proximity of the two thought systems, Freud as the conjunctive component, and the emergence of a school of treatment for the mentally troubled reflects the role and mission of mysticism, addressing the troubled mind in search of inner tranquility. It all fit together, says Bakan.

****

In the case of psychoanalysis, its development is closely related to the ethnicity of its originator. For there has hardly been a scientific pursuit which was so spun out of the being of the investigator. The images which Freud uses to describe his work on dream interpretation are pertinent in this connection. He writes of it: "None of my works has been so completely my own as this; it is my own dung-heap, my own seedling and a *nova species mihi*." Freud's major work, *The Interpretation of Dreams,* is unique in the history of science and medicine in that it draws so heavily and directly on the most intimate features of the investigator himself.

Another astounding phenomenon characterizing the emergence and development of psychoanalytic theory and the whole school of thought and practice which evolved from Freud's insights is the fact that the ethnicity of the research scientist himself is crucial to the character of the discovery. Bakan suggests that in no other scientific endeavor -- in biology, medicine, chemistry, physics, etc. -- has the ethnicity of the scientist been relevant to the discovery. With Freud and psychoanalysis, it was not only relevant but actually indispensable to the discovery itself.

****

Freud believed that anti-Semitism was practically ubiquitous in either latent or manifest form; the broad masses in England were anti-Semitic "as everywhere;" he was of the opinion that the book on Moses (*Moses and Monotheism*) would anger the Jews; he expressed a love for Hebrew and Yiddish, according to Freud's son; he refused to accept royalties on Hebrew and Yiddish translations of his works; he was sympathetic to Zionism from the first days of the movement and was acquainted with and respected Herzl; he had once sent Herzl a copy of one of his works with a personal dedication; Freud's son was a member of Kadimah, a Zionist organization, and Freud himself was an honorary member of it.

To further elevate the centrality of Freud's Jewishness, Bakan points out that for Freud everything was colored by his ethnicity -- his studies, his research, his writing, his treatment by colleagues, his patients, his work -- all reflected and demonstrated his Jewishness. Freud, though an avoid non-believer, was forever the practicing Jew, waving fees from Jewish organizations, supporting Zionism in every way permissible, and befriending Herzl, the father of Zionism. Not willing to publicly link psychoanalysis and Hasidism, Freud never veered from his alignment with Judaism as a Jewish physician.

****

Freud, explains his biographer Ernest Jones, "felt himself to be Jewish to the core, and it evidently meant a great deal to him. He had the common Jewish sensitiveness to the slightest hint of anti-Semintism and he made very few friends who were not Jews." On one occasion he announced that he was a Jew and neither an Austrian nor a German. He was extremely fond of telling Jewish stories and jokes and sometimes demonstrated an extreme sensitivity about expressing Jewish character publicly, a prudence which appears to be highly relevant to our present thesis.

Ever the teller of tales, Freud emulated the rabbinic tradition by using stories to illustrate a point and to provide insight into relationships. He was first and last a Jew, even denying on occasion to be Austrian or German, preferring always to be thought of and perceived as a son of Israel. His use of Talmudic and rabbinic tales in his practice and in his instruction was important to him, whether he realized just how closely his psychological interpretation and practice came to the interpretation and practice of Jewish mysticism. To read Jewish mystics was like reading stories taken from Freud's clinical case studies, and he often pointed out their similarities.

****

It is important to distinguish between Freud's sense of identity as a Jew and his acceptance of Jewish religious doctrines. The intensity of his feelings on his Jewish identify was matched by his rejection of religious doctrine and practice. His works on religion are *against* the classical Judaeo-Christian religious doctrines. Yet his sense of Jewish identity was so strong that we might consider his *genetic* conception of the Jew, most clearly asserted in his *Moses and Monotheism*, as the theoretical counterpart of his deep feeling of Jewish identity.

Though rabbinic in technique, Freud was not a believer in the theological constructs of Jewish thought. He was an experiential Jew, born and reared under the umbrella of the Talmud and the Torah, not a believer in the "truth" of the biblical stories, but rather in their metaphorical value. He fought religious practices which demeaned the human spirit, whether they were Christian or Jewish teachings, but he always valued the rabbinic and Hasidic stories of relationships as illustrative of how tradition offers aid in uncovering the mysteries of life. The unconscious is likewise uncovered through these metaphorical tales dreamed in the dreams of the mentally ill.

****

Freud spent his whole life in a virtual ghetto, a world made up almost exclusively of Jews. ... Both of Freud's parents cam from Galacia, a region whose atmosphere was saturated with Chassidism, a late and socially widespread form of Jewish mysticism. Freud says explicitly that his father came from a Chassidic milieu, and we know that the birthplace of Jakob Freud, Freud's father, was filled with Chassidic lore and learning. ... What it was that moved Freud to interest himself in Kabbala and Chassidism is not hard to understand. He must have felt himself to be spiritually at home in these worlds.

Bakan makes it clear that Freud was attracted to that which he knew best, that for which he was reared to uphold, namely, the Hasidic traditions of the Baal Shem Tov and the teachings of the Kabbala and the *Zohar*. That he held on tightly to that tradition and those mechanisms of cultural conveyance in the face of modern scientific psychology is a credit to Freud's creative capacity to hold on to what was of value and to mobilize those insights to the benefit of modern science and mental health.

****

PART TWO THE MILIEU OF JEWISH MYSTICISM

The most important document in the Kabbalistic tradition is the *Zohar*. It is ostensibly the work of Simeon ben Yohai in the first half of the second century. The major part of the *Zohar* consists of a lengthy commentary on passages from the Torah. Besides, various other writings are included within it. Gersham Scholem (the leading 20th century Jewish mysticism scholar) enumerates the contents of the *Zohar* under twenty headings in addition to the main one. The work was first brought to light by Moses de Leon in the latter years of the thirteenth century. There has been much speculation about the problem of its authorship. Scholem believes that it was written in its entirety by Moses de Leon. For about two centuries the work remained relatively obscure, but then its influence flowered. It became one of the most significant writings in Jewish thought, an expression of the deepest currents in the history of Judaism. ... Besides its singular emphasis on sexual and family relationships, the *Zohar* shares with Freud's psychoanalytic writings the following characteristics: views on anti-Semitism, the conception of man as bisexual, a theory of sexual-social development, and, perhaps most important, a set of techniques for the interpretation of linguistic productions.

The strongest argument, says Bakan, for his contention that Freud drew from the Jewish mystical tradition, wittingly or not, is irrelevant, and is best illustrated in the kabbalastic writings found in that classic text, the *Zohar*. This book was thought of as sacred, a product of a great mystic himself and a text that draws from the Talmud and the Torah but provides a mystical understanding of man's relationship to God presented in sexual and familial terms as man's relationship to his wife and children. The points of similarity in dealing with these issues with psychoanalysis is more than astounding, they are strikingly similar in ethos and worldview. In some instances psychoanalytic analysis seems to be a re-write of illustrative materials in this great mystical classic.

****

It is one of the more important characteristics of psychoanalysis that it views evil as a distortion of love. ... (Furthermore), sexuality as the locus for the expression of personal freedom has deep roots. In the *Zohar* the sexual metaphor is used very freely. The orthodox tradition sharply restricted sexual expression, perhaps, as has been suggested by some writers, as a result of the effort of the Jews to dissociate themselves from religious practices involving sexual rites. The sexual is also a temptation which is ever-present and sometimes pressingly so; and it offers the most accessible sins. Perhaps the most important reason for the sexual excesses is to be found in the contribution of Freud himself, that sexuality is at the core of human personality.

A careful reading of the *Zohar* leads one to understand the influence it would have had, either directly through Freud's exposure to the text itself, or indirectly, through Freud's emersion in the Jewish milieu of rabbinic and synagogue culture of the ghetto in which he matured to adulthood. The sexual metaphors of man and woman were used by the mystical writers to speak of man's relationship to God. Sin and evil, goodness and righteousness, all are reflected in sexuality, and when speaking of God and Man, or Man and Woman, the sexual metaphors were powerfully indicative of Jewish law and custom. Sexuality is the core of human relationships and is the center of human personality development. Freud said it and the Jewish mystics had taught it for centuries before him.

****

PART THREE THE MOSES THEME IN THE THOUGHT OF FREUD

(As we have been saying), Jewish history we believe can help us to illuminate Freud's contributions. The line-up within Jewish history was that of the mystical versus the orthodox, the former advancing varieties of approaches against the domination of thought and life associated with the classical disciplined approach of the latter. We believe that viewing Freud's works in the light of this classical struggle increases their intelligibility. ... We believe that the primary key to the understanding of Freud is contained in his concern with Moses. In his autobiography Freud tells us, "My early familiarity with the Bible story (at a time almost before I had learnt the art of reading), had, as I recognized much later, an enduring effect upon the direction of my interest." We have two essays on Moses by Freud.

Bakan is no newcomer to Jewish thought and history, and his perceptive insights into both the mystical and the classical tradition of rabbinic teaching are outstanding. He believed, and documented the reasons for his belief, that Freud himself was exposed to both the mystical and classical traditions within Judaism and that Freud's struggle with his own Jewishness stemmed from this internal struggle, the struggle between keeping the law in compliance with rabbinic instruction and following one's heart as it was nurtured and instructed through the Kabbalistic teachings of the Zohar handed down from the Baal Shem Tov within Hasidism. Freud's fascination with the life story of Moses, Bakan suggests, gives us a clue as to this historic struggle.

****

The hostility which he had towards religion was not to religion as such. It has, for example, been quite appropriately argued that Freud's whole psychoanalytic contribution shares many of the characteristics which we generally subsume under the rubric of religion. Rather, what Freud opposes is religion in the Mosaic tradition, most fully expressed in Jewish orthodoxy. His resistance to law and his tendency towards the violation of the commandment against idolatry, as manifested in his jocular yet passionate "having of other gods before" the Mosaic God, expressed his rebellion against orthodox Jewish religion. The "grubby old gods" lessened Moses' magic power.

Those who would criticize and discount Freud's attack upon religion often miss the point of his attack, an attack designed to challenge the fostering and perpetuation of immaturity and irresponsibility taught by traditional and institutional religious leaders. That was the focus of Freud's discontent. Religious law was the bane of both Freud and psychoanalysis because such law held the individual hostage to a world view and ethos built upon the necessity of obedience and compliance with dictates touted by the purveyors of religious authority, dominance, and control.

****

Freud's most revelatory work with respect to our hypothesis is his book, *Moses and Monotheism.* It was the last book Freud wrote and, in our opinion, expresses some of his deepest impulses, impulses which were operative throughout his life. The book is the only one written by Freud which directs itself avowedly to the problem of Judaism and the meaning of being Jewish. ... Some of the followers of Freud have tended to dismiss it; and by some, it is regarded as the product of senility, with the suggestion, perhaps, that respect to Freud's genius is best paid by ignoring it. If this book had not come from the hand of Sigmund Freud, one would seriously doubt whether it would ever have seen the light of day. ... If the book is one which is in the Kabbalistic tradition, and if it was written under the sense of persecution, that it should be deliberately obscure is completely understandable.

It was Freud's *Moses and Monotheism*, moreso than any other of his books, which convinced Bakan of the accuracy of his suspicion with regard to the Jewish mystical origins of psychoanalytic insight and practice. Though most of Freud's followers, and many of his colleagues, chose to discount the value of Freud's book, owing to its radical Jewishness and its attack upon the historic figure of Judaism itself, Bakan believes that Freud was at his

Jewish best when writing this book, attempting to vindicate his own work by comparing it to the Jewish struggles implicit in the story of Moses, who may or may not have been Jewish!

****

Modern psychoanalysis plays a "religious" role in people's lives, especially with respect to their "sins" as sins are defined by the Mosaic code. The deepest violations of the Mosaic code -- aggression, murder, sexuality, incest, etc., --- are the very subject matter of psychoanalysis. The psychoanalyst stands first as a representative of the superego, as Freud so well recognized when he discussed the transference relationship; and second as a non-punishing superego. In the course of psychoanalysis the patient learns that the expected punishment will not materialize. The transference is essential; for unless the patient identifies the figure of the psychoanalyst with the superego, then the permissiveness is essentially ineffectual. The psychoanalyst listens to the patient's discussion of his deepest "sins" and does not blame. As a matter of fact, if there is any blame which is implicitly or explicitly contained within the psychoanalytic mood, it is directed against the patents of the patient in their treatment of him when he was an infant and a child. The psychoanalyst presents himself as a better parent, in the patient's struggle with the "other" parent.

That psychoanalysis has filled the need which the fall of religion has left is Bakan's argument in reading Freud, for Freud was fixated upon expunging "sin" from the mentally ill patient. Therapy is designed to remove the sin which religion has fostered within the consciousness of the reflective person. Whereas God promises punishment for disobedience and his clergy fulfill that role in dealing with religious adherents, Freud suggests that the psychoanalyst assumes the role of the superego (in place of God and his clergy) but with a difference; the psychoanalytic superego forgives and permits sin rather than condemns it; forgives the individual's weaknesses and encourages the individual on toward maturity and responsibility rather than what the clergy do on behalf of the God-superego who condemns, punishes, and demands retribution for such sins.

****

Freud's whole effort at the creation of psychoanalysis may be viewed as Messianic in this respect. The aim of psychoanalytic thought is the production of greater freedom for the individual, releasing him from the tyranny of the unconscious, which is, in Freud's view, the result of social oppression. That psychoanalysis should have grown up in the context of the healing of the sick who were incurable by orthodox medical means accords with the Messianic quality of the psychoanalytic movement. For Messianism characteristically proves itself first by miraculously healing the sick. Thereafter it reaches out to large-scale social reform. So Freud's psychoanalysis reached out from the healing of individuals to the healing of society.

Freud suggests that not only is psychoanalysis the best substitute for religion and fulfills the role of the superego, which is forgiving and empowering, but psychoanalysis also fulfills the role of the Messiah (in the Jewish and Christian traditions) in that the Messianic role of psychoanalysis is to heal the individual and thereby heal society at large. This Messianic role of psychoanalysis is that of bringing the good news of forgiveness and empowerment, maturity and responsibility, without the condemnation and damnation of the religious establishment.

****

PART FOUR THE DEVIL AS SUSPENDED SUPEREGO

Freud made contact with the Jewish mystical tradition as it was part and parcel of his personality and culture. The problem of how the transition was effected, what the dynamics involved were, is still an open one. It is of course axiomatic that each person draws upon his culture for the determination of his social role. But in the case of an individual who has one foot in one culture and the other foot in another culture the problem of why he should put his weight on one foot rather than the other does not submit to solution very readily. And even if we accept a simpler idea of cultural determination, we have still to decide on the factors which make for the particular adaptation of the cultural elements.

Bakan is consistent to a fault in reminding us of the actual absence of any verifiable proof of this connection between the origins of psychoanalysis and Jewish mysticism in the thought of Freud. Bakan contends as both anthropologist and psychologist that Freud, being a member of two cultures concurrently -- Jewish and Austrian/Gentile -- that it was inevitable that he should draw from each in the formation of his theoretical constructs. That he was a Jewish psychiatrist living and working in Gentile Vienna inevitably presented him with materials from each culture relevant to the development of his own system of thought. That he did not, by choice or oversight, choose to identify the sources of his thought is understandable, given the complex situation in which he lived and practiced his profession.

****

The Jewish mystical tradition has always maintained that mystical concerns are properly reserved for later life. The reason for this is that if the person is too young he will misunderstand what he learns and will fall into infidelity. ... There is some tradition that the year of transition is thirty-six. It was in his thirty-sixth year that the Baal Shem Tov is said to have revealed himself to the world. And it is about this time that Freud begins to show himself to the world, emerging from the “latency” of his previous years. Freud completed his thirty-sixth year on May 6, 1982. That the significance of the thirty-sixth year may not have been completely lost to Freud is indicated by the gift his father gave him on his thirty-fifth birthday, I.e., the beginning of his thirty-sixth year -- the Bible Freud had studied in his youth.

Bakan has ventured here, surprisingly, to recount a Jewish

mystical tradition regarding the number 36, the age when men become susceptible to the inner stirrings of the spiritual life. It happened to the Baal Shem Tov at age 36 and it seemed to have happened to Freud at age 36 as well. That Bakan would resort to employing such a story to attempt to validate his carefully- argued position regarding the origins of Freud's theories is surprisingly Jewish itself. It was the Bible of Freud's youth, which Freud's father gave him on his 36th birthday. This, Bakan would have us believe, was relevant to Freud's new self-understanding. Freud never mentioned it.

****

During this transition period Freud seems to have moved very quickly in his medical practice from the role of physician to "healer." He soon abandoned the traditional methods of the physician and turned to the time-honored devices of the "healer," suggestion and hypnosis. One of the most significant of Freud's therapeutic discoveries was the transference. Freud recognized in the deeply affective involvement of the patient with the therapist a major vehicle for the cure of the patient. The phenomenon of the transference had caused Breuer to hesitate. Yet Freud had within his personality the means to cope with and control its consequences. Perhaps it was his apparently excellent marital relationship that made the temptation of sex relations so remote that it was essentially an impersonal event as far as his own libidinous experiences were concerned. Furthermore, his desire to play magician, or healer, or Devil may have made mastery of the transference phenomenon positively rewarding.

The significance in terms of the history of psychoanalysis of Freud turning 36 years of age and its relationship to the Baal Shem Tov is that from about this time in Freud's practice he moved conspicuously away from his role as a physician and medical practitioner and became quite decidedly a therapist or "healer" in the more traditional Jewish sense of rabbinic counseling. It was during this transition that he hit upon what was to become one of the building blocks of psychoanalytic theory, namely, the concept of the "transference," the shifting of the patient's love and attention on to the therapist. This phenomenon, Freud argued, was crucial to the healing process, and its recognition was necessary in order for therapy to proceed to a fruitful and happy conclusion.

****

In the transference relationship Freud discovered that which he had yearned for in his earlier years, "a master key to open with ease all female hearts," and he no longer stood ""helpless at the strange design of the lock," forced to "torment" himself "to discover a suitable key to it." ... The "magic" involved was one of the features of classical magic, the trick or art of making people fall in love. By turning this magic into a therapeutic device Freud made one of the great contributions to modern knowledge.

The magic key of Jewish mystical thought was, for Freud, found in the discovery of "transference" in the therapeutic relationship. This hermeneutical mechanism became the tool Freud insisted upon using in ferreting out the cause of mental illness. Every patient must succumb to the trials of transference in order to move on towards emotional health and personal maturity.

****

PART FIVE PSYCHOANALYSIS AND KABBALA

Despite the similarities of psychoanalysis to Kabbala as a doctrine and method, we are unable to hypothesize that Freud actually read in Kabbalistic literature. The point is actually a minor one. The Kabbalistic spirit pervaded the culture out of which Freud arises. This much is evident: Freud was opened up to Kabbalistic feelings within himself, and this may be a sufficient explanation of the close similarities. ... What Freud was, of course, demonstrating with the lengthy scholar section of *The Interpretation of Dreams* was that he was capable of that kind of disciplined scholarship. ... Generally speaking, there are two principal areas in which Kabbala and psychoanalysis show striking similarity: techniques of interpretation and the importance and meaning attached to sexuality.

Bakan, even at the end of the book, was still insisting that though there is no record of Freud ever actually reading the Kabbalistic literature, there is every evidence in his psychological writings of the sensitivities and insights which the Kabbalistic literature fosters. Freud could not have grown up in an Hasidic milieu without at some point or another, in some fashion or another, having been exposed to the stories of the Baal Shem Tov, the writings of the Kabbala, and the book of the *Zohar*. Did Bakan prove it? No. Could his argument be disproven? No. He made the case and the case stands unchallenged, though still unproven.

****

CHAPTER TEN

Abraham Maslow and *Religion, Values, and Peak-Experiences*

With Bakan's analysis of Freud having precipitated a raging national debate, the stage was set for a frontal attack upon the institution of religion itself, an attack which simultaneously condemned the institutionalization of religion while affirming the efficacy of the religious experience. That task was eagerly embraced by Abraham Harold Maslow (1908 - 1970). Maslow was born in Brooklyn, New York, the first of seven children, to parents who were uneducated Jews from Russia. Because he was intellectually gifted, he distinguished himself at the Brooklyn Borough High School. His father's ambition for him to study law lasted only a few weeks at the City College of New York and, after transferring to Cornell for a few courses, Maslow returned to CCNY but failed to complete his degree. Maslow married his high school sweetheart when he was 20 and his bride 19. He then applied to and was accepted at the University of Wisconsin, where he earned his B.A. in 1930, his M.A. in 1931, and his Ph.D. in 1934, all in psychology. After serving on the Wisconsin faculty as Assistant Instructor in Psychology (1930-1934) and Teaching Fellow in Psychology (1934-1935), Maslow was back in New York at Teacher's College, Columbia University, where he became interested specifically in research on human sexuality. At Columbia, he served as a Carnegie Fellow from 1935-1937. Unlike Freud, Jung, and Adler, Maslow was disinclined to focus his attention and research upon the mentally ill, preferring to study why and how people are mentally healthy, happy, and fulfilled. Eventually, he would develop a whole psychodynamic schema of theoretical constructs and a conceptual framework called the "hierarchy of needs." From 1951 to 1969, he taught at Brandeis University where he developed the concept of "self-actualization." Maslow was elected president of the American Psychological Association and became the founding editor of both the *Journal of Humanistic Psychology* and the *Journal of Transpersonal Psychology*. The recognized head of what became known as the Third Force in psychology, that is, the humanistic school *vis a vis*

Freudian psychology and behaviorism, Maslow ended his teaching carrier as the first Resident Fellow of the W. P. Laughlin Charitable Foundation in Menlo Park, where he died on the 8th of June, 1970, at the age of sixty-two.

Not religion itself but the institutionalization of religion, rather than the experience and value of religious sentiment, was the victim of Maslow's systematic dissection. Maslow contended unabashedly that "man has a higher and transcendent nature, and," he pointed out, "this is part of his essence," even suggesting that it is actually part of his biological nature as a member of a species which has evolved through history. The book which made it all come together was his 1970 *Religions, Values, and Peak-Experiences,* published by Penguin of New York. Maslow's criticism suggested that the institutionalization of religious experience had cost the individual severely. An instant bestseller, Maslow's opening statement set the tone for the whole book: "Organized Religion, the churches, finally may become the major enemies of the religious experience and the religious experiencer. This is a main thesis of this book" (1970:4). Whereas David Roberts had attempted to show how psychotherapy and Christian theology could compliment each other, and Allport had argued for the "value" of religious experience, whether true or not, and whereas Bakan had shown the influence of Hasidic mysticism upon the theories of Freud's psychoanalysis, Maslow was the first of the leading psychologists to frontally attack "organized religion" itself, and he did it by simultaneously affirming and vindicating the meaning and value of the religious experience as valid and true for the individual. This was transformative in the field of psychology, for now the science was able to demonstrate a capacity at social criticism without posturing as an atheistic endeavor designed to dislodge religion from the individual. Rather, it was a demonstration of how the institutions of religion could meaningfully and effectively be dislodged from the authentic religious experience itself. This Maslow did in his *Religions, Values, and Peak-Experiences,* thereby empowering both the science of psychology to proceed with its analytical agenda as well as validating and authenticating members of society who thought of themselves as "spiritual" without being "religious." His two previous books, *Toward a Psychology of*

Being (1962) and *The Psychology of Science: A Reconnaissance* (1966) set the scholarly standard for the writing of this book on religious values. His final work, *The Farther Reaches of Human Nature* (1971) assured Maslow of a place in the history of psychology. Today, the whole secular spirituality movement of individuals who seek to affirm and nurture their feelings of spirituality while denying any attraction for or subjectivity to religious institutions is in line with Maslovian psychology. Spirituality without the church, synagogue, or mosque was what came out of Maslow's analysis, and that sentiment still persists throughout modern western society today.

Selections from *Religions, Values, and Peak-Experiences,* by Abraham Maslow, with commentary.

NOTE: In the following, the original text will be printed in *Arial Unicode MS* typestyle (as is this note itself to illustrate) as an easy and aesthetically pleasing way of identifying the primary source paragraphs. The author's commentary will be in *Times New Roman.* It is hoped that this differentiation between the "primary source" and the "commentary" made by use of differing typestyles will prove helpful and not disruptive to the reader. *I have also chosen to use a quadruple asterisk (****) to separate the primary text from the commentary.*

CHAPTER ONE INTRODUCTION

I am very much in favor of a clear separation of church and state … I want to demonstrate that spiritual values have naturalistic meaning, that they are not the exclusive possession of organized churches, that they do not need supernatural concepts to validate them, that they are well within the jurisdiction of a suitably enlarged science, and that, therefore, they are the general responsibility of *all* mankind. If all of this is so, then we shall have to re-evaluate the possible place of spiritual and moral values in education. For, if these values are not exclusively identified with churches, then teaching values in the schools need not breach the wall between church and state. The Supreme Court decisions on prayer in the public schools were seen (mistakenly, as we shall see) by many Americans as a rejection of spiritual values in education. Much of the turmoil was in defense of these higher values and eternal verities rather than of the prayers as such.

In the work of Abraham Maslow, the psychology of religion comes into its own, for he, more than others before him, had a gift of taking the best from the best and combining it into a system of analysis, making the combination greater than any one of its parts. Sympathetic but not susceptible to the religious urges of the common person, Maslow showed in his work that those urges are legitimate and real and can be addressed and nurtured without requiring an allegiance to a religious faith tradition, a church, or synagogue, with its religious leaders seeking to dominate and exercise power over an individual's authentic feelings regarding the transcendent reality of life. A strong supporter of the separation of Church and State, Maslow did not believe in the separation of the emotional feelings of awe, wonder, and mystery from science. In his system, religion and science go hand-in-hand even though religious establishments and science do not and cannot. The spirituality of the human person is not, must not be, defined by his allegiance to a faith community, for both feelings of transcendent reality and spirituality are and must be exercised outside the perimeters of institutional controls put in place by religious leaders.

****

Very many people in our society apparently see organized religion as *the* locus, *the* source, *the* custodian and guardian and teacher of the spiritual life. Its methods, its style of teaching, its content are widely and officially accepted as *the* path, by many as the *only* path, to the life of righteousness, of purity and virtue, of justice and goodness, etc. This is also true, paradoxically enough, for many orthodoxy positivistic scientists, philosophers, and other intellectuals. Pious positivists as a group accept the same strict dichotomizing of facts and values that the professional religionists do. Since they exclude values from the realm of science and from the realm of exact, rational, positivistic knowledge, all values are turned over by default to non-scientists and to non-rationalists (I.e., to "non-knowers") to deal with.

Maslow challenges the religious population who presume that only within the confines (and confinements) of religious institutions can the spiritual life of individuals live and grow. More disturbing even than that imperialistic position, Maslow believes that the non-religious community has regrettably reconciled itself to relinquishing any rights to value-speaking to the self-styled religious establishment, thereby divesting itself of both its right and responsibility to address issues of value and ethics within its own arena of work. This divestment of responsibility for dealing with spiritual and value issues on the part of the non-religious establishment to the religious establishment is the great tragedy facing modern society today. Religious institutions are quite pleased with the relinquishment of oversight regarding values and spirituality by the non-religious community, thereby, by default, investing in the religious establishment sole authority in matters of values and ethics, spirituality, and authentic feelings of transcendence. The religious right today exercises an unchallenged sense of entitlement to moral pontification, while the secular left stands impotent to either defend or assert itself.

****

Something of this sort is certainly true for many psychologists and many educators. It is almost *Universally* true for the positivistic psychologists, the behaviorists, the neo-behaviorists, and the ultra-experimentalists, all of whom feel values and the life of value to be none of their professional concern, and who casually renounce all consideration of poetry and art and of any of the religious or transcendent experiences. Indeed, the pure positivist rejects any inner experiences of *any* kind as being "unscientific," as not in the realm of human knowledge, as not susceptible of study by a scientific method, because such data are not objective, that is to say, public and shared.

The divestiture of responsibility (and accountability) in matters regarding values and ethics, within the psychological community specifically, and the scientific community generally, is a cause of great concern, explains Maslow. Though religious institutions and traditions do not have a right to exclusive dominion in matters of values and ethics, they have assumed such a role and the scientific community has easily permitted it without protestations. Value-free education is a contradiction in terms, explains Maslow, and to allow the religious community to assume full responsibility for value education is a travesty, and ultimately an abiding danger to the well-being of society. The ignoring of or even the abandoning of the legitimate and authentic experiences of awe, wonder, and mystery on the part of the educational and scientific community has left the religious establishment in complete control of defining and monitoring what it has chosen to call ethical and moral, using its own confining and restricting definitions set by theologians and religious leaders. The discounting, by default, of true inner experience of spiritual value has left society having to choose between conforming to religious mandates or to a one-dimensionality to personal experience. To say that spiritual feelings are either the domain of the church, or that they do not exist is a failure of leadership on the part of the education establishment, says Maslow.

****

The other dominating theory of psychology, the Freudian, coming from a very different compass direction winds up at a similar terminus, denying that it has anything much to do with spiritual or ethical values. Freud himself and H. Hartman after him say something like this: "The only goal of the psychoanalytic method is to undo repressions and all other defenses against seeing unpleasant truth; it has nothing to do with ideologies, indoctrinations, religious dogmas or teaching of a way of life or system of values." And so official, orthodox, Freudian psychoanalysis remains essentially a system of psychopathology and of cure of psychopathology. It does not supply us with a psychology of the higher life or of the "spiritual life," of what the human being should grow *toward,* of what he can become (although I believe psychoanalytic method and theory is a necessary substructure for any such "higher" or growth psychology. Freud came out of nineteenth-century, mechanistic, physical-chemical, reductionistic science; and there his more Talmudic followers remain, at least with respect to the theory of values and everything that has to do with values.

Representing the Third Force school in psychology, i.e., the humanistic school of thought within psychotherapy, Maslow is critical of Freud and the psychoanalysts who have totally abdicated responsibility for either nurturing authentic spirituality within an individual or providing counsel and guidance in matters of values and ethics. Moral behavior falls outside their domain, as Freud would say. Not condemning Freud outright for abdication of leadership responsibilities in this arena, Maslow believes that the substructure of psychoanalysis carries within it the components needed to foster a legitimizing sense of personal spirituality, influenced, as Bakan would agree, by the Talmud and Kabbala of Freud's upbringing.

****

This reductionism goes so far sometimes that the Freudians seem almost to say that the "higher life" is just a set of "defenses against the instincts," especially denial and reaction-formation. Were it not for the concept of sublimation, that is what they would have to be saying. Unfortunately, sublimation is so weak and unsatisfactory a concept that it simply cannot bear this huge responsibility. Thus, psychoanalysis often comes perilously close to being a nihilistic and value-denying philosophy of man.

Not ready to exonerate the Freudians, nor even to let them off lightly for having abandoned what is rightfully their domain, viz., the raising of human life to a higher level of spiritual maturity, Maslow is tempted to dismiss the supposed "sublimation" phenomenon of psychoanalysis, for there in lies the justification for their willingness to relinquish ethical counsel to the mentally disturbed and troubled.

****

Neither are the humanistic scholars and artists of any great help these days. They used to be, and were supposed to be, as a group, carriers of and teachers of the eternal verities and the higher life. The goal of humanistic studies was defined as the perception and knowledge of the good, the beautiful, and the true. Such studies were expected to refine the discrimination between what is excellent and what is not (excellence generally being understood to be the true, the good, and the beautiful). They were supposed to inspire the student to the better life, to the higher life, to goodness and virtue. What was truly valuable, Matthew Arnold said, was "the acquainting ourselves with the best that has been known and said in the world." And no one disagreed with him. Nor did it need to be spelled out that he meant knowledge of the classics; these were the universally accepted models.

Not one to just castigate the opposition in psychiatric and psychotherapeutic practice, Maslow turns on his own kind, the humanistic school known as the Third Force, by charging them with a too ready willingness to divest themselves of moral responsibility in counseling the spiritually deprived. Humanists of all varieties have historically been both charged with the responsibility and capable of assuming that charge to teach the value of the true, the good, and the beautiful, and to do so without apology. It was assumed, it was expected, it was, in a word, demanded of society that those in leadership roles embracing the highest expressions of human culture were themselves charged with the responsibility and, indeed, obligation of passing that appreciation of the finer things of life along to subsequent generations. It truly went without saying in earlier times, but, laments Maslow, we can no longer make that assumption.

****

We can no longer rely on tradition, on consensus, on cultural habit, on unanimity of belief to give us our values. These agreed-upon traditions are all gone. Of course, we never should have rested on tradition -- as its failures must have proven to everyone by now -- it never was a firm foundation. It was destroyed too easily by truth, by honesty, by the facts, by science, by simple, pragmatic, historical failure. Only truth itself can be our foundation, our base for building. Only empirical, naturalistic knowledge, in its broadest sense, can serve us now.

But, complains Maslow, those blissful days are gone. Tradition was not a solid foundation, for much of what was held "by tradition" was not true, was blatantly false, and/or was perpetrated by religious leaders who aspired, more than anything, to exercise power and jurisdiction over the lives and thoughts of the broader society. Assuming themselves to be the arbiters and purveyors of truth, goodness, and beauty, they spoiled everything they touched -- they corrupted the truth with doctrines, they replaced goodness with fascist directives, and corrupted beauty with images of their own demented worldview. But now, says Maslow, the truth is out. Science has come, and come to stay. It has taken up residence in the house that tradition built and religion managed, and is now in charge.

****

CHAPTER TWO
DICHOTOMIZED SCIENCE AND DICHOTOMIZED RELIGION

My thesis is, in general, that new developments in psychology are forcing a profound change in our philosophy of science, a change so extensive that we may be able to accept the basic religious questions as a proper part of the jurisdiction of science, once science is broadened and redefined. It is because both science and religion have been too narrowly conceived, and have been too exclusively dichotomized and separated from each other, that they have been seen to be two mutually exclusive worlds. To put it briefly, this separation permitted nineteenth-century science to become too exclusively mechanistic, too positivistic, too reductionistic, too desparately attempting to be value-free. It mistakenly conceived of itself as having nothing to say about ends or ultimate values or spiritual values.

Maslow is, at the end of the day, optimistic. A Jewish psychologist with hope is a refreshing sight, and Maslow is just the fellow to fill that role. The dismantling of our modern tendency to dichotomize science and religion has led to the present miserable state of non- and mis-communication between the two schools of thought. It is religion that is of interest to true science, not religious institutions, not churches, not synagogues, not colleges of theologians arguing over man-made doctrines about this and that belief. Religious sentiment is real, Maslow proposes, for the sense of awe, wonder, and mystery is endemic to the human experience and human consciousness. A mature science, a science fully cognizant of its social responsibilities, is a science that is eager to embrace these fundamentally human characteristics, needs, and aspirations. In the 19th century, science was eager to move forward, and saw religion (defined almost exclusively as "the church") as a restraint, a deterrent, a block to scientific research. And, thus, mistaken, science chose to turn its back on its rightful duty in dealing with values and ethics, morals and conduct. The time has come for science to reclaim its rightful place in this regard.

****

This dichotomizing of knowledge and values has also pathologized the organized religions by cutting them off from facts, from knowledge, from science, even to the point of often making them the enemies of scientific knowledge. In effect, it tempts them to say that they have nothing more to learn. But something is happening now to both science and religion, at least to their more intelligent and sophisticated representatives. These changes make possible a very different attitude by the less narrow scientist toward the religious questions, at least to the naturalistic, humanistic, religious questions. It might be said that this is simply one more instance of what has happened so often in the past, I.e., of snatching away another territory from the jurisdiction of organized religion.

The unanticipated and tragic cost of the 19th century scientific abandonment of morals and ethics, of values in education, was the setting free of religious ideologies from the truths being daily discovered by the sciences. When religion and its institutions and spokespersons were set free from accountability in addressing the truths being revealed daily in the science laboratories of the world, religion was left to its own devices, without science, without access to verifiable facts. Religion then became its own validation, without science, without authentication, and thus, "mystery" because the stock in trade answer when religious ideologies were questioned, when asked for explanations. Religion was a mystery and, therefore, beyond and outside the domain of scientific enquiry and investigation. The price has been severe for all of society as a result.

****

This relation between religion and science could be stated in such a dichotomous, competitive way, but I think I can show that it need not be, and that the person who is deeply religious -- in a particular sense that I shall discuss -- must rather feel strengthened and encouraged by the prospect that his value questions may be more firmly answered than ever before. Sooner or later, we shall have to redefine both religion and science.

Ever the optimist in believing that truth will eventually prevail and that the human community is able to handle the truth, Maslow looks to a promising day of convergent realities where religion (not the church or its establishments), as the purveyor of the human emotions of awe, wonder, and mystery, can hold hands with science (not the positivists who dismiss the legitimacy of these human emotions), as the purveyor of demonstrable truth, verifiable facts, and validation of authentic human experiences of spiritual encounter with transcendent reality, a reality that does not require or demand a deity from "outside" the universe but a transcendent sense of the greater depth and height of human experience in confronting the great wonders and mysteries of the physical universe.

****

When all that could be called "religious" (naturalistically as well as super naturalistically) was cut away from science, from knowledge, from further discovery, from the possibility of skeptical investigation, from confirming and disconfirming, and, therefore, from the possibility of purifying and improving, such a dichotomized religion was doomed. It tended to claim that the founding revelation was complete, perfect, final, and eternal. It had the truth, the whole truth, and had nothing more to learn, thereby being pushed into the position that has destroyed so many churches, of resisting change, of being *only* conservative, of being anti-intellectual and anti-scientific, of making piety and obedience exclusive of skeptical intellectuality -- in effect, of contradicting naturalistic truth.

The decline, the inevitable and long-awaited decline of religious establishmentarianism is predicated upon the dominance of scientifically-verified human experiences of awe, wonder, and mystery, experiences not the domain of churches or synagogues or faith communities touting religious ideologies requiring compliance and obedience at the peril of one's everlasting soul. Religion of this kind with its institutional forms, is doomed in the face of a scientific understanding of the nature of human experience, human personality, human needs and the value of each in relationship to our understanding the universe in which we live. True science validates true religion, for true religion is the purveyor of authentic human experience of awe, wonder, and mystery (devoid of the necessity of a deity found outside the universe as institutionalized forms of religious expression demand and promote). These human experiences are validated by science -- awe, wonder, mystery -- and they are the true expressions of an authentic religious encounter with the universe. This is true religion, and true science.

****

We have seen often enough throughout history the church whose pieties are mouthed in the middle of human exploitation and degradation as if the one had nothing to do with the other ("Render unto Caesar that which is Caesar's"). this pie-in-the-sky kind of religion, which often enough has turned into an actual *support* of daily evil, is almost inevitable when the existence has no intrinsic and constant connection with the ideal, when heaven is off some place far away from the earth, when human improvement becomes impossible in the world but can be achieved only by renouncing the world. "For endeavor for the better is moved by faith in what is possible, not by adherence to the actual," as John Dewey pointed out.

Maslow is ruthlessly honest in assailing religious establishmentarianism, a religious institutionalization that is self-promoting and self-serving, that seeks to dominate the human will by demanding compliance with an ideology constructed precisely to stifle human enquiry, human initiative, human creativity. This kind of religion is to be denied, denounced, and destroyed, with a science of human emotions which values enquiry, initiative, and creativity.

****

But what the more sophisticated scientist is now in the process of learning is that though he must disagree with most of the answers to the religious questions which have been given by organized religion, it is increasingly clear that the religious questions themselves -- and religious questions, the religious yearnings, the religious needs themselves -- are perfectly respectable scientifically, that they are rooted deep in human nature, that they can be studied, described, examined in a scientific way, and that the churches were trying to censor perfectly sound human questions. Though the answers were not acceptable, the questions themselves were and are perfectly acceptable, and perfectly legitimate. As a matter of fact, contemporary existential and humanistic psychologists would probably consider a person sick or abnormal in an existential way if he were NOT concerned with these "religious" questions.

This posture of Maslow's is precisely what the scientific community needed in facing the criticism of the religious establishment, for the defensive or dismissive science of the past failed to address the legitimacy of human emotions, and all of the weight was on the side of religion. Unfortunately, those defending religion were the purveyors of religious establishmentarianism, a religious entity built upon the foundation of ideology and the exercise of power. With the coming of Maslow and his re-definition of religion (rather than religious institutions and ideologies) as fully authentic expressions of human emotions, true science, a science of accountability and responsibility, was now in a position to respond positively to an encounter, a convergence of interests.

****

CHAPTER THREE THE "CORE-RELIGIOUS," OR "TRANSCENCENT," EXPERIENCE

The very beginning, the intrinsic core, the essence, the universal nucleus of every known high religion (unless Confuciainism is also called a religion) has been the private, lonely, personal illumination, revelation, or ecstasy of some acutely sensitive prophet or seer. The high religions call themselves revealed religions and each of them tends to rest its validity, its function, and its right to exist on the codification and the communication of this original mystic experience or revelation from the lonely prophet to the mass of human beings in general. But it has recently begun to appear that these "revelations" or mystical illuminations can be subsumed under the heading of the "peak-experiences" or "ecstasies" or "transcendent" experiences which are now being eagerly investigated by many psychologists.

In demonstrating the effectiveness of psychological enquiry into religious experience and behavior, Maslow was eager to promote the notion of a core experience which embodied a sense of the transcendent. Though all great religions of the world are adhered to by large masses of people, the core experience was that of a single individual, a person who had a peak experience which gave rise to a deepening understanding of the world and our relationship to it. And, within each of these great religions, there are individuals who also have these peak experiences. These experiences constitute data worthy of and accessible to investigation and study. This is where the psychologist, says Maslow, can provide a great service to both religion and science.

****

In a word, we can study today what happened in the past and was then explainable in supernatural terms only. By so doing, we are enabled to examine religion in all its facets and in all its meanings in a way that makes it a part of science rather than something outside and exclusive of it. Also this kind of study leads us to another very plausible hypothesis: to the extent that all mystical or peak-experiences are the same in their essence and have always been the same, all religions are the same in their essence and always have been the same. They should, therefore, come to agree in principle on teaching that which is common to all of them, I.e., whatever it is that peak-experiences teach in common.

With this scientifically sympathetic approach to religious data provided by the founders and their mystical followers involving the peak experience of transcendence, Maslow believes that the research psychologist can come to a better and deeper understanding of the meaning and nature of religious experience. Furthermore, if, as expected, these data all reflect upon and refer to a single reality of transcendence, then the commonality of all religions can be affirmed and confirmed. This, in a sense, is the first example in the psychology of religion of a research psychologist proposing a kind of an *ecumenical psychology of religion*, wherein all religions converge into one reality.

****

Much theology, much verbal religion through history and throughout the world, can be considered to be the more or less vain efforts to put into communicable words and formulae, and into symbolic rituals and ceremonies, the original mystical experience of the original prophets. In a word, organized religion can be thought of as an effort to communicate peak-experiences to non-peakers, to teach them, to apply them, etc. Often, to make it more difficult, this job falls into the hands of non-peakers. On the whole we now would expect that this would be a vain effort, at least so far as much of mankind is concerned. The peak-experiences and their experiential reality ordinarily are not transmittable to non-peakers, at lest not by words alone, and certainly not by non-peakers.

Maslow's brilliance in his assessment of religious ideologies and institutions is no more clear in evidence than in his characterization of the theological enterprise of established religions. Theology, at the end of the day, is an attempt on the part of religious leaders to verbalize the nature of the formative experience (peak) of the founder of the religious system to those who have not had and/or will not have such a peak experience. And, to make matters more difficult, if not worse, the theologians themselves are too often members of that group of religious followers who have not had the peak experience themselves. It is like having someone who has never tasted ice cream trying to explain what ice cream tastes like to someone else who has also not tasted ice cream. It cannot really be done effectively, no matter the sincerity or genuineness of the effort.

****

To summarize, it looks quite probable that the peak-experience may be the model of the religious revelation or the religious illumination or conversion which has played so great a role in the history of religions. But, because peak-experiences are in the natural world and because we can research with them and investigate them, and because our knowledge of such experiences is growing and may be confidently expected to grow in the future, we may now fairly hope to understand more about the big revelations, conversions, and illuminations upon which the high religions were founded.

Maslow would have us understand that as we come to a greater understanding of the nature and function of the peak experience in religious encounters by not only the founders of the great religions but those of a mystical bent who take up the peak experience as their own reality, we can anticipate growing in our understanding of this experience, its commonality among all religions, and how it functions in human growth and development. Diverting our attention from the non-peakers (!) such as theologians and religious establishment leaders and directing our attention to those who have had the peak experience, we are closer to the real thing. Though this may not please the non-peaking administrators of religious institutions, it may very well serve to better understand the true nature of religious experience.

****

To approach this whole discussion from another angle, in effect what I have been saying is that the evidence from the peak-experiences permits us to talk about the essential, the intrinsic, the basic, the most fundamental religious or transcendent experience as a totally private and personal one which can hardly be shared (except with other "peakers"). As a consequent, all the paraphernalia of organized religion -- buildings and specialized personnel, rituals, dogmas, ceremonials, and the like -- are to the "peaker" secondary, peripheral, and of doubtful value in relation to the intrinsic and essential religious or transcendent experience.

Maslow is blatantly dismissive of the non-peak paraphernalia used by non-peakers to perpetuate the religions which have, as a matter of fact, been created and established by those who have had the peak experience. The motivation of the non-peakers to perpetuate a religion of which they themselves had not had the core experience is an interesting phenomenon within itself, and may draw in sociologists and anthropologists, as well as psychopathologists, in attempting to understand who these non-peakers really are and what is their motivation. To have had the core experience is sufficient grounds to justify the perpetuation of the experience, but for non-core experiencers to take up the cause constitutes another study all together.

****

CHAPTER FOUR ORGANIZATIONAL DANGERS TO TRANSCENDENT EXPERIENCES

It has sometimes seemed to me as I interviewed "non-theistic religious people" that they had *more* religious (or transcendent) experiences than conventionally religious people. (This is, so far, only an impression but it would obviously be a worthwhile research project.) Partly this may have been because they were more often "serious" about values, ethics, life-philosophy, because they have had to struggle away from conventional beliefs and have had to create a system of faith for themselves individually.

The observation by Maslow that in his own research he has found that often the non-religious person proves, at the end of the day, to actually be more religious than the purported religious person is quite a profound insight into the nature of religious identity, affiliation, and function. Allport, as we have seen earlier, spent a great deal of time identifying those central characteristics of religious people, finding often that what motivated them were social and personality issues rather more than specifically religious feelings. Maslow pushes this insight further in his own work. A person who is particularly responsive and susceptible to transcendent feelings of awe, wonder, and mystery, but who finds that institutional expressions of religious feelings are rather outside their field of interest may, says Maslow, have been forced into a deeper cognizance of their own religious experience owing to this non-institutional affiliation. They have been forced to become more intentional in their religious understandings of the world and their experience in the absence of religious institutions which often tout pre-set explanations to confirm their authenticity.

****

The reason I now bring up this impression (which may or may not be validated, may or may not be simply a sampling error, etc.) is that it brought me to the realization that for most people a conventional religion, while strongly religionizes one part of life, thereby also strongly "de-religionizes" the rest of life. The experiences of the holy, the sacred, the divine, of awe, of creatureliness, of surrender, of mystery, of piety, thanksgiving, gratitude, self-dedication, if they happen at all, tend to be confined to a single day of the week, to happen under one roof only of one kind of structure only, under certain triggering circumstances only, to rest heavily on the presence of certain traditional, powerful, but intrinsically irrelevant, stimuli, e.g., organ music, incense, chanting of a particular kind, certain regalia, and other arbitrary triggers. Being religious, or rather feeling religious, under these ecclesiastical auspices seems to absolve many (most?) people from the necessity or desire to feel these experiences at any other time. "Religionizing" only one part of life secularizes the rest of it.

Maslow's profoundly insightful understanding of the relationship between sacred and secular would be of great benefit to the sociologists of religion, like Peter Berger, in fully appreciating the dynamic nature of the relationship, within an individual, of these two components of life, viz., sacred and secular or, in Maslow's terms, religious and non-religious. Conspicuously religious people (individuals defining themselves and being defined by others as religious owing to their behavior in relationship to religious practices such as worship, etc.) are able to differentiate their religious life from their secular life in a way that non-conspicuously religious persons (individuals who have a deeply abiding sense of the spirituality of life and their relationship to it as experienced in awe, wonder, and mystery but decidedly not institutionally expressed by "going to church") are able to do. The former religious person knows when he is being religious and doing religious things -- going to church, etc. -- whereas the non-religious person, who is perpetually conscious of the spirituality of his life, does not. This is a profoundly insightful understanding.

****

This is in contrast with my impression that "serious" people of all kinds tend to be able to "religionize" *any* part of life, *any* day of the week, in *any* place, and under all sorts of circumstances, I.e., to be aware of Tillich's "dimension of depth." Of course, it would not occur to the more "serious" people who are non-theists to ut the label "religious experiences" on what they were feeling, or to use such words as "holy," "pious," "sacred," or the like. By my usage, however, they are often having "core-religious experiences" or transcendent experiences when they report having peak-experiences. In this sense, a sensitive, creative working artist I know who calls himself an agnostic could be said to be having many "religious experiences," and I am sure that he would agree with me if I asked him about it.

Maslow is joined by the Protestant liberal theologian of the 20th century, Paul Tillich, in disallowing non-religious persons from being atheists just because of an apparent inability to identify their core experiences as religious. If they sense the spirituality of the world, its depth of meaning, the validity of awe, wonder, and mystery, they are, by Maslow and Tillich's understanding, "religious" because they are having core or peak experiences of the meaning of life. These "non-religious" people are often more religious than the "religious" people who never have such core experiences.

****

Apparently it is one danger of the legalistic and organizational versions of religion that they may tend to suppress naturalistic peak-, transcendent, mystical, or other core-religious experiences and to make them less likely to occur, I.e., the degree of religious organization may correlate negatively with the frequency of "religious" experiences. Conventional religions may even be used as defenses against and resistances to the shaking experiences of transcendence.

As the Church did in the Middle Ages, mystics were often incarcerated (referred to as being put into monasteries and convents) because of the danger the core or peak-experiencers bring to the established religious traditions. There is little control or governance over these mystics whereas those who are religious without ever having had a core experience can be controlled quite easily by the "teachings and doctrines" of the Church, which are used by the establishmentarians as mechanisms of control.

****

There may also be another such inverse relationship -- between organizationism and religious transcendent experiencing -- at least for some people. (For however many this may be, it is a *possible* danger for all.) If we contrast the vivid, poignant, shaking, peak-experience type of religious or transcendent experience, which I have been describing, with the thoughtless, habitual, reflex-like, absent-minded, automatic responses which are dubbed "religious" by many people (only because they occur in familiar circumstances semantically labeled "religious"), then we are faced with a universal, "existential" problem. Familiarization and repetition produces a lowering of the intensity and richness of consciousness, even though it *also* produces preference, security, comfort, etc. familiarization, in a word, makes it unnecessary to attend, to think, to feel, to live fully, to experience richly. This is true not only in the realm of religion but also in the realms of music, art, architecture, patriotism, even in nature itself. ... Clearly the aim of education in this realm must be phrased in terms of inner, subjective experiences in each individual. Unless these experiences are known to have occurred, value-education cannot be said to have succeeded in reaching its true goal.

The danger of religious institutions is that they persist without the core experience! The same may be said of all social institutions, and the real danger in this phenomenon is the absence of the core experience which motivates the individual in the first place. Habit-forming religion is the worst kind, for it does not draw from the source of its strength, the core experience. The same is true of all expressions of creativity and understanding, and in the world of value-based education, the danger of rote learning of values rather than experiencing the core of moral guidance leads to a susceptibility to fascism, whether political or religious, blind obedience without the guiding experience of self-understanding.

****

CHAPTER FIVE HOPE, SKEPTICISM, AND MAN'S HIGHER NATURE

The point of view that is rapidly developing now -- that the highest spiritual values appear to have naturalistic sanctions and that supernatural sanctions for these values are, therefore, not necessary -- raises some questions which have not been raised before in quite this form. For instance, why were supernatural sanctions for goodness, altruism, virtue, and love necessary in the first place?

Maslow is asking questions in 1964 which have been substantially addressed in the 21st century by such thinkers/researchers as the famous Harvard sociobiologist, Edward O. Wilson. Julian Huxley, of course, addressed these earlier, but without the full benefit of DNA and James Watson's work. However, we do know that Maslow was then asking the right questions, namely, since there is an erosion of the security of religious dogmatism in the face of the advance of research science, why did these characteristics of human growth and development, both individually and socially, have to have religious approval and sanction back then now that we know they are endemic to human evolution. Whereas religious institutions and their establishmentarians would have us believe that these qualities of moral behavior were derived from an outside source, namely a transcendent God of the Bible, we now know that this is not so and that the human community, in the absence of any knowledge of such an outside deity, has developed the same moral understanding of human relationships.

****

One important characteristic of the new "third" psychology is its demonstration of man's "higher nature." As we look back through the religious conceptions of human nature -- and indeed we need not look back so very far because the same doctrine can be found in Freud -- it becomes crystal clear that any doctrine of the innate depravity of man or any maligning of his animal nature very easily leads to some extra-human interpretation of goodness, saintliness, virtue, self-sacrifice, altruism, etc. If they can't be explained from within human nature -- and explained they must be -- then they must be explained from outside of human nature. The worse man is, the poorer a thing he is conceived to be, the more necessary becomes a god. ... Explanation from the natural is more parsimonious and therefore more satisfying to educated people than is explanation from the supernatural.

An outspoken and well-respected proponent of the Third Force School of Psychology (behaviorism and psychoanalysis being the second and first type), Maslow contends rather persuasively that the doctrine of Original Sin is the culprit in demeaning our self-image. This Christian doctrine, a mainstay of the faith, teaches the total depravity of the human person. Our depravity is explained in the biblical story of the fall of Adam from the grace of God due to

Adam's disobedience brought on by the wife God himself gave Adam, namely, Eve. Because of this pervasive doctrine, coloring all of Christian theology and the western world's conception of humanity, the human community has paid a great price and continues to suffer considerably from its implications. This doctrine, more than any other, makes it absolutely necessary that there be a Loving God who forgives and redeems the depraved human community. This is a terrible state for modern society to imagine itself to be in, and the rise of modern science and the new psychology has come to exonerate and liberate society from this religious oppression.

****

The faith that ethical progress was an inevitable by-product of advances in knowledge of the natural world and in the technological by-products of these advances died with World War I, with Freud, with the depression, with the atom bomb. Perhaps even more shaking, certainly for the psychologist, has been the recent discovery that affluence itself throws into the clearest, coldest light the spiritual, ethical, philosophical hunger of mankind. This is so because striving for something one lacks inevitably makes one feel that a life has a meaning and that life is worthwhile. But when one lacks nothing, and has nothing to strive for, then ….")

If Freud is acclaimed to be the most insightful social critic of modern times as a psychotherapist, Maslow cannot be far behind, for Maslow has identified the core of our social malaise in the modern world. When once we had nothing except our belief in a better world, now we seem to have everything, except a belief in a better world. We are driven to get and hold and keep and hoard but to what end? Maslow would have us move towards seeking meaning akin to Viktor Frankl's "will to meaning." Maslow suggests that we are in a spiritual slump, a wasteland of possessions without meaning, world (for western modern man) of affluency without value.

****

Thus we have the peculiar situation in which many intellectuals today find themselves skeptical in every sense, but fully aware of the yearning for a faith or a belief of some kind and aware also of the terrible spiritual (and political) consequences when this yearning has no satisfaction. And so we have a new language to describe the situation, words like anomie, anaerobia, rootlessness, value pathology, meaninglessness, existential boredom, spiritual starvation, other-directedness, the neuroses of success, etc. Most psychotherapists would agree that a large proportion of the population of all affluent nations -- not only America -- are now caught in this situation of valuelessness, although most of these therapists are still speaking superficially and symptomatically of character neuroses, immaturity, juvenile delinquency, over-indulgences, etc.

Skepticism, cynicism, despair, have not, says Maslow, expunged our deeply abiding need for a spirituality of self and relationships. We have, as intellectuals are all prone to do, created a whole vocabulary of descriptive terms to characterize our present plight, our having everything while feeling as if we have nothing. That traditional religious institutions have now lost their attractiveness is confirmed by all statistical studies, but where to turn in a world of affluency yet full of spiritually starving people? Help, suggests Maslow, is on the way.

****

A new approach to psychotherapy, existential therapy, is evolving to meet this situation. But on the whole, since therapy is impracticable for mass purposes, most people simply stay caught in the situation and lead privately and publicly miserable lives. A small proportion "returns to traditional religion," although most observers agree that this return is not part to be deeply rooted. But some others, still a small proportion, are finding in newly available hints from psychology another possibility of a positive, naturalistic faith, a "common faith" as John Dewey called it, a "humanistic faith" as Erich Fromm called it, humanistic psychology as many others are now calling it.

The Third Force School of Psychology, in a word, is going to be the answer, a kind of psychology broadly defined and sensitive to the human eagerness for a spiritual depth to life's experiences. Religious institutions have failed in continuing ineffectively to promote their canned responses to deep and new questions about life and its meaning. A secular spirituality, one that values deeply the eagerness modern society feels for the nurture of awe, wonder, and mystery in their lives, seems to be on the horizon. A spirituality that does not deny the core of religious need and experience but which affirms and nurtures it -- feelings of creativity, initiative, justice, spirituality, beauty, etc., all bespeak a spiritual depth not dependent upon an external deity but reliant upon an appreciation for the endemic qualities of the human person. This seems to offer promise to the modern world.

****

CHAPTER SIX SCIENCE AND THE RELGIOUS LIBERALS AND NON-THEISTS

Nineteenth-century objectivistic, value-free science has finally proven to be also a poor foundation for the atheists, the agnostics, the rationalists, the humanists, and other non-theists, as well as for the "liberal" religionists, e.g., the Unitarians and the Universalists. Both of them, orthodox science and liberal and non-heuristic religion, leave out too much that is precious to most human beings. In their revolt against the organized, institutionalized churches, they have unwittingly accepted the immature and naive dichotomy between traditional religion (as the only carrier of values), on one hand, and, on the other, a totally mechanistic, reductionistic, objectivistic, neutral, value-free science. To this day, liberal religionists rest heavily, even exclusively, on the natural sciences which seem to them to be somehow more "scientific" than the psychological sciences upon which they should base themselves but which they use almost not at all (except in positivistic versions).

Modern liberal thinkers have fallen victim, says Maslow, to the baby-and-the-bath syndrome, having thrown over as ineffective and blatantly dysfunctional the institutional expressions of religious sensibilities, namely, the churches and their institutional cognates: Modern individuals have embraced a naturalistic science which provides answers to the functional questions of development and advancement but which has, unfortunately and unnecessarily, disregarded the spiritual depth of the human quest for meaning in the world. Science has the capacity, when employed within the context of a value-based agenda which values the "core" experiences of the human person encountering awe, wonder, and mystery to speak to our condition. Technology-driven science is good but it does not do the whole job -- it gets things done but does not nourish the soul (to use a phrase from Otto Rank). The modern person has fallen victim to a reductionistic perception of the benefits of science. To elevate science to a level of sensitivity to the hunger driving the human quest for meaning is what is called for now.

****

Like positivistic psychologists, they feel much more at home with the cognitive than they do with the emotional and the impulsive and volitional. They make no basic place in their systems for the mysterious, the unknown, the unknowable, the dangerous-to-know, or the ineffable. They pass by entirely the old, rich literature based on the mystical experiences. They have no systematic place for goals, ends, yearnings, aspirations, and hopes, let alone will or purpose. They don't know what to do with the experiential, the subjective, and the phenomenological that the existentialists stress so much, as do also the psychotherapists. The inexact, the illogical, the metaphorical, the mythic, the symbolic, the contradictory or conflicted, the ambiguous, the ambivalent are all considered to be "lower" or "not good," I.e., something to be "improved" toward pure rationality and logic.

Antiseptic is the term Maslow needs to describe what modern science has allowed itself to become. And it need not have done so, for a scientific understanding of the human personality will bring into play an appreciation for emotion, an appreciation for the depth of human experience of the good and the beautiful. The loss of spontaneity in human relationships and creative endeavors need not be lost in a scientific world. Rather, spontaneity needs to be fostered, nurtured, and encouraged.

****

This is also true for the experiences of surrender, of reverence, of devotion, of self-dedication, of humility and oblation, of awe and the feeling of smallness. These experiences, which organized religions have always tried to make possible, are also common enough in the peak-experiences ... including even impulses to kneeling, to prostration, and to something like worship. But these are all missing from the non-theisms and from the liberal theisms. This is of especial importance today because of the widespread "faultlessness" in our society, I.e., people having nothing to admire, to sacrifice themselves for, to surrender to, to die for. This gap calls for filling. Perhaps, even, it may be an "instinctual" need. Any onto-psychology or any religion, it would seem, must satisfy this need.

Organized religion, the religious establishment, the institutionalization of religious sensibilities, has always attempted to own and govern these emotions of reverence and devotion, of awe, wonder, and mystery. And, up until modern science came onto the scene, institutional expressions of religion maintained dominance over the majority of individuals, particularly those who were devoid of the core experience and were mere satisfied followers. It seems to have worked for a very long time, and the institutional church has benefited immensely from it. However, those days seem to be numbered now, as those with core experiences of deep spirituality who are outside the organized institutional expressions of religious awareness are beginning to outnumber those without the core experience who continue to patronize the church and its cognates. A true psychology of religion, Maslow points out, will embrace and affirm this experience of secular spirituality. It is already doing so in many ways.

****

A rather bleak, boring, unexciting, unemotional, cool philosophy of life which fails to do what the traditional religions have tried to do when they were at their best, to inspire, to awe, to comfort, to fulfill, to guide in the value choices, and to discriminate between higher and lower, better and worse, not to mention to produce Dionysiac experiences, wildness, rejoicing, impulsiveness is the result. Any religion, liberal or orthodox, theistic or non-theistic, must be not only intellectually credible and morally worthy of respect, but it must also be emotionally satisfying (and I include here the transcendent emotions as well). No wonder that the liberal religions and semi-religious groups exert so little influence even though their members are the most intelligent and most capable sections of the population. Some perceptive liberals and non-theists are going through an "agonizing reappraisal" very similar to that which the orthodox often go through, namely a loss of faith in their foundation beliefs. Just as many intellectuals lose faith in religious orthodoxy, so do they also lose faith in positivistic, nineteenth-century science as a way of life. Thus they too often have the sense of loss, the craving to believe, the yearning for a value-system, the faultlessness and the simultaneous longing for values which marks so many in this "Age of Longing."

Eighteenth-century Deism will not do it. The intellect is only half of the reality of the core experience. For a new day to dawn, the scientific community will need to affirm the whole person, mind and spirit, body and soul, and by doing so elevate an appreciation of the core experience of encounter with the spirituality of life. The liberal expressions of religious awareness, Maslow points out, is so very ineffective, owing precisely to its failure to address the whole person's sense of both rational explanation and emotional affirmation. Reason and emotion are the combined components of the human quest for spiritual meaning.

****

I am myself uneasy, even jittery, over the semantic confusion which lies in store for us -- indeed which is already here -- as all the concepts which have been traditionally "religious" are redefined and then used in a very different way. Even the word "god" is being defined by many theologians today in such a way as to exclude the conception of a person with a form, a voice, a beard, etc. If God gets to be defined as "Being itself," or as "the integrating principle in the universe," or as "the whole of everything," or as "the meaningfulness of the cosmos," or in some other non-personal way, then what will atheists be fighting against? They may very well agree with "integrating principles" or "the principle of harmony."

Maslow is fully aware of the problem of language, for if the liberals (modern non-religionists) are allowed to redefine the terminology employed by the conservatives (traditional religionists), then how is a conversation to occur when both sides are using the same words but with different meanings? Julian Huxley attempted a glossary of old terms defined in the new way, and little came of it. To speak of God as the "God of the Bible" is quite different than speaking of God as "the principle of integration" in the universe. Whatever might be said in such a dialogue between a liberal and a conservative in which reference to God is central would, of course, be completely valueless if not counter productive.

****

I think it best to define a psychologist, not as one who knows the answers, but rather as one who struggles with the questions. Perhaps it is because he is so innocently unaware of his smallness, of the feebleness of his knowledge, of the smallness of his playpen, or the smallness of his portion in the cosmos and because he takes his narrow limits so for grated that he reminds me of the little boy who was seen standing uncertainly at a street corner with a bundle under his arm. A concerned by passer asked him where he was going and he replied that he was running away from home. Why was he waiting at the corner? He wasn't allowed to cross the street!

Maslow is humble as a psychotherapist and this is not a common phenomenon. He has suggested that the psychologist functions as a philosopher in asking the key questions without proposing to provide the right answers. It is in the questioning that we find our way -- Do I go this way or that? here or there? up or down? -- and in the asking, we seem to have the capacity to move forward. Religious institutions have too long proposed the answers to all human questions, even when it was clear they had no answers. The result has been the decline of religious institutions as meaningful contexts within which to seek for meaning and purpose in life.

****

Another consequence of accepting the concept of a natural, general, basic, personal religious experience is that it will also reform atheism, agnosticism, and humanism. These doctrines have, on the whole, been simply a rejection of the churches; and they have fallen into the trap of identifying religion with the churches, a very serious mistake as we have seen. They threw out too much, as we are now discovering. The alternative that these groups have rested on has been pure science of the nineteenth-century sort, pure rationalism insofar as they have not relied merely on negative attacks upon the organized churches. This has turned out to be not so much a solution of the problem as a retreat from it.

That religion can be defined as a naturalistic phenomenon is liberating in that it brings religion and its experience into the matrix of being human. It is not an alien and foreign phenomenon which has to be interpreted by duly designated individuals appointed and approved by the institutionalized forms of religious establishments. With this understanding, those groups that have for so long thought of themselves as outside the religious discussion, protesting the domain assumptions of the religious establishment, may now think of themselves as full participants in the exploration of a viable spirituality for the entire human community, based upon what is natural to us rather than foreign.

****

CHAPTER SEVEN VALUE-FREE EDUCATION?

These dichotomizing trends -- making organized religions the guardian of all values, dichotomizing knowledge from religion, considering science to be value-free, and trying to make it so -- have wrought their confusion in the field of education, too. The most charitable thing we can say about this state of affairs is that American education is conflicted and confused about its far goals and purposes. But for many educators, it must be said more harshly that they seem to have renounced far goals altogether or, at any rate, keep trying to. It is as if they wanted education to be purely technological training for the acquisition of skills which come close to being value-free or amoral (in the sense of being useful either for good or evil, and also in the sense of failing to enlarge the personality).

Maslow is the avowd enemy of a naïve concept called "value-free education," for, says he, all things of importance imply a value system. Making established institutional religion the keepers of the value system of society, separating, intentionally, scientific knowledge from religious ideology, proposing something as preposterous as a "value-free" science, and even trying to create a kind of value-free educational system, all bespeak a simplicity of thought bordering on the irresponsible. The current problem in American education, explains Maslow, is that it is singularly devoid of an identifiable sense of purpose -- goals are conspicuously absent, especially long-term goals which affect the way an individual establishes priorities and the way a society envisions its future. Technology is a good thing, but can quickly turn evil if there is no sense of an abiding value-system operative in the decision-making process of social development.

****

According to the new third psychology (Allport, Fromm, Rogers, and others), the far goal of education --- as of psychotherapy, of family life, of work, of society, of life itself -- is to aid the person to grow to fullest humanness, to the greatest fulfillment and actualization of his highest potentials, to his greatest possible stature. In a word, it should help him to become the best he is capable of becoming, to become *actually* what he deeply is *potentially*. What we call healthy growth is growth toward this final goal. And if this is the vectorial direction of education -- the quarter of the compass toward which ti moves, the purpose which gives it worth and meaning and which justifies it -- then we are at once also supplied with a touchstone by which to discriminate good instruments from bad instruments, functional means from non-functional means, good teaching from bad teaching, good courses from bad courses, good curricula from bad curricula. The moment we can clearly distinguish instrumental goods from instrumental bads, thousands of consequences start to flow.

These far-reaching goals, which are so desperately needed and so conspicuously absent are no secret, they are not mysterious, and they do not elude a reflective-thinking society. The goals are to enhance humanity, to foster social responsibility, and to nurture well-balanced individual personalities. The intent of every society in the formation of its far-reaching goals is to aspire to actualize what it perceives to be latent virtues and gifts within its people. By identifying these principles of well-being, for individuals and society at large, there is a measuring rod for determining social and public policy, implementation of virtuous initiatives and stifling negative ones.

****

Trying to be value-free, trying to be purely technological (means without ends), trying to rest on tradition or habit alone (old values in the absence of living values), defining education simply as indoctrination (loyalty to ordained values rather than to one's own) -- all these are value-confusions, philosophical and axiological failures. And inevitably, they breed all the value-pathologies, e.g., such idiocies as the four-year college degree, three-credit courses, required courses from which there is no exception, etc. Clarity of end-values makes it very easy to avoid these mismatching of means and ends. The better we know which ends we want, the easier it is for us to create truly efficient means to those ends. If we are not clear about those ends, or deny that there are any, then we are doomed to confusion of instruments.

Social pathology is the result of a wrong-headed notion of a value-free technology and value-free educational system. Confusion reigns as to what is the right thing to do and why it is right to do it. Far-reaching goals and "end-values" should be the agenda for a well-balanced society, and to rely upon an antiquated religious entity or a naïve scientism devoid of a sense of ethics and morals is the recipe for disaster, for individuals, and for society at large. Fascism, both political and religious, is the alternative to a well-thought-out value system designed to foster creativity, nurture individuality, and encourage social responsibility.

****

The final and unavoidable conclusion is that education -- like all our social institutions -- must be concerned with its final values, and this in turn is just about the same as speaking of what have been called "spiritual values" or "higher values." These are the principles of choice which help us to answer the ago-old "spiritual" (philosophical? Religious? Humanistic? Ethical?) questions: What is the good life? What is the good man? The good woman? What is the good society and what is my relation to it? What are my obligations to society? What is best for my children? What is justice? Truth/ Virtue? What is my relation to nature, to death, to aging, to pain, to illness? How can I live a zestful, enjoyable, meaningful life? What is my responsibility to my brothers? Who are my brothers? What shall I be loyal to? What must I be ready to die for? It used to be that all these questions were answered by organized religions in their various ways. Slowly these answers have come more and more to be based on natural, empirical fact and less and less on custom, tradition, "revelations," sacred texts, interpretations by a priestly class.

A well-balanced educational system, driven by a deeply-abiding sense of values, will inevitably produce a "spiritual" society of deeply valued individuality and social accountability. The fundamental questions of life, for individuals as well as for society at large, derive from a well-nurtured sense of spiritual depth within the culture, a depth which values the ultimate questions of the meaning and purpose of life, the goals and ambitions of a responsible society, and the destiny of all peoples committed to service to others. The answers, no longer produced or tenable from religious institutions which have abdicated their responsible commitment to the maturity of individuals and society, must now come from the naturally endemic source, the human spirit itself. It is within humankind ourselves, Maslow points out, that our answers must come. They will not come from an imagined external source called God. The God of the Book is no longer operative in a scientific worldview, where facts rather than myth and fiction are the controlling ingredients in human decision-making. That humankind is naturally good has been established in the face of a religious ideology that played upon the false notion of human depravity. Now we know. We hold the answers to the meaning and purpose and direction of life ourselves. We are to determine the outcome of our efforts, not an external force conjured in the minds of would-be power brokers in the religious establishments of by-gone days.

****

What I have been pointing out in this lecture is that this process of a steadily increasing reliance on natural facts as guides in making life decisions is now advancing into the realm of "spiritual values." Partly this is so because of new discoveries, but partly it is so because more and more of us realize that nineteenth-century science has to be redefined, reconstructed, enlarged, in order to be adequate to this new task. This job of reconstruction is now proceeding. And insofar as education bases itself upon natural and scientific knowledge, rather than upon tradition, custom, the unexamined beliefs and prejudices of the community and of the conventional religious establishment, to that extent can I foresee that it, too, will change, moving steadily toward these ultimate values in its jurisdiction.

Nature provides the answers to our dilemmas of how to live and why. We need not look to tradition or myth or concocted potions to produce the answer. They have been tried and have been found wanting. Power is no longer brokered by those running the religious establishments. It is science, a science of accountability and responsibility, a science of facts, a science which recognizes the spiritual depth of the human personality which is now in control.

****

CHAPTER EIGHT CONCLUSIONS

There is, then, a road which all profoundly "serious," "ultimately concerned" people of good will can travel together for a very long distance. Only when they come almost to its end does the road fork so that they must part in disagreement. Practically everything that, for example, Rudolf Otto defines as characteristic of the religious experience -- the holy; the sacred; creative feeling; humility; gratitude and oblation; creature feeling; thanksgiving; awe before the *mysterium tremendous;* the sense of the divine, the ineffable; the sense of littleness before mystery; the quality of exaltedness and sublimity; the awareness of limits and even of powerlessness; the impulse to surrender and to kneel; a sense of the eternal and of fusion with the whole of the universe; even the experience of heaven and hell -- all of these experiences can be accepted as real by clergymen and atheists alike.

The commonality we all share -- religious and scientific alike -- is so much greater than our differences. And, when we define religion as the natural human propensity to pursue our spiritual depths through the fostering and nurturing of awe, wonder, and mystery, there is little room to distinguish between those who prefer to seek this spiritual depth through traditional forms of religious institutionalism, and those who prefer the freedom of scientific enquiry. The goal is the same -- fullness of life and purpose for living. That religious establishmentarians are eager to promote their worldview must be countered by the scientifically-attuned members of society who seek personal freedom and liberation from institutional oversight. The road eventually diverges, but not nearly so soon as many would think. We all, both groups, share the same long-term goals of fullness of life and service to others. Only at the end of the day must we part, with one claiming a scientific worldview while the other adheres to a theistically-driven view of the world and our place in it.

****

These two groups (sophisticated theologians and sophisticated scientists) seem to be coming closer and closer together in their conception of the universe as "organism," as having *some* kind of "meaning." Whether or not to call this integration "God" finally gets to be an arbitrary decision and a personal indulgence determined by one's personal history, one's personal revelations, and one's personal myths. John Dewey, an agnostic, decided for strategic and communicative purposes to retain the word "God," defining it in a naturalistic way. Indeed, these "serious" people are coming so close together as to suggest that they are becoming a single party of mankind, the earnest ones, the seeking, questioning, probing ones, the ones who are not sure, the ones with a "tragic sense of life," the explorers of the depths and of the heights, the "saving remnant." The other party then is made up of all the superficial, the moment-bound, the here-bound ones, those who are totally absorbed with the trivial, those who are "plated with piety, not alloyed with it," those who are reduced to the concrete, to the momentary, and to the immediately selfish. Almost, we could say, we wind up with adults, on the one hand, and children, on the other.

For those who truly seek the well-being of human society and our responsible place in the universe, whether theologians or scientists, whether religionists or secularists, both groups can travel together. Only those who would have it all their way, allowing for no divergence of worldviews, are to be excluded from this journey. They must go it alone, abiding in their demented sense of the worthlessness of the human person in the absence of a salvation provided by an alien being called God. The rest, those who seek to know and serve to the best of their ability, while believing in science or in an external God, their work is clearly laid out before them. That work is progress and well-being for the human person, society, and the earth itself.

****

What is the practical upshot for education of all these considerations? We wind up with a rather startling conclusion, namely, that the teaching of spiritual values of ethical and moral values definitely does (in principle) have a place in education, perhaps ultimately a very basic and essential place, and that this in no way needs to controvert the American separation between church and state for the very simple reason that spiritual, ethical, and moral values need have nothing to do with any church. Or perhaps, better said, they are the common core of all churches, all religions, including the non-theistic ones. As a matter of fact, it is possible that precisely these ultimate values are and should be the far goals of all education, as they are and should be also the far goals of psychotherapy, of child care, of marriage, the family, of work, and perhaps of all other social institutions. I grant that this may turn out to be an overstatement, and yet there is something here that we must all accept. We reject the notion of distance value goals in education under the penalty of falling into the great danger of defining education as mere technological training without relation to the good life, to ethics, to morals, or for that matter to anything else.

Spiritual values, those values that nurture the human spirit by feeding our aspirations and ambitions, our desire to foster justice and to seek new heights of understanding and service, these are the values which a responsible education system must embrace and perpetuate. Education is more than facts; it is more than mere information; it is certainly more than technological skills for building and doing. Education is the mechanism whereby the human community becomes and remains human, becomes and remains responsible and accountable for our individual and corporate actions, and the medium through which we foster these goals and aspirations for every forthcoming generation of well-meaning people in society. Education is the core and embodiment of our value system and it is the means whereby we prove and validate our humanity.

****

CONCLUDING COMMENT

From William James to Abraham Maslow is a sixty-year span of time commencing with a call to investigate religious experience and concluding with a clarion call for theology and psychology to converge upon the phenomenon of religious experience with scientific integrity and theological responsibility. The ten books considered in this essay are all iconic and epic in the contributions they have made to the subjects they have covered. That eighteen of the top theological institutions in the United States were asked to collaborate in identifying just what ten books would be credited with contributing to the development of the discipline of the psychology of religion was, itself, a unique event. It is hoped that the task set before us at the outset has been met and discharged with integrity and credibility.

GLOSSARY OF TERMS

Accusation Used by Adlerians as a safeguarding tendency whereby one protects magnified feelings of self-esteem by blaming others for one's own failures.

Activity The degree of activity is the level of energy or interest with which one moves toward finding solutions to life's problems as used in Adlerian psychology.

Actualizing tendency A Rogerian term referring to the tendency within all people to move toward completion or fulfillment of potentials.

Aesthetic needs A term used by Maslow which refers to human needs for art, music, beauty, etc. though they may be related to the basic conative needs, aesthetic needs are a separate dimension.

Aggression An Adlereian term referring to safeguarding tendencies that may include depreciation or accusation of others, as well as self-accusation, all designed to protect exaggerated feelings of personal superiority by striking out against other people.

Aggression A Freudian term referring to one or two primary instincts or drives that motivate people. Aggression is the outward manifestation of the death instinct and is at least a partial explanation for wars, personal hostility, sadism, masochism, and murder.

Analytical Psychology Theory of personality and approach to psychotherapy founded by Carl Jung.

Anima Jungian archetype that represents the feminine side in the personality of males and originates from men's inherited experiences with women.

Animus Jungian archetype that represents the masculine component in the personality of females and originates from women's inherited experiences with men.

Anticathexis A Freudian term referring to a check or restraint upon an instinctual drive.

Anxiety A felt, affective, unpleasant state accompanied by physical sensation.

Apathy A term used by Sullivan to refer to the dynamism that reduces tensions of needs through the adoption of an indifferent attitude.

Archetypes Jung's concept that refers to the content of the collective unconscious.

Attitude Jung's specialized usage referring to a predisposition to act or react in a characteristic manner, that is, in either an introverted or an extraverted direction.

Autistic language A term used by Sullivan to refer to private or parataxic language, which makes little or no sense to other people.

Autoeroticism Self-gratification and in Freudian terms, infants are seen as exclusively autoerotic since their interest in pleasure is limited to themselves.

Aversive stimulus A painful or undesired stimulus which, when associated with a response, decreases the tendency of that response to be repeated in similar situations.

B-love A concept developed by Maslow to refer to love between self-actualizing people characterized by the love for the "being of the other."

B-values A concept developed by Maslow that refers to the values of self-actualizing people, including beauty, truth, goodness, justice, wholeness, etc.

Basic anxiety A term from Maslow suggesting that anxiety arises from the inability to satisfy physiological and safety needs.

Behaviorism A school of psychology that limits its subject matter to observable behavior. John B. Watson is usually credited with being the founder of behaviorism, with b. F. Skinner its most notable proponent.

Castration complex Freudian suggesting a condition that accompanies the Oedipus complex, but takes different forms in the two sexes. In boys it takes the form of castration anxiety, or fear of having one's penis removed, and it is responsible for shattering the Oedipus complex. In girls it takes the form of penis envy, or the desire to have a penis, and precedes and instigates the Oedipus complex.

Cathexis A Freudian term referring to a driving or urging force.

Client-centered therapy Approach to psychotherapy originated by Carl Rogers, which is based on respect for the person's capacity to grow within a nurturing climate.

Cognitive needs A Maslovian term suggesting needs for knowledge and understanding; related to basic or conative needs, yet operate on a different dimension.

Collective unconscious Jung's idea of an inherited unconscious. He believed that many of our acts are motivated by unconscious ideas that are beyond our personal experiences and originate with repeated experiences of our ancestors.

Complex A Jungian term suggesting an emotionally toned conglomeration of ideas, which comprise the contents of the personal unconscious. Jung originally used the Word Association Test to uncover complexes.

Compulsion neurosis Neurotic reaction characterized by phobias, obsessions, and compulsions.

Conditions of worth A term employed by Rogers to suggest

restrictions or qualifications attached to one person's regard for another.

Congruence Rogers' term for the matching of organismic experiences with awaeness, and with the ability to express those experiences. One of three "necessary and sufficient" therapeutic conditions.

Conscience As used by Freud, that pat of the superego which results from experience with punishment and which, therefore, tells a person what is wrong or improper conduct. As used by Frankl, conscience "is that capacity which empowers a person to seize the meaning of a situation in its very uniqueness."

Conscious As used by Freud, a term referring to those mental elements in awareness at any given time.

Consensual validation The agreement of two or more people on the meaning of experiences, especially language. In Sullivan's thought, consensually validated experiences are said to operate on the syntaxic level of cognition.

Constructing obstacles Adler developed this term to suggest the safeguarding tendency characterized by a person creating a barrier to success so that self-esteem can be protected by either using the barrier as an excuse or by overcoming it.

Conversion hysteria Neurotic reaction characterized by the transformation of repressed psychological conflicts into overt physical symptoms.

Counter transference A Freudian concept referring to the strong undeserved feelings the therapist develops toward the patient during the course of treatment. These feelings can be either positive or negative and are considered by most writers to be a hindrance to successful psychotherapy.

D-love A term developed by Maslow to refer to deficiency love or affection (attachment) based on the lover's specific deficiency and the loved one's ability to satisfy that deficit.

Death instinct A Freud concept which suggests one of two primary drives or impulses, the death instinct is also known as Thanatos or agression.

Deductive method Approach to factor analytical theories of personality that gathers data on the basis of previously determined hypotheses or theory. Reasoning from the general to the particular.

Defense mechanisms A Freud concept referring to techniques such as repression, reaction formation, sublimation, etc., whereby the ego defends itself against the pain of anxiety.

Defensiveness Rogers's term for the protection of the self-concept against anxiety and threat by denial and distortion of experiences inconsistent with it.

Denial Roger's term for the blocking of an experience or some aspect of an experience from awareness because it is inconsistent with the self-concept.

Depreciation Adlerian safeguarding tendency whereby another's achievements are undervalued and one's own are overvalued.

Dereflection According to Frankl, dereflection focuses attention away from the situation. "…on two essential qualities of human existence, namely, man's capacities of self-transcendence and self-detachment."

Desacralization Maslow suggests that this is the process of removing respect, joy, awe, rapture, etc., from an experience resulting in the purification or objectifying of that experience.

Dissociation A term used by Sullivan to suggest the process of separating unwanted impulses, desires, and needs from the self-system.

Dynamisms Sullivan's terms for the relatively consistent patterns of action which characterize the person throughout a lifetime. Similar to traits or habit patterns.

Ecclesiogenic damage According to Frankl, damage caused by the clergy.

Ego A term used extensively by Freud and Freudians to refer to the province of the mind that refers to the "I" or those experiences which are owned (not necessarily consciously) by the person. As the only region of the mind in contact with the real world, the ego is said to serve the reality principle.

Ego A term used extensively by Jung and the Jungians to refer to the center of consciousness. In Jungian psychology the ego is of lesser importance than the more inclusive self and is limited to consciousness.

Ego-ideal In Freud terms, that part of the superego which results from experiences with reward and which, therefore, teach a person what is right or proper conduct.

Eidetic personifications Sullivan's concept for imaginary traits attributed to real or imaginary people in order to protect one's self-esteem.

Empathy Roger's term for the accurate sensing of the feelings of another and the communication of these perceptions. One of three "necessary and sufficient" therapeutic conditions.

Empathy Sullivan's term for an indefinite process through which anxiety is transferred from one person to another, for example from mother to infant.

Empirical Based on experience, systematic observation, and experiment rather than logical reasoning or philosophical speculation.

Energy transformations Sullivan's term for the overt or covert actions designed to satisfy needs or reduce anxiety.

Enhancement needs Roger's term for the need to develop, to grow, and to achieve.

Erogenous zones Organs of the body that are especially sensitive to the reception of pleasure. In Freudian theory, the three principal erogenous zones are the mouth, anus, and genitals.

Excuses Adlerian safeguarding tendencies whereby the person, through the use of reasonable sounding justifications, becomes convinced of the reality of self-erected obstacles.

Existential As used by Frankl, "...may be used in three ways: to (a) existence itself, I.e., the specifically human mode of being; (b) the meaning of existence; and © the striving to find a concrete meaning in personal existence, that is to say, the will to meaning."

Existential Analysis As used by Frankl, psychotherapy whose starting-point and whose particular concern is making man conscious of his responsibility. It is the "analysis of the responsibility aspects of being human."

Existential frustration In Frank's terms, a "frustration of the will-to-meaning which may lead to neurosis. ... It is in itself neither pathological nor pathogenic. A man's concern, even his despair, over the worthwhile ness of life is a spiritual distress but by no means a mental disease."

Existential vacuum A general sense of meaninglessness sand emptiness, an "inner void," an "abyss-experience" according to Frankl and Logotherapists, and it manifest itself "mainly in a state of boredom."

External evluation A Rogerian term for the conditions of worth placed on a person, which may then serve as a criterion for evaluating one's own conduct. Conditions of worth block growth and interfere with one's becoming fully functioning.

Extraversion A Jungian concept which refers to an attitude or type characterized by the turning outward of psychic energy so that the person is oriented toward the objective.

Feeling A Jungian concept which refers to a rational function that tells us the value of something. The feeling function can be either extraverted (directed toward the objective world) or introverted (directed toward the subjective world).

Fiction An Adlerian term used to refer to a belief or expectation of the future, which serves to motivate present behavior. The truthfulness of a fictional idea is immaterial since the person acts as if the idea were true.

Fixation A defense mechanism that arises when psychic energy is blocked at one stage of development, thus making change or psychological growth difficult.

Formative tendency A term used by Rogers to refer to the tendency in all matter to evolve from simpler to more complex forms.

Genital stage A period of life recognized in Freudian psychology beginning with puberty and continuing through adulthood. This second sexual stage of the person's life should not be confused with the phallic phase, which takes place during the first sexual stage, that is, during infancy.

Hesitating A terms used by Alderian psychologists applied to the safeguarding tendency characterized by vacillation or procrastination designed to provide a person with the excuse, "It's too late now."

Heuristic Pertaining to a method or theory that leads to the discovery of new information.

Hierarchy of needs A major concept in the work of Maslow which refers to the realization that needs are ordered in such a manner that those on a lower level must be satisfied before higher level needs become activated.

Holistic-dynamic Maslow's theory of personality, which streses both the unity of the organism and the motivational aspects of personality.

Humanistic psychology Ill-defined term referring to those theories and systems of psychology which, in general, emphasize the power of the individual to make conscious rational decisions and which stress the primacy of humans to other beings.

Hyperintention In Franklian psychology, attempts to escape the existential vacuum by focusing on the pursuit of pleasure. The direct attention on pleasure defeats itself. "The more an individual aims at pleasure, the more he misses the aim."

Hysteria A Freudian term used to refer to a mental disorder characterized by conversion of repressed psychical elements into somatic symptoms such as impotency, paralysis, or blindness, where no physiological bases for these symptoms exist.

Id A key term in Freudian psychoanalytic theory which refers to that region of personality which is alien to the ego in that it includes experiences that have never been owned by the person. The id is the home base for all the instincts and its sole function is to seek pleasure, regardless of consequences.

Ideal self A Rogerian terms used for one's view of self as one would like to be.

Idealization An Adlerian safeguarding tendency whereby the individual, in order to maintain exaggerated feelings of inferiority, sets up an ideal model so that any real person, by comparison, will inevitably fall short and thus be depreciated.

Incongruence A term used by Rogers to suggest the perception of discrepancies between organism self, self-concept, and ideal self.

Individual Psychology Theory of personality and approach to psychotherapy founded by Alfred Adler.

Individuation Jung's term for the process of becoming a whole perso, that is, an individual with a high level of psychic development. Similar to Maslow's concept of self-actualization.

Inductive method Approach to factor analytic theories of personality that gathers data with no preconceived hypotheses or theory in mind. Reasoning from the particular to the general.

Infantile state Freud's term for the first four or five years of life characterized by autoerotic or pleasure-seeking behavior and consisting of the oral, anal, and phallic substages.

Inferiority complex A term used by Adler to suggest the exaggerated or abnormally strong feelings of inferiority, which usually interfere with socially useful solutions to life's problems.

Instinct From the German "trieb" meaning drive or impulse, Freud used this term to refer to an internal stimulus that impels action or thought. The two primary instincts are sex and aggression.

Instinctoid needs Maslow developed this term to mean the needs that are innately determined, but can be modified through learning. The frustration of instinctoid needs leads to pathology. The use of the word "instinctual" would have served his system better as there was always confusion regarding this term.

Intimacy Sullivan used this term to refer to the conjunctive dynamism characterized by a close personal relationship with another person who is more or less of equal status.

Introversion Jung used this term to apply to an attitude or type characterized by the turning inward of psychic energy with an orientation toward the subjective.

Intuition Jung used this term to apply to an irrational function that involves perception of elementary data that are beyond our awareness. Intuitive people "Know" something without understanding how they know.

Irrational functions Methods of dealing with the world without evaluation or thinking. Sensing and intuiting are the two irrational functions.

Isolation A Freudian term used to characterize a defense mechanism; also a type of repression, whereby the ego attempts to isolate an experience by establishing a period of black-out affect immediately following that experience.

Latent dream content A term used by Freud for the underlying, unconscious meaning of a dream. Freud held that the latent content, which can only be revealed through dream interpretation, was more important than the surface, or manifest, dream content.

Libido Freud used this term to refer to the psychic energy of the life instinct; sexual drive or energy.

Life instinct Freud used this term for one or two primary drives or impulses, the life instinct is also called Eros or sex.

Logotherapy According to Frankl, "focuses on the meaning of human existence as well as on man's search for such a meaning. ... the striving to find a meaning in one's life is the primary motivational force in man. ... It is a psychotherapy which not only recognizes man's spirit, but actually starts from it."

Lust A term used by Sullivan for the isolating dynamism characterized by impersonal sexual interest in another.

Maintenance needs A Rogerian term for those basic needs which protect the status quo. They may be either physiological (e.g., food), or interpersonal (e.g., the need to maintain the current self-concept).

Malevolence Sullivan's term for those destructive behavior

patterns characterized by the attitude that people are evil and harmful and that the world is a bad place to live.

Manadala A symbol, says Jung, that represents the striving for unity and completion. It is often seen as a circle within a square or a square within a circle.

Manifest dream content A central Freudian concept referring to the surface or conscious meaning of a dream. The manifest content of a dream is the story the dreamer can describe to others. Freud believed that the manifest level of a dream has no deep psychological significance and that the unconscious or latent level holds the key to the dream's true meaning.

Masculine protest Adler's term for the neurotic and erroneous belief held by some men and women that males are superior to females.

Maturity Freud used this term to mean the final psychosexual state following infancy, latency, and the genital period. Maturity would be characterized by a strong ego in control of the id and superego and by an ever-expanding realm of consciousness. Though we all strive for maturity, Freud believed that only a very few individuals ever reach it.

Metamotivation Maslow's terms for the motives of self-actualizing people including especially the B-values.

Metapathology Maslow's terms for the illness characterized by absence of values, lack of fulfillment, and loss of meaning of life and resulting from deprivation of self-actualization needs.

Moving backward Adler used this term to apply to the safeguarding of inflated feelings of of superiority by reverting to a more secure period of life.

Neurasthenia Neurotic condition characterized by excessive fatigue, chronic aches and pains, and low motivational level.

Neurosis A term signifying mild personality disorders, as opposed to the more severe psychotic reactions. Neuroses are generally characterized by one or more of the following: anxiety, hysteria, phobias, obsessive-compulsive reactions, depressing, chronic fatigue, and hypochondriacal reactions.

Noetic dimension The dimension of the human spirit containing our healthy core, where can be found such uniquely human attributes as will to meaning, ideas and ideals, creativity, etc.

Noogenic A logo therapeutic term which refers to anything having to do with the "spiritual" core of one's personality. The word spiritual does not mean religious but rather it refers to the specifically human dimension of being human. Noetic phenomena is a dimension above the somatic and psychic.

Oedipus compex The classic concept in Freudian psychoanalysis used to indicate the situation where the child of either sex develops feelings of love and/or hostility for the parent. In the smiple male Oedipus complex, the boy has incestuous feelings of love for the mother and hostility toward the father. The simple female Oedipus complex exists when the girl feels hostility for the mother and sexual love for the father.

Operational definition A definition of a concept in terms of specific operations to be carried out by the observer.

Oral phase Freud used this term to refer to the earliest phase of the infantile period. This stage is characterized by attempts to gain pleasure through the activity of the mouth, especially sucking, eating, and biting; corresponds roughly to the first 12 - 18 months of life.

Organ dialect Adlerian term referring to the expression of a person's underlying intentions or style of life through a diseased or dysfunction bodily organ.

Organismic self Roger used this concept as a more general term than self-concept, the organismic self includes the entire person, including those aspects of existence beyond awareness.

Paradoxical intention In Franklian terms, it "means that the patient is encouraged to do, or wish to happen, the very things he fears. … It lends itself to the short-term treatment of obsessive-compulsive and phobic patients."

Paranoia Mental disorder characterized by unrealistic feelings of persecution, grandiosity, and suspicious attitude toward others.

Parataxic Sullivan's terms for the mode of cognition characterized by attribution of cause and effect when none is present; private language not consensually validated (I.e., not able to be accurately communicated to others).

Parsimony Criterion of a useful theory, which states that when two theories are equal on other criteria, the simpler one is preferred.

Peak experience A classic concept of Maslow used to refer to an intense, mystical experience often characteristic of self-actualizing people, but not limited to them.

Perceptual-conscious In Freud's thought, the system that perceives external stimuli through sight, sound, taste, etc., and communicates them to the conscious system.

Person of tomorrow Rogers used this phrase to refer to the psychologically healthy individual in the process of evolving into all that he or she can become.

Person-centered The teory of personality founded by Carl Rogers as an outgrowth of his client-centered psychotherapy.

Persona Jungian archetype that represents that side of personality one shows to the rest of the wold. Also, the mask worn by ancient Roman actors in the Greek theater, and thus the root of the word "personality."

Personal unconscious Jung's term for those repressed experiences which pertain exclusively to one particular individual; opposed to the collective unconscious which pertains to unconscious experiences that originate with repeated experiences of our ancestors.

Personality A universal concept referring to all those relatively permanent traits, dispositions, or characteristics within the individual, which give some degree of consistency to that person's behavior. Traits may be unique, common to some groups or culture, or shared by the entire species. At present, no one definition of personality is accepted universally and every major school of psychotherapy has produced its own.

Personifications Sullivan used this term to apply to images a person has of self or others, such as "good-mother," "Bad-mother," "good-me," and "bad-me."

Phallic phase Freud's term for the third and latest stage of the infantile period, this period is characterized by the Oedipus complex. Though anatomical differences between the sexes are responsible for important differences in the male and female Oedipal periods, Freud used the term phallic phase to signify both the male and the female developmental stage. He has been roundly criticized by the feminist psychoanalists of the day.

Pleasure principle Freud used this term to refer to the motivation of the id to seek immediate reduction of tension through the gratification of instinctual drives.

Positive regard Rogers used this term to refer to the need to be loved, liked, or accepted by another.

Positive reinforcer Any stimulus which, when added to a situation, increases the probability that a given behavior will occur.

Preconscious Freud meant by this term those mental elements which are currently not in awareness, but which can become conscious with varying degrees of difficulty.

Primary narcissism Freud meant the infant's investment of libido upon its own ego; self-love or autoerotic behavior of the infant.

Primary process Freud's term which refers to the id, which houses the primary motivators of behavior called instincts.

Progression Jung's term for the forward flow of psychic energy. Involves the extraverted attitude and movement toward adaptation to the external world.

Projection A defense mechanism whereby the ego reduces anxiety by attributing an unwanted impulse to another person or object.

Phototoxic Primitive, presymbolic, undifferentiated mode of experience which cannot be communicated to others.

Psychoanalysis Theory of personality, developed by Freud and the Freudian school called by this name, and a recognized mode of psychotherapy.

Psychodynamic Loosely defined term usually referring to those psychological theories which heavily emphasize unconscious motivation. The theories of Freud, Adler, Jung, and Sullivan are usually considered to be psychodynamic.

Psychoid unconscious Jung's term for those elements in the unconscious which are not capable of becoming conscious.

Psychopathology General term referring to various levels and types of mental disturbances or beahvior disorders, including neuroses, psychoses, and psychosomatic ailments.

Psychosis Severe personality disorders, as opposed to the more mild neurotic reactions. Psychoses interfere seriously with the usual functions of life and include both organic brain disfunctions and functional or learned condictions.

Quaternary A Jungian term used to refer to an archetype symbolized by figures with four equal dies or four elements.

Rational functions Jung's term for the methods of dealing with the world which involve thinking and feeling, i.e., valuing.

Reaction formation A defense mechanism characterized by the repression of one impulse and the adoption of the exact opposite form of behavior. Reactive behavior is ordinarily exaggerated and ostentatious.

Reality principle Freud's term used to refer to the go, which must realistically arbitrate the conflicting demands of the id, the superego, and the external world.

Regression Freud's term for a defense mechanism whereby the person returns to a stage previously catheter by libido in order to protect the ego against anxiety; return to an earlier time in life, usually childhood.

Regression Jung's term for the backward flow of psychic energy. Regression involves the introverted attitude and movement towards adaptation to the internal world.

Repetition compulsion Freud used this concept to refer to the tendency of the instinct, especially the death instinct, to repeat or recreate an earlier condition, particularly one that was frightening or anxiety-arousing.

Repression Freud's term for the forcing of unwanted, anxiety-laden experiences into the unconscious in order to defend the person against the pain of that anxiety.

Resacralization Maslow developed this concept for the process of returning respect, joy, awe, rapture, etc., to an experience in order that the experience is more subjective and personal.

Sadistic-anal phase Freud used this concept to refer to the anal phase, this is the second stage of the infantile period and is characterized by attempts to gain pleasure from the execretory function and such related behaviors as destroying or losing objects, stubbornness, neatness, and miserliness. Corresponds roughly to the second year of life.

Safeguarding tendencies A dominant concept in Adlerian psychology, the term is used to refer to the protective mechanisms such as aggression, withdrawal, etc., which maintain exaggerated feelings of superiority.

Schizophrenia Psychotic disorder characterized by fundamental disturbances in perception of reality, severe apathy, and loss of affect.

Secondary narcissism Freudian concept referring to self-love or autoerotic behavior in an adolescent.

Secondary reinforcement Learned reinforcement. If a previously ineffective event, for example money, increases the likelihood that learning will take place, then that event is a secondary reinforcer.

Selective inattention A classic term developed by Sullivan to refer to the control of focal awareness, which involves a refusal to see those things one does not wish to see or a refusal to hear things wishes not to hear.

Self In Jungian psychology, the most comprehensive of all archetypes, including the whole of personality, though it is mostly unconscious. The self is often symbolized by the mandala motif.

Self-accusation Adlerian safeguarding tendency whereby the person aggresses indirectly against others through self-torture and guilt.

Self-actualization Maslow's classic concept referring to the highest level of human motivation characterized by full development of all one's capacities.

Self-regard Roger developed this term to refer to the need to accept, like, or love oneself.

Self-system Sullivan's term for the complex of dynamisms that protect the person from anxiety and maintain interpersonal security.

Self-transcendence In Franklian psychology, "self-transcendence is our ability to reach beyond ourselves to people we love or to causes that are important to us (Lukas)." "Self-transcendence is the essence of existence. Being human is being directed to something other than itself" according to Frankl.

Shadow Jungian archetype representing the inferior or dark side of personality.

Social interest An Adlerian term for the translation of the German, *Gemeinschaftsgefuhl,* meaning a community feeling or a sense of feeling at one with all human beings.

Solicitude Adlerian safeguarding tendency whereby the individual depreciates others and receives an inflated feeling of superiority by acting as if other people are incapable of caring form themselves.

Somnolent detachment Sullivan's term for the dynamism that protects the person from increasingly strong and painful effects of severe anxiety.

Standing still Adlerian term for the safeguarding tendency characterized by lack of action as a means of avoiding failure.

Stereotypes Sullivan used this term to refer to imaginary traits attributed to a group of people.

Style of life Adler's terms for a person's individuality expressing itself in any circumstance or environment; the "flavor" of a person's life.

Subception A term developed by Rogers to refer to the process of perceiving stimuli without an awareness of the perception.

Sublimation A defense mechanism that involves the repression of the genital aim of Eros and its substitution by a cultural or social aim.

Successive approximations Procedure used to shape an organism's behavior; entails the rewarding of behaviors as they become closer and closer to the target behavior.

Superego Freud's classic term for that province of the mind which refers to the moral or ethical processes of personality. The superego has two subsystems -- the conscience, which tells us what is wrong, and the ego-ideal, which tells us what is right.

Superiority complex Adler's terms used to refer to the exaggerated and unrealistic feelings of personal superiority as an overcompensation for unusually strong feelings of inferiority.

Suppression the blocking or inhibiting of an activity by either a conscious act of the will or by an outside agent such as parents or other authority figures. Not to be confused with *repression*, which is the unconscious blocking of anxiety-producing experiences.

Syntaxic Sullivan's well-developed concept used to refer to the consensually validated experiences. As the highest level of cognition, syntaxic experiences can be accurately communicated to others, usually through language.

Taoist attitude An adapted term developed by Maslow to refer to the no interfering, passive, receptive attitude that includes awe and wonder toward that which is observed.

Tenderness Sullivan used this term to refer to the tension within the mothering one, which is aroused by the manifest needs of the infant. Within the child tenderness is felt as the need to receive care.

Terror Sullivan's term for the experience of absolute or complete tension.

Theory A scientific theory is a set of related assumptions from which, by logical deductive reasoning, testable hypotheses can be drawn.

Thinking By this term, Jung meant a rational function that tells us the meaning of a sensation that originates either from the external world (extraverted) or from the internal or subjective world (introverted).

Third force Somewhat vague terms referring to those approaches to psychology which have reacted against the psychodynamic and behaviorist theories of Freud, Jung, Adler and Skinner and all those in between them. Rogers and Frankl belong to the Third Force but some would argue that Erikson and Maslow belong to the psychodynamic school. Since no one pays dues to belong to one or the other, the question is essentially mute.

Threat Roger's term for the results from the perception of an experience that is inconsistent with one's organismic self.

Transference Freud developed the term but many schools now use it to refer to the strong, underserved feelings the patient develops towad the analyst during the course of treatment. This feeling may be either sexual or hostile and stems from the patient's earlier experiences with parents.

Transformation Psychotherapeutic approach used by Jung wherein the therapist is transformed into a healthy individual who can aid the patient in establishing a philosophy of life.

Types Jung's classification of people based on the two-dimensional scheme of attitudes and functions. The two attitudes of extraversion and introversion and the four functions of thinking, feeling, sensing, and intuiting combine to produce eight possible types.

Unconditional positive regard   A Rogerian term for the need to be accepted and prized by another without any restrictions or qualifications. One of three "necessary and sufficient" therapeutic conditions.

Unconscious   Freud meant all those mental elements of which a person is unaware. Two levels of the unconscious are the unconscious proper and the preconscious. Unconscious ideas can become conscious only through great resistance and difficulty.

Undoing   A Freudian defense mechanism, closely related to repression, involving the ego's attempt to do away with unpleasant experiences and their consequences by an expenditure of energy on compulsive ceremonial activities.

Vulnerable   A Rogerian term for a condition that exists when people are unaware of the discrepancy between their organism selves and their experiences. Vulnerable people often behave in ways incomprehensible to themselves and to others.

Will-to-meaning   "According to logo therapy," says Frankl, "the striving to find a meaning in one's life is the primary motivational force in man."   This is in opposition to the will-to-pleasure in Freudian psychology and the will-to-power in Adler's thought.

Withdrawal   Adler's term for safeguarding one's exaggerated sense of superiority by establishing a distance between oneself and one's problems.

BIBLIOGRAPHY

PRIMARY SOURCES

Note: These primary sources are major works written by the authors of the ten books considered here as pivotal in the establishment of the discipline of the psychology of religion.

Allport, Gordon W. (1937) *Personality: A Psychological Interpretation.* N.Y.: Holt.

Allport, Gordon W. (1950) *The Individual and His Religion.* New York: Macmillan.

Allport, Gordon W. (1955) *Becoming: Basic Considerations for a Psychology of Personality.* New Haven, CT: Yale University Press.

Bakan, David (1958) *Sigmund Freud and the Jewish Mystical Tradition.* Princeton, NJ: D.Van Nostrand Company.

Freud, Sigmund (1927 German/ 1953 Vienna) *The Future of an Illusion.* N.Y.: Liveright Publishing Company.

Freud, Sigmund (1939) *Moses and Monotheism.* N.Y.: Vintage Books Edition.

Freud, Sigmund (1930) *Civilization and Its Discontents.* London: Hogarth Press Edition.

Freud, Sigmund (1918) *Totem and Taboo: Resemblances Between the Psychic Lives of Savages and Neurotics* N.Y.: Vintage Books Edition.

Fromm, Eric (1950) *Psychoanalysis and Religion.* New Haven: Yale University Press.

Fromm, Eric ((1941) *Escape from Freedom.* New York: Rinehart & Company.

Fromm, Eric (1956) *The Art of Loving.* New York: Bantam Books.

Fromm, Eric (1973) *The Anatomy of Human Destructiveness.* N.Y.: Rinehart & Winston.

James, William (1890) *The Principles of Psychology, Volumes 1 and 2.* New York: Holt, Rinehart and Winston.

James, William (1902) *The Varieties of Religious Experience.* N.Y.: Longmans, Green and Company.

Jung, Carl (1938) *Psychology and Religion.* New Haven: Yale University Press.

Jung, Carl (1912) *The Psychology of the Unconscious.* Leipzig: Franz Deuticke.

Jung, Carl (1963) *Memories, Dreams, Reflections.* (London: Collins & Routledge &
Kegan Paul.

Jung, Carl (1933) *Modern Man in Search of a Soul* New York: Harcourt, Brace and Company.

Leuba, James H. (1896) A Study in the Psychology of Religious Phenomenon. *American Journal of Psychology* 5:309-335.

Leuba, James H. (1915) *The Psychological Origin and Nature of Religion.* London: Constable and Company.

Leuba, James H. (1926a) Psychology of Religion. *Psychological Bulletin* 23:714-722.

Leuba, James H. (1926b) Notes on Meetings and Conferences for the Discussion of the Psychology of Religion. *Psychological Bulletin* 23:729.

Maslow, Abraham H. (1970) *Religions, Values, and Peak-Experiences.* N.Y.: Penguin.

Maslow, Abraham H. (1962) *Toward a Psychology of Being.* N.Y.: Van Nostrand.

Maslow, Abraham H. (1966) *The Psychology of Science: A Reconnaisance.* N.Y.: Harper & Row.

Maslow, Abraham H. (1971) *The Farther Reaches of Human Nature.* N.Y.: Viking.

Rank, Otto (1907) *Art and Artist.* N.Y.: W. W. Norton.

Rank, Otto (1924) *The Trauma of Birth.* N.Y.: W. W. Norton.

Rank, Otto (1950 *English Trans.*) *Psychology and the Soul.* New York: A. S. Barnes & Company.

Roberts, David E. (1950) *Psychotherapy and A Christian View of Man.* New York: Charles Scribner's.

SECONDARY SOURCES

Note: These secondary sources are illustrative of the proliferation of scholarship and publishing which the rise of the discipline of the psychology of religion has caused.

Ames, E. S. (1910) *The Psychology of Religious Experience.* Boston: Houghton Mifflin.

Anderson, V. (2002). "Pragmatic Theology and the Natural Sciences at the Intersection of Human Interests." *Zygon: Journal of Religion & Science*, 37(1), 161.

Argyle, Michael, and Benjamin Beit-Hallahmi. (1975) *The Social Psychology of Religion.* Boston: Beacon Press.

Atran, S. (2002). *In Gods We Trust: The Evolutionary Landscape of Religion*, New York, Oxford University Press.

Aziz, Robert (1990). *C.G. Jung's Psychology of Religion and Synchronicity* (10 ed.). The State University of New York Press.

Aziz, Robert (1999). "Synchronicity and the Transformation of the Ethical in Jungian Psychology". In Becker, Carl. *Asian and Jungian Views of Ethics*. Greenwood.

Aziz, Robert (2007). *The Syndetic Paradigm: The Untrodden Path Beyond Freud and Jung*. The State University of New York Press.

Batson, C.D., Schoenrade, P. & Ventis, L. (1993). *Religion and the Individual*, New York, Oxford University Press.

Beit-Hammahmi, B. (1977). "Psychology of religion 1880-1930: The rise and fall of a psychological movement." in H. Newton Malony (Ed.), *Current Perspectives in the Psychology of Religion.* (pp. 17-26). Grand Rapids, MI: Wm. B. Eerdmans Publishing Company.

Belzen, J. (2000). "The future of the psychology of religion." *Pastoral Psychology* 49(1), 3-12.

Belzen, J. (2005). "The symposia for European psychologists of religion, 1979-2003--A retrospective." *International Journal for the Psychology of Religion*, 15(4), 297-313.

Calvin, S. S. (1902) "The Psychological Necessity of Religion." *American Journal of Psychology* 15: 10-15.

Coe, G. A. (1916) *The Psychology of Religion.* Chicago:

University of Chicago Press.

Dunlap. K. (1946). *Religion: Its Functions in Human Life*. New York: McGraw-Hill Book Company, Inc.

Emmons, R.,&Paloutzian, R. (2003). "The psychology of religion." *Annual Review of Psychology*, 54(1), 377.

Flower, J. C. (1927) *An Approach to the Psychology of Religion.* N.Y.: Harcourt.

Fontana, D., *Psychology, Religion and Spirituality*. (2003). Oxford, Blackwell.

Fuller, R. (2006). "American Psychology and the Religious Imagination." *Journal of the History of the Behavioral Sciences*, 42(3), 221-235.

Fuller, A. R. (1994). (3rd ed.). *Psychology & Religion: Eight Points of View.* Lanham, MD: Littlefield Adams.

Gargiulo, Gerald J. (1971) "Review of Peter Homans' *Theology After Freud.*" *American Imago,* Vol. 28, No. 1, 99-103.

Genia, V. (1997). "The Spiritual Experience Index: Revision and Reformulation" *Review of Religious Research*, 38, 344-361.

Glock, C.Y. & Stark, R. (1965). *Religion and Society in Tension*, Chicago: Rand McNally.

Gorsuch, R. & Venable (1983). "Development of an Age-Universal I-E Scale." *Journal for the Scientific Study of Religion.*

Haber, J., Jacob, R. & Spangler, J.D.C. (2007) Dimensions of religion and their relationship to health. *The International Journal for the Psychology of Religion*, 17 (4) 265-288 .

Harre, Rom, and Roger Lamb, Editors (1983) *The Encyclopedic Dictionary of Psychology* (Cambridge, MA: The MIT Press.

Henry, E. R. (1938) "A Survey of courses in Psychology Offered by Undergraduate Colleges of Liberal Arts." *Psychological Bulletin* 35:420-435.

Hill, P. C. & Hood, R. (1999). *Measures of Religiosity*, Birmingham, Alabama: Religious Education Press.

Hill, P. C. & Pargament, K. (2003). *Advances in the Conceptualisation and Measurement of Spirituality. American Psychologist*, 58, p64-74.

Hood, R. (2000). "American Psychology of Religion and the Journal for the Scientific Study of Religion." *Journal for the Scientific Study of Religion*, 39(4), 531-543.

Hood, R. W. Jr., Spilka, B., Hunsberger, B., & Gorsuch, R. (1996). *The Psychology of Religion: An empirical approach.* New York: Guilford.

Homans, Peter (1970) *Theology After Freud: An Interpretive Inquiry.* Indianapolis: The Bobbs-Merrill Company.

Homans, Peter (1984) *The Ability to Mourn: Disillusionment and the Social Origins of Psychoanalysis.* Chicago: University of Chicago Press.

Hunsberger, B. (1991). "Empirical work in the psychology of religion." *Canadian Psychology*, 32(3), 497-507.

Johnson, P. (1945). *Psychology of Religion.* New York: Abingdon-Cokesbury Press.

Kendler, Howard H. (1987) *Historical Foundations of Modern Psychology* (Chicago, IL: The Dorsey Press).

Leak, G.,&Fish, S. (1999). "Development and Initial Validation of a Measure of Religious Maturity." *International Journal for the Psychology of Religion*, 9(2), 83.

Leuba, J. (1900). "The psychology of religion: An empirical study of the growth of religious consciousness." *Psychological Review*, 7(5), 509-516.

Levin, J. (2001). *God, Faith and Health: Exploring the Spirituality-Health Connection*, New York, Wiley.

Loewenthal. K. M. (2000). *The Psychology of Religion: A Short Introduction.* Boston, MA: Oneworld Publications.

Main, R. (2008). *Psychology of Religion: An Overview of its History and Current Status*
Essex: University of Essex Press.

McNamara, R. (Ed.) (2006), *Where God and Science Meet [3 Volumes]: How Brain and Evolutionary Studies Alter Our Understanding of Religion.* Westport, CT: Praeger/Greenwood.

Meissner, W., (1984) *Psychoanalysis and Religious Experience*, London and New Haven, Yale University Press.

Miller, W., & Thoresen, C. (2003). "Spirituality, religion, and health: An emerging research field." *American Psychologist*, 58(1), 24-35.

Morgan, John H. (2010) *Beginning With Freud: The Classical Schools of Psychotherapy.* Lima, OH: Wyndham Hall Press.

Morgan, John H. (2010) *Clinical Pastoral Psychotherapy: A Practitioner's Handbook for Ministry Professionals* (Mishawaka, IN: GTF Books).

Morgan, John H. (1987) *From Freud to Frankl: Our Modern Search for Personal Meaning.* (Bristol, IN: Wyndham Hall Press).

Morgan, John H. (2006) *In the Absence of God: Religious Humanism as Spiritual Journey with special reference to Julian Huxley* (South Bend, IN: Cloverdale Books).

Morgan, John H. (2007) *"In the Beginning..." The Paleolithic Origins of Religious Consciousness* (South Bend, IN: Cloverdale Books).

Morgan, John H. (2005) *Naturally Good: A Behaviaoral History of Moral Development (from Charles Darwin to E. O. Wilson).* South Bend, IN: Cloverdale Books.

Morgan, John H. (1978) *In Search of Meaning: From Freud to Teilhard de Chardin.* Washington, DC: University Press of America.

Page, F. H. (1951) The Psychology of Religion after Fifty Years. *Canadian Journal of Psychology* 5:60-67.

Paloutzian, R. (1996). *Invitation to the Psychology of Religion*, 2nd Ed. New York: Allen and Bacon.

Pargament, K. (1999). "The Psychology of Religion and

Spirituality? Yes and No." *International Journal for the Psychology of Religion*, 9(1), 3.

Pratt, J. B. (1907) *The Psychology of Religious Belief.* N.Y.: Macmillan.

Pratt, J. B. (1905) Psychology of Religion. *Harvard Theological Review* 1:435-454.

Reber, Arthur S. (1985) *The Penguin Dictionary of Psychology.* New York: Viking Penguin.

Richardson, Robert D. (2006) *William James: In the Maelstrom of American Modernism.* Boston: Houghton Mifflin.

Rieff, Philip. (1966) *The Triumph of the Therapeutic: Uses of Faith After Freud.* N.Y.: Harper & Row.

Schaud, E. L. (1923) "The Present Status of the Psychology of Religion." *Journal of Religion* 3:362-379.

Schaud, E. L. (1924) "The Psychology of Religion in America during the Past Quarter Century." *Journal of Religion* 4:113-134.

Starbuck, E. D. (1899) *Psychology of Religion.* N.Y.: Scribner's.

Strunk, Oscar. (1957) "The Present Status of the Psychology of Religion." *The Journal of Bible and Religion* 26:387-392.

Strunk, O. Jr. (1977). "Humanistic religious psychology: A new chapter in the psychology of religion." In H. Newton Malony (Ed.), *Current Perspectives in the Psychology of Religion.* (pp. 27-35). Grand Rapids, MI: Wm. B. Eerdmans Publishing Company.

Vande Kemp, H. (1992). "G. Stanley Hall and the Clark School of Religious Psychology." *American Psychologist*,

47(2), 290-298.

Weiman, H. N., & Wescott-Weiman, R. (1935). *Normative Psychology of Religion*. New York: Thomas Crowell Company.

Wells, G. (1936). "Normative Psychology of Religion." *Psychological Bulletin*, 33(4), 300-302.

White, S. (1992). "G. Stanley Hall: From philosophy to developmental psychology." *Developmental Psychology*, 28(1), 25-34.

Wulff, D. M. (1997). *Psychology of Religion: Classic and Contemporary* (2nd ed.). New York: John Wiley.

APPENDIX

*The eighteen institutions approached were Andover Newton Theological School, Boston University School of Theology, Candler School of Theology (Emory University), Catholic Theological Union, Duke University Divinity School, General Theological Seminary, Graduate Theological Foundation, Harvard University Divinity School, Lutheran School of Theology (Chicago), Perkins School of Theology (Southern Methodist University), Princeton Theological Seminary, San Francisco Theological Seminary, St. John's University School of Theology, St. Joseph's Seminary (New York), Union Theological Seminary (New York), University of Chicago Divinity School, Yale University Divinity School.

ABOUT THE AUTHOR

John H. Morgan, Doctor of Philosophy (Hartford Seminary), Doctor of Science (London College of Applied Sciences), Doctor of Psychology (Foundation House/Oxford), is the Karl Mannheim Professor of the History and Philosophy of the Social Sciences at the Graduate Theological Foundation and the Sir Julian Huxley Distinguished Research Professor at Cloverdale College in Indiana. He is a Senior Fellow of Foundation House/Oxford and has held postdoctoral appointments to Harvard, Yale, and Princeton, and has been the National Science Foundation Science Faculty Fellow at the University of Notre Dame and a Visiting Scholar in the Center for Near Eastern Studies at New York University. A member of the American Psychological Association, American Anthropological Association, and the American Sociological Association, he has been a member of the Board of Studies of the theology summer program of Oxford University since 1995 where he has regularly taught a doctoral-level seminar since 1998. He is the author/editor of many books and his latest include *Beginning With Freud: The Classical Schools of Psychotherapy (2010); Beyond Divine Intervention: The Biology of Right and Wrong (2009); "In the Beginning...": The Paleolithic Origins of Religious Consciousness (2009); In the Absence of God: Religious Humanism as Spiritual Journey (with special reference to Julian Huxley) (2008);* and *Naturally God: A Behavioral History of Moral Development (From Charles Darwin to E. O. Wilson) (2008).* In 2009, he was elected to membership on the Advisory Board of the Centre for Religion in Public Life at Oxford University and in 2011 he was appointed Visiting Scholar at Harvard University for the second time in his career.